Critical Essays in Modern Literature

CRITICAL ESSAYS IN MODERN LITERATURE

The Fiction and Criticism of Katherine Anne Porter (revised)
Harry L. Mooney, Jr.

Entrances to Dylan Thomas' Poetry
Ralph Maud

Joyce Cary: The Comedy of Freedom
Charles G. Hoffmann

The Fiction of J. D. Salinger (revised)
Frederick L. Gwynn and Joseph L. Blotner

James Agee: Promise and Fulfillment
Kenneth Seib

Chronicles of Conscience: A Study of George Orwell and Arthur Koestler
Jenni Calder

Richard Wright: An Introduction to the Man and His Work
Russell Carl Brignano

Dylan Thomas' Early Prose: A Study in Creative Mythology
Annis Pratt

The Situation of the Novel
Bernard Bergonzi

D. H. Lawrence: Body of Darkness
R. E. Pritchard

The Hole in the Fabric: Science, Contemporary Literature, and Henry James
Strother B. Purdy

Tragic Realism and Modern Society: Studies in the Sociology of the Modern Novel
John Orr

Reading the Thirties: Texts and Contexts
Bernard Bergonzi

The Romantic Genesis of the Modern Novel
Charles Schug

The Great Succession: Henry James and the Legacy of Hawthorne
Robert Emmet Long

The Great Succession

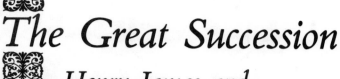

The Great Succession

*Henry James and
the Legacy of Hawthorne*

Robert Emmet Long

UNIVERSITY OF PITTSBURGH PRESS

Published by the University of Pittsburgh Press, Pittsburgh, Pa. 15260
Copyright © 1979, University of Pittsburgh Press
Feffer and Simons, Inc., London
Manufactured in the United States of America

Library of Congress Cataloging in Publication Data

Long, Robert Emmet.
  The great succession.

  (Critical essays in modern literature)
  Includes bibliographical references and index.
  1. James, Henry, 1843–1916—Criticism and interpretation. 2. Hawthorne, Nathaniel,
1804–1864—Influence—James. I. Title.
  PS2124.L6   813'.4   79-922
  ISBN 0-8229-3398-5

Several of the chapters in this book contain material previously published in the following essays. It is reprinted by permission of the journal editors, to whom acknowledgment is gratefully made. "Transformations: *The Blithedale Romance* to Howells and James," *American Literature* 47 (January 1976), 552–71; "Henry James's Apprenticeship—the Hawthorne Aspect," *American Literature* 47 (May 1976), 194–216; "James's *Roderick Hudson:* The End of the Apprenticeship —Hawthorne and Turgenev," *American Literature* 48 (November 1976), 312–26; all copyright 1976 by Duke University Press. "The Society and the Masks: *The Blithedale Romance* and *The Bostonians,*" *Nineteenth-Century Fiction* 19, no. 2 (September 1964), 105–22; copyright 1964 by The Regents of the University of California. "James's *Washington Square:* The Hawthorne Relation," *The New England Quarterly* 46 (December 1973), 573–90; copyright 1973 by *The New England Quarterly.*

For my sister Carolyn

1951

Contents

Acknowledgments

The beginnings of this study go back to a graduate seminar (on Melville and Hawthorne) given by Walter Sutton, a model professor of the humanities whose many kindnesses shown to me at that time and since it is a pleasure to acknowledge. I would like to acknowledge, too, the usefulness of Lewis Leary's doctoral seminar on Henry James at Columbia; and the stimulation received from the late Marius Bewley, in the course of our conversations about James and other American writers. Donald David Stone, a colleague of mine while I was teaching in the English department at Queens College (City University of New York), is another Jamesian whose intelligence and accomplishment have left a strong impression. Nearer at hand, I am indebted to John W. Crowley for reading the manuscript of this book (and other manuscripts of mine); and to my sister Carolyn, whose loyalty and many services have been extraordinary.

I would like to express my thanks, also, to the Byrd Library, Syracuse University, for use of their research facilities; and to Penfield Library, State University of New York, College at Oswego—and particularly to Mr. George Scheck and the Interlibrary Loan department, for extensive use of their services.

The Great Succession

"My study is man," said he. And, looking at me, "I do not know your name," he said, "but there is something of the hawkeye about you, too."

—Nathaniel Hawthorne, *American Notebooks*

But already I feel that this Hawthorne has dropped germinous seeds into my soul.

—Herman Melville, "Hawthorne and His Mosses"

For the moral was that an American could be an artist, one of the finest, without "going outside" about it, as I liked to say; quite in fact as if Hawthorne had become one by being American enough.

—Henry James, *Notes of a Son and Brother*

1   The Earlier James:
The Question of Hawthorne

What has been called "the Hawthorne tradition," Hawthorne's effect on younger American writers, began even in his own lifetime. In the early summer of 1850, Hawthorne retired to the Berkshires, where he met Herman Melville, a neighbor of six miles' distance, and a friendship developed between them. Hawthorne had just completed *The Scarlet Letter,* which he described to Horatio Bridge as "positively a hell-fired story, into which I found it almost impossible to throw any cheering light"; and in Pittsfield, Melville was writing *Moby Dick,* about which, in a letter to Hawthorne and in a phrase curiously similar to the latter's own, he referred to "the hell-fire in which the whole book is broiled."[1] It was a meeting and friendship unusually important to the younger Melville, who had just written anonymously a lengthy and brilliantly appreciative review of *Mosses from an Old Manse.* In the review Melville stresses the "power of blackness" of Hawthorne's vision, his "short, quick probings of the very axis of reality" (phrases that suggest his own fiction as well as Hawthorne's). Near the end of the article he remarks: "To what infinite height of loving wonder and admiration I may yet be borne, when by repeatedly banqueting on these Mosses I shall have thoroughly incorporated their whole stuff into my being, that, I cannot tell. But already I feel that this Hawthorne has dropped germinous seeds into my soul."[2]

The Great Succession

Moby Dick was not completed for more than a year after Melville met Hawthorne (to whom it was dedicated), and there is some reason to think that Hawthorne was influential upon it—in its more strongly gothic architecture than in Melville's previous writing; its theme of a damnation pact; and its night-world atmosphere of Ahab's lonely estrangement. In *Pierre,* which immediately follows *Moby Dick* and extends its themes in a more social context, there are also traces of Hawthorne, particularly of *The House of the Seven Gables* —in the symbolic portraits of Pierre's father; in the ancestral house, used to frame the hero's experience; and in the pervasive sense Melville gives of the hero's psychic and communal dislocation. But more important than any specific borrowing is the certitude Hawthorne gave Melville, the "shock of recognition" he experienced on reading him that a tragic art of a high order had come into being in America. Hawthorne's fiction was proof that a time of ripeness had arrived, confirming the rightness of his own subterranean exploration of reality. The bond between them is revealed in Melville's affiliated preoccupation with the darkly inscrutable and deeply ambiguous underside of life, which could be expressed in no form more effectively than in the morally probing and poetic prose romance in which they both wrote.

The fiction of Hawthorne and Melville in the 1850s represents the high tide of the American assimilation of European romanticism. Both called their books *romances,* and by comparison with English novels of the same decade, such as Thackeray's *Vanity Fair,* their writing does indeed belong to a genre that is quite different from English realism. One feature of the cultural conditioning of Hawthorne and Melville that worked against a commitment to realism was the Calvinist imagination, which places the individual and his spiritual condition at the center of the universe and tends to regard the physical world as a symbolic chart containing concealed meanings that are relevant to him. Hawthorne and Melville have their roots in the theology of the seventeenth century, in writers like Bunyan, and hence the tendency of their imaginations is toward emblem, fable, and allegory. Their characters are not free to belong wholly to the world; they are idealized, in the sense that they belong largely to a realm of moral abstraction.

Their probing of the individual's subterranean life, largely in his isolation from a fully particularized society, also marks off their fiction from that of the literary generation that came into being after the Civil War, the generation of James, Twain, and Howells, for whom social actuality is a primary context of the individual's experience. In a cultural sense there is an immense distance from the Old Manse to Newport, where James came of age in an environment of European art and travel. In the years of James's growing up his family moved back and forth between Europe and Newport several times, since James, senior, was anxious to liberate his children from the orthodoxies and ways of thinking of a single environment; and the unanchored upbringing he gave them was to have an indelible effect on the relativistic thinking of both William and Henry. Its effect on Henry immediately was to make him a kind of Europeanized American, a young man who regarded his homeland with a continental bias, and looked away from Concord and Boston toward Europe.

Considering the post–Civil War perspectives of James's early manhood (the scaling down of romantic assumptions, the emphasis away from religion toward science, the new spirit of critical scrutiny), it is not surprising that James's fiction has a different orientation than Hawthorne's. Yet despite this difference, Hawthorne was to have unique importance to James as a founder of a native tradition who established the contours of American psychological experience. James frequently referred to Hawthorne in forming his own fictional conceptions and eventually entered into a complex relationship with him.[3] Hawthorne was of crucial importance as the only previous writer of stature James knew of who had shown how American psychological experience could be treated in imaginative literature. This was true particularly of the "matter" of New England, in respect to which Hawthorne's imagination was authoritative. It is surprising how frequently, in setting a tale in New England or in treating New Englanders abroad, James gravitates to

5

Hawthorne. Hawthorne was as important to James as he had been earlier to Melville, even though the novels of James and Melville have extremely different orientations.

In 1879 James published his critical biography of Hawthorne, which remains even today an informative and fascinating document of their relationship.[4] In this work James's sense of his own difference from Hawthorne as an American writer is immediately apparent. It is implied even in the book's style, its urbane and cosmopolitan tone. James criticizes Hawthorne for his "national consciousness" and at one point even reminds himself that he must not be guilty of cherishing such a restricted point of view. (The conflict between his allegiance to a cosmopolitan perspective and his gravitation to a national consciousness, represented in American literature by Hawthorne, runs throughout James's career.) He makes significant allusions to French writers like Taine, employs French terms, and uses locutions that defer to French clarity—"what the French call" and "as the French say." He doubts in a telling comment if Hawthorne had ever read Balzac.

In his interpretation of Hawthorne, James is influenced by Taine and his method of examining how a writer is molded by his environment. Of Hawthorne's religious and metaphysical background James says relatively little; but he is extremely conscious of his social milieu, the small, insular democracy that produced him. James stresses how small that world was, and how democracy affected Hawthorne's habits of observation, or rather, his comparative lack of observation of the world around him. He notes how democracy creates a sense of social vagueness, which he finds in Hawthorne's *Notebooks* and other writing. The most frequently used word in *Hawthorne* is *observer,* and it is as an observer, whose vision has been trained upon the actual world, that James is most often critical of Hawthorne.

Certain themes keep reappearing in James's criticism of Hawthorne, all of them related to the effect on Hawthorne of his milieu —his democratic social vagueness, the smallness of his New England world (and its lack of acquaintance with European standards), his national consciousness, which kept him from participating very fully

6

in cultures different from his own. All these things conspire to create an intensity but also a narrowness and constriction in Hawthorne's imaginative response to the world. "If Hawthorne had been a young Englishman," James writes, "or a young Frenchman of the same degree of genius, the same cast of mind, the same habits, his consciousness of the world around him would have been a very different affair; however obscure, however reserved, his own personal life, his sense of his fellow-mortals would have been almost infinitely more various" (p. 34).

James stresses not the benefit to Hawthorne's art of his New England milieu, but the many limitations this milieu imposed upon it. *Our Old Home* has a "serious defect" produced by Hawthorne's "national consciousness": "It is the work," James remarks, "of an outsider, of a stranger, of a man who remains to the end a mere spectator (something less even than an observer)" (p. 120). That Hawthorne's imagination does not extend out to embrace life in its multiplicity and many-sidedness can also be seen in works set on American soil— in *The Scarlet Letter,* with its comparative absence of variation in its historical coloring and its characters' states; and in *The Blithedale Romance,* with its absence of satire that would have given a distinct impression of the idiosyncrasies of its bohemian reformers. Its human background is vague because Hawthorne's democratic conditioning did not equip him with an alertness to social discriminations and distinctions. The same kind of democratic indistinctness accounts for the defect of Holgrave in *The House of the Seven Gables.* Holgrave, James comments, "is not sharply enough characterized; he lacks features; he is not an individual, but a type" (p. 103).

At the heart of the biography is one principal limitation of Hawthorne's art, part of the limitations of his American environment, that distinguishes his work from James's. Living as he did so single-mindedly in his insular New England world, Hawthorne was unacquainted with European realism. "It cannot be too often repeated," James writes, "that Hawthorne was not a realist. . . . he never attempted to render exactly or closely the actual facts of the society that surrounded him. . . . His shadowy style of portraiture never suggests a rigid standard of accuracy" (pp. 98, 3). Hawthorne's romance mode, at odds with realistic representation, led him at times in the direction of a too-fanciful allegory, or to conceptions too unclearly specified, such as the conceit of Priscilla as the Veiled Lady in *The Blithedale Romance,* with her cloudy relationships to Zenobia, Hollingsworth, and Westervelt. James speaks of a "want of substance and cohesion in the latter portions of *The Blithedale Romance*" (p. 108) and of a failure of cohesion in *The Marble Faun* between Hawthorne's literal notation of the streets of Rome and the "moonshiny romance," as Hawthorne himself referred to it, of his principal characters. "The story," James notes, "straggles and wanders, is dropped and taken up again, and towards the close lapses into an almost fatal vagueness" (p. 134).

Two terms James uses are particularly revealing—the distinction he makes between *picture* and *characterization,* and what he calls *real psychology.* Of the characters in *The House of the Seven Gables,* James observes that they are "all pictures rather than persons" (p. 99). Hephzibah Pyncheon "is a picture, as her companions are pictures; she is a charming piece of descriptive writing, rather than a dramatic exhibition" (p. 100). What James seems to mean is that Hawthorne has captured all her traits, rather than having revealed her through steadily unfolding dramatic incident. She remains at the end what she was at the beginning. Judge Pyncheon, too, is unvaryingly "a picture rather than a character" (p. 101), an image in Hawthorne's mind. The realist would have given close and careful attention to his character's interaction with others, accounting for every reaction and response as, taken together, they build toward a completeness of characterization. Isabel Archer develops in this way, slowly and steadily, by the revelation of her psychology through social experience.

Hawthorne's failure at many points in his fiction to account for sharply specified motivation grows out of the limitations of the romance mode itself. His use of the letter A in *The Scarlet Letter* is at times too allegorical, and has, James says, nothing to do with "real psychology." In *The Marble Faun* Donatello is a charming conceit in his ambiguous representation as partly faun and partly modern-day Italian youth; but he is chiefly picturesque, being neither quite one thing nor the other, is "impalpable," and lacks psychological credibility. By "real psychology," of course, James refers to psychological realism, which engaged his own allegiances. The psychological realist, which James was, is a historian of motivation; the large plausibility he is concerned with is, almost of necessity, not achieved in Hawthorne's romances.

But although James asserts that Hawthorne was not in the least a realist, he seems to imply that, at various points in his career, Hawthorne made some effort to approach realism, or may have entertained some notion of realism as an alternative to romance. He remarks on the struggle in Hawthorne between his shyness and his desire to know something of life; Hawthorne's preface to *Twice-Told Tales,* in which he speaks of his attempt to open an intercourse with the world, is cited as an illustration. "We are speaking here," James observes, "of small things, it must be remembered—of little attempts, little sketches, a little world. But everything is relative, and this smallness of scale must not render less apparent the interesting character of Hawthorne's efforts" (p. 44). James seems conscious of *The House of the Seven Gables* and *The Blithedale Romance* as an effort to move at least part way into realism. He describes *The House of the Seven Gables* as reading more like a prologue to a great novel than a great novel itself, as if Hawthorne had some complicated purpose that reached beyond it and could have been achieved only in a fully realistic literature. While noting that there is too little of the interest of manners in *The Blithedale Romance,* James does acknowledge that the novel is now and then touched with the "light of the profane world—the vulgar, many-coloured world of actuality" (p. 105). Its most interesting characters are Miles Coverdale, who is no longer a disembodied spirit but a "particular man, with a certain human grossness" (p. 105); and Zenobia, who is the nearest approach Hawthorne made to the complete creation of a *person.* She is more "concrete" than Hawthorne's other heroines, and has been produced by a "greater multiplicity of touches." (p. 106). In such remarks James implies that Hawthorne had made some effort (which must have involved struggle) to revise his own romance mode into realism, a prophetic prelude to James's revision of Hawthorne's romance into realism, with which I will be concerned.

In the modern period, T. S. Eliot was one of the first to call attention to Hawthorne as James's "real progenitor." According to Eliot, Hawthorne's progenitor role did not have to do with influence specifically, but with a continuation of sensibility, "their indifference to religious dogma at the same time as their exceptional awareness of spiritual reality." In *American Renaissance* (1941) F. O. Matthiessen considers the relationship in more detail, remarking that James "began where Hawthorne left off" and carried his effects further. Matthiessen touches on the relationship lightly, although suggestively, and characterizes James's late trilogy of novels, in which his highly developed skills of representation were subordinated to the inner meanings they could symbolize, as being indebted to Hawthorne. Hawthorne, he comments, "is the direct ancestor of *The Golden Bowl*."[5]

More recently, in three chapters devoted to Hawthorne and James in *The Complex Fate*, Marius Bewley makes a considerably larger claim for Hawthorne's influence. "The influence of Hawthorne on James," he asserts, "is not only demonstrably far greater than in the case of [Flaubert, Turgenev, Maupassant, and Zola]: it was an influence that persisted to the end. . . . Its importance for James is to be gauged by the fact that Hawthorne was the great American predecessor, the only one through whose art he approached his own native tradition. . . . Hawthorne's methods of work, his moral preoccupations, the fundamental problems that confronted him as an artist in America, his attraction to a kind of allegory that was akin to symbolism, even to some extent the actual scenes and materials and types he chose to deal with, made a deep and lasting impression on James's 'fictions'." Bewley is emphatic in placing James's moral and esthetic concerns within the Hawthorne tradition. "To focus James's art against a background of continental writers," he remarks, "is not to focus it at all."[6]

Yet apart from the critical comments of Eliot, Matthiessen, and Bewley, less has been written on the relationship of Hawthorne and James than might be assumed. Hawthorne's relevance to James is generally acknowledged, but instead of the extended study or short book which Matthiessen, in *American Renaissance,* surmised could be written on the subject, there have been only a few essays and notes, and relatively brief passages in books (such as Buitenhuis's *The Grasping Imagination*)[7] generally dealing with other topics. The closest approach to an extended study is the Hawthorne and James section of Bewley's *The Complex Fate*, which has been disputed by other critics, particularly Leon Edel and Peter Buitenhuis. Both Edel and Buitenhuis find Bewley's claims for Hawthorne's influence exaggerated, often obscuring what seems to them the more significant effect on James of French realism. These critical disagreements do not begin to provide an adequate perspective on Hawthorne and James, but they raise some issues which I would like to consider. They raise the question of how deeply James was affected by an "internal" American tradition, represented by Hawthorne, and the question of how, if James's allegiances were with continental realism, he could have been affected by Hawthorne at the same time. It is, I think, possible to show how James responded to Hawthorne without slighting the role of European realism; and, without exaggerating, to claim for Hawthorne a major role in James's formative period. The relationship of Hawthorne and James is an elusive subject (at least until it has been brought into focus), and it will be necessary, in clarifying it, to be specific, to notice the evolution of James's conceptions and how these conceptions bear upon Hawthorne, ultimately revealing a steady pattern of confrontation and response.

11

In a letter of 1867 to Thomas Sergeant Perry, James wrote of his future direction as a writer, as it seemed to him then, in the following way:

When I say that I should like to do as Ste. Beuve has done, I don't mean that I should like to imitate him, or reproduce him in English; but only that I should like to acquire something of his intelligence and his patience and vigour. One feels—I feel at least, that he is a man of the past, of a dead generation; and that we young Americans are (without cant) men of the future. . . . We are Americans born. . . . I look upon it as a great blessing; and I think that to be an American is an excellent preparation for culture. We have exquisite qualities as a race, and it seems to me that we are ahead of the European races in the fact that more than either *[sic]* of them we can deal with forms of civilization not our own, can pick and choose and assimilate and in short (aesthetically etc.) claim our property wherever we find it. . . . We must of course have something of our own—something distinctive and homogenous—and I take it that we shall find it in our moral consciousness.[8]

The vocabulary James uses is revealing—*pick* and *choose, assimilate*. A letter written eight years later, on his return to England in 1875, begins: "I take possession of the old world—I inhale it—I appropriate it!"[9] Appropriation and assimilation are essential features of James's formative period. He drew upon different traditions at once, and in such a manner, that rather than cancelling each other out, they combined to form an art distinctively James's own.

James's assimilation of romance and realism appears throughout his earlier period—a period in which he undergoes his apprenticeship as an imaginative writer and achieves his first mastery in the novel; and in which Hawthorne's effect on him can be demonstrated in its most dramatic and revealing phase. This assimilation of romance and realism can be noticed not only in tales like "The Last of the Valerii" and "The Madonna of the Future," with their Hawthornesque quality and realistic observation, but also in his novels. It is a steady pattern that can be observed from the beginnings of James's career to *The Bostonians*. The pattern is not always obvious, particularly in view of the great differences that exist between Hawthorne's more primitive conceptions, and thinly specified social contexts, and James's characters and situations belonging to the world of the drawing room. But these differences are not absolute. Northrop Frye has described Hawthorne's characters as "stylized figures which expand into psychological archetypes,"[10] and it is because these conceptions were archetypal, providing prototype models of American experience, that they proved of irreplaceable value to James. Hawthorne's archetypes, or prototype models, could be and indeed were transformed by James repeatedly into social and psychological realism. These transformations reveal James's interpretive mind, but most of all they provide outline and definition to the relationship of Hawthorne and James.

12

2 James's Apprenticeship: The Hawthorne Aspect

Hawthorne's influence on James during his apprenticeship period has sometimes been assumed, but it has never been well outlined. In her early study *Henry James*, Rebecca West describes Hawthorne's influence on young James as "not altogether happy." "It was due to him," she points out, "that Mr. James's characters have 'almost wailed' their way from *The Passionate Pilgrim [sic]* to *The Golden Bowl* —but he certainly shepherded Mr. James into the European environment and lent him a framework on which to drape his emotions until he had discovered his own power to build an imaginative structure." Miss West does not examine any of the early stories in particular; her remarks are confined to a number of generalizations about them which are shrewd but rather oversimplified. In *The Great Tradition*, published during the James revival after World War II, F. R. Leavis regards Hawthorne's influence on the early James as being both formative and constructive. He believes that Hawthorne led James away from the English tradition, represented by Thackeray, into an American mode of poetic fiction that probes the moral and psychological. "The more we consider James's early work," he writes, "the more important does Hawthorne's influence appear."[1] Leavis's reading of James is better informed than Miss West's, but it lacks what James once called "solidity of specification." He does not demonstrate where and how Hawthorne's influence can be seen in the early stories. More recently, in *The Grasping Imagination*, Peter Buitenhuis has discussed some of James's early stories and attempted to be specific about Hawthorne's effect on them. In a seven-page chapter devoted to Hawthorne and James, he treats three stories which reveal Hawthorne's influence and touches very lightly on three others. Buitenhuis's criticism is clear and intelligent, but as a survey of Hawthorne and the early James, his brief chapter still leaves much unsaid.

As I will be considering it, James's apprenticeship covers a period of approximately ten years, from the end of the Civil War to 1875, when he published *Roderick Hudson*, his first "real" novel. He wrote prolifically during this period, but much of what he produced was travel writing and literary criticism. In all, he published twenty-seven stories during the ten-year period, an average of two or three stories a year, which suggests a rather hesitant beginning. His stories during the later 1860s are his feeblest, carefully written and constructed, but rather prim and pale. They have a French lucidity, an accuracy of psychological observation, and are all concerned with social relationships. Relationships between the sexes have a primary importance, and often James's male characters face various hazards, including death itself, in their contact with women. Such hazards of encounter are present in "The Story of a Year" (1865), which is narrated realistically but has an elusive kinship with Hawthorne.[2]

"The Story of a Year" begins in a Hawthornesque manner, as James refers to his tale as a "romance" and proceeds to speak of "a certain young couple I wot of." The story is set during the Civil War, although the war does not have a very strong reality, even as a distant background. What is more real is the small group of four characters, and their psychological relationships to one another. As the story opens, John Ford and Elizabeth Crowe take a "sunset walk" that foreshadows Ford's later death, ostensibly as the result of wounds received in the war. Elizabeth waits in their New England village while Ford is in the army, but she is not emotionally or intellectually deep, and later she feels the attraction of another man, Robert Bruce. The wounded Ford returns to the village gravely ill

and dies, although not entirely of his physical wounds, after he recognizes that Elizabeth has changed. He wishes to be disinterested
and self-sacrificing, and asks her not to mourn for him, but rather to
marry and lead a normal life. In the final passage, calling at the Ford
house, Bruce is described as "a tall figure beneath the budding trees
of the garden" (p. 97), and is thus linked with germination and the
natural world. By contrast, Ford is compared to a "wounded Greek,
who at falling dusk has crawled into a temple to die, steeping the
last dull interval in idle admiration of sculptured Artemis" (p. 96).
Artemis, associated with chastity and the moon (imagination), is
Ford's *real* lover, not Miss Crowe, who belongs to the world. Engagement and withdrawal or renunciation, a theme prominent in
James's later career, is present at the very beginning.

James had not read *Fanshawe* when he wrote "The Story of a
Year," but it is worth noting that the theme of the first story to
which he signed his name is quite similar to that of Hawthorne's in
his first attempt at fiction. Both of their heroes seem disqualified
from participation in the active world and eventually retire into
death. Fanshawe at one point rescues Ellen Langton, but instead of
marrying her, as he could easily do, withdraws to his solitary
studies; pale and wasted, he sinks poignantly into an early grave.
Ellen later marries the "normal" man, Edward Walcott. Mysteriously inward, Fanshawe is the first of Hawthorne's male characters
who, with a puritan fastidiousness, shrink from a coarse exposure to
life, retire into a strange solitude, or become socially alienated artists
of the exquisite or detached spectators who observe others whose
lives seem more real to them than their own. In "The Story of a
Year" James's first hero, although more realistically dressed, comes
from this same cultural stock. Moreover, the interest of the story is
psychological, and involves the use, somewhat primitive as yet, of
dream psychology, symbolism, and light versus dark imagery
(Ford's pallor, and Lizzie Crowe's dark hair and name). James bores
into Lizzie's mind and inner states and probes her rudimentary soul.
Her soul is searched also by the two "conscious" characters in the
story, Ford and his mother. "Of the full extent of Mrs. Ford's observation," James remarks, "I think Lizzie was hardly aware. She

was like a reveller in a brilliantly lighted room, with a curtainless window. . . . And Mrs. Ford may not inaptly be compared to the chilly spectator on the dark side of the pane" (p. 65). Much of the interest of the story, as in Hawthorne, is with the inner mind rather than the outward life.

In two other of the earliest stories, James appears to have derived his characters' names from Hawthorne. In "A Landscape-Painter" (1866) the young woman's name is Miriam, and there is about her a hint of the "dark lady" quality of Miriam in *The Marble Faun*. She is described as having "a great deal of wavy black hair, which encircles her head like a dusky glory, a smoky halo" (p. 107). By the end, she outwits her male counterpart and secures his fortune by marrying him. In "Poor Richard" (1867) Richard Maule has hopes that never prosper, and his adverse fate is underscored by his name Maule, like that of the afflicted Maule line in *The House of the Seven Gables*. Another of the earliest tales, "The Story of a Masterpiece" (1868), resembles Hawthorne's work in more than names since its most likely source is his story "The Prophetic Pictures." In "The Prophetic Pictures" an artist with the power of seeing into "the inmost soul" of those he represents on canvas paints the portraits of a young couple about to be married. It is intimated, ambiguously, that he may possess prophetic powers, so that what he paints will alter and influence the future of his models. As Elinor and Walter first see the portraits, they are pleased; but on a second viewing Elinor is aware of a sadness in her portrait, and Walter of something rather ominous in his. As time goes on the portrait expressions deepen and confirm an impending act of violence of Walter upon Elinor. At the romantic center of the story is the notion of the painting as having a magical property, and of the painter as a wizard or possessor of souls, a conception that is held in check, however, by Hawthorne's ambiguity. In "The Story of a Masterpiece" James begins with an opening similar to Hawthorne's; a young couple is about to be married, and an artist paints a portrait of the bride-to-be, Miss Marian Everett. Her fiancé, John Lennox, is disturbed by the portrait, and wonders if the painter has not revealed her soul, exposing a heartlessness in her that he had not suspected. The question is raised as to the reliability of

16

the painter's vision; and later it comes out that he had known Miss Everett in Europe and been jilted by her for a man with better prospects. The probing of her character continues until there is little doubt left that she is less than what Lennox had hoped. He goes through with the marriage, but slashes the mocking portrait to shreds with a knife. There is a romantic insinuation in the story that the painting has assumed Marian's soul, but James has explained the portrait's grip on Lennox in a realistic way, making it fix a suspicion already lodged in his mind until it becomes an obsession. The story, and its prophetic portrait idea, may have had a romantic source in Hawthorne, yet James's treatment is distinctively realistic.

James's next two stories, however, are written in a romantic, indeed, a gothic mode. "The Romance of Certain Old Clothes" (1868) begins with the sentence: "Toward the middle of the eighteenth century there lived in the Province of Massachusetts a widowed gentlewoman" (p. 297), and is strikingly reminiscent of Hawthorne's colonial fables. "Indeed," Matthiessen has remarked, "you can hardly see anything else [except Hawthorne] in it."[3] Like Hawthorne, James creates a middle ground between the solidly real and the spectral, playing one off against the other in an atmosphere of unsettling eeriness. The story is skillfully narrated, but it reads too much like a highly adept imitation of another writer's work, and the ending, with the ghostly fingerprints on the throat of the usurper bride, seems forced.

Its companion story, "De Grey: A Romance" (1868), is set in America during the Federal period, and deals with an ancestral curse upon a house. Here, too, James's conception belongs to a received mode and has all the trappings of the gothic romance—an ancient family line afflicted by a strange curse, a large secluded house in the country dominated by an atmosphere of impending doom, the introduction of a young woman as the bride of the youth who is the last of his line, and who dies at the climax of mounting suspense crying, "I belong, by I don't know what fatal, inexorable ties, to darkness and death and nothingness" (p. 427). James has one of his characters assert at the end that Paul De Grey's death was the result merely of a fall from his horse, and occurred under no "supernatural pressure";

17

by this means he attempts to conclude on a note of ambiguity, somewhat like Hawthorne, but his ambiguity is weak since his gothicism has already passed beyond qualification. "The Romance of Certain Old Clothes" and "De Grey: A Romance" may have been attempts to reach a larger audience; but they appear also to suggest James's doubt that he had found an adequate emotional richness in his rather stiffly proficient stories of the later 1860s. There seems some uncertainty in his mind as to how he ought to proceed. He next writes "Osborne's Revenge," a fully realistic story set in contemporary America, and then "Gabrielle de Bergerac," a lush historical romance reminiscent of George Sand, set in eighteenth-century France.

The stories of the 1860s seem somewhat like exercises, or experiments in form, first attempts in different modes of fiction. "A Light Man" (1869), however, is a step forward, and shows a new boldness of conception.[4] In it James addresses himself as a realist to psychological oddity. There is a French influence on "A Light Man," for the story is written in the form of a self-revealing diary, but at the same time Hawthorne's influence can be detected, since James's protagonist derives from one of Hawthorne's great character types, the egotist-violator. He is present here as Maximus Austin, but will appear again, in more mature form, as Austin Sloper in *Washington Square,* and again as Gilbert Osmond in *The Portrait of a Lady*. The plot of "A Light Man" might suggest a stage melodrama—a malleable patron, the destruction of a will, a trusting friend betrayed and disinherited, Maximus at the end contemplating a mercenary marriage. Yet James deals with this material in a way that reverses melodramatic expectations. The expectation his situation arouses of fierce and exaggerated passions is undercut ironically by the passionlessness of all the characters, particularly the narrator. Maximus continually mocks the melodramatic role he plays, so that he seems an archvillain only in a make-believe way. He speaks, for example, of "my villainous self grinning at [the old man's] bedside" (p. 91), and describes himself as a crafty "egotist."

The psychological interest of the story stems from James's ambiguous treatment of Maximus, whose wit deflates the notion of a moral universe, but who is yet judged morally by James. He is a ver-

18

sion of Hawthorne's intellectual investigator who violates the sanctity of another's being for the sake of a psychological experiment; yet his romance villain role is subjected to such irony that his manipulation of the other characters seems at times more mirthful than terrible. In his younger days the human spectacle had provided him with what he calls "a certain entertainment" (p. 73), but he is now so jaded that he can amuse himself only by manipulating old Sloane and Theodore, both of whom have made personal sacrifices for him. At one point he describes Sloane in his library as he "rose from his chair—the man of fancy, to greet me—the man of fact" (p. 66). What is implied by his being a man of "fact," however, is that he has no soul, and can discern none in anyone else.

As the story progresses Maximus confides to his diary that Sloane "amuses me"; having gained his affection, he tells him that he is going away—to see how he will react, and particularly whether he will be jolted into altering his will. Sloane suffers a stroke in his bed upon hearing that Maximus is leaving, after which Maximus makes an entry in his diary recording the new "sensation" Sloane has afforded him: "I shall probably never again have such a sensation as I enjoyed tonight—actually feel a heated human heart throbbing and turning and struggling in my grasp; know its pants, it spasms, its convulsions, and its final senseless quiescence" (p. 89). What his entry actually records is Maximus's enactment of Hawthorne's Unpardonable Sin, intellectual pride or the separation of the head from the heart, together with his violation in cold blood of another's being. Yet James's irony prevents Maximus from becoming a "fiend," for he is capable neither of passion nor of recognition. He is worldliness reduced·to an essence of negativity, and his fate will be to remain always a "light man," or what Dostoyevsky calls "a moral idiot." James's irony in the story shows considerable sophistication. Sloane and Theodore, characters who lack awareness of evil (interestingly, Sloane is an inveterate reader of Emerson), are played off against the protagonist, who represents consciousness and knowledge but has no use for them except to injure others. Moreover, the readers's response is complicated by James's having manipulated him to feel an identification with Maximus, the man of superior intellect—a strat-

19

egy James later refines upon with Austin Sloper. Even more to the point, James's incorporation of a romance conception of Hawthorne's into a realistic story concerned with differing perspectives, and edged with irony, begins a pattern of mutation that can be noticed in the next stories he writes.

James's next story, "Travelling Companions" (1870), draws upon his travel impressions of Europe during his Grand Tour of 1868–1869, and has a special interest insofar as it is his first realistic story set on European soil and his first attempt to portray the American girl abroad. In this richly sensuous Italian setting (distinctly different from the cold Protestant North), James's American characters seem never completely at ease. Charlotte Evans, from Araminta, New Jersey, is accompanied by her father, and in Milan she meets the narrator, Mr. Brooke, an American who has lately been educated in Germany. The story begins in Milan, then moves to Vincenza, Venice, Padua, and finally Rome. Charlotte is described as having the "frankness and freedom" of the American girl, and in Milan she goes about unescorted. She becomes involved in a *contretemps* in Padua when she misses the last train and stays overnight at a local inn, where Brooke stays also; according to the custom of the country, her virtue has been compromised by their staying at the inn together. At approximately the same time, Brooke has been reading Hawthorne. He points out to Charlotte with unobtrusive casualness, that "Rappaccini's Daughter" is set in Padua, an allusion that underscores the idea of a maiden's purity despite outward appearances which seem to condemn her. The allusion, however, involves more than a witty comparison, for Hawthorne is present in the story in another way, in James's conception of Charlotte Evans. She is a serious-minded American girl who responds with appreciation to the sensuous richness of Italy, and yet also resists it, fearing its tendency to pervert the stern truths of her native Protestantism. Following a series of disturbing experiences, including the death of her father, she is seen at a prayer bench in St. Peter's in Rome, offering up "half-prayers." What is striking about James's depiction of Charlotte is her similarity, on a realistic level, to Hawthorne's Hilda in *The Marble Faun*. She has many essential likenesses to Hilda—her going about alone and unchaperoned, her morally guarded response to Italy, her half-way gesture to Catholicism in St. Peter's while yet retaining her American Protestant beliefs. In his first attempt to envision the American girl abroad, James refashioned an earlier model in Hawthorne.

"A Light Man" and "Travelling Companions" may seem to have little relation to one another, but they are related in James's concern with alternative modes of perception. In "A Light Man" James brings a character who possesses worldly consciousness into close proximity with two other characters who are innocent of the world or of evil; in "Travelling Companions" he places an American girl in a context of worldly knowledge implied in the Italian setting. She is an American innocent, and touches upon the experience of Europe only lightly. Yet there is a lurking sense of its danger; her "safe" marriage at the end to Mr. Brooke is a kind of rescue. In both of these encounters between innocence and knowledge, James refers to psychological models in Hawthorne. He brings a sharper focus to his material than he had in the early stories of the 1860s and at the same time begins to develop his powers of subtlety and irony. Approaching closer to Hawthorne than he had previously, James begins to find a new certainty of direction.

21

Interestingly, all of James's best stories of the 1870–1875 period, introduced by "Travelling Companions," have a quite definite relation of some kind to Hawthorne. "A Passionate Pilgrim" (1871), which immediately follows "Travelling Companions," derives from Hawthorne's experience in England. In his *English Notebooks* Hawthorne remarks on the inn where he stays, and the countryside around it, that "it is entirely English, and like nothing in America; and yet I feel as if I might have lived here a long while ago, and had now come back because I retained pleasant recollections of it." In *Our Old Home* he elaborates further on the phenomenon of "American appetite for English soil," citing a number of cases which came to his attention, as the American consul at Liverpool, of Americans who "cherished a fantastic notion" of a rightful claim to an English estate. One such man was confirmed in his notion by his own striking resemblance to a portrait in the picture gallery of the estate to which he believed he had a claim. Another was a New England shopkeeper who had traveled impetuously to England to pursue his claim, a pathetic figure with a "foolish kind of pathos" entangled in his delusion. Hawthorne concludes that "after all these . . . vindictive animosities, we have still an unspeakable yearning toward England."[5]

James's Clement Searle is an American claimant of the kind Hawthorne describes, with a "foolish kind of pathos" entangled in his delusion. He yearns for England and feels that his life in America has been a mistake, making him an exile from his rightful home. His claim to an English estate, however, is so improbable that he seems like a dreamer caught between two worlds, one which he rejects and the other which rejects him. "I have always fancied," Searle remarks to the narrator, "that I was meant for a gentler world. . . . I was born with a soul for the picturesque" (p. 245). In fact, it is the picturesqueness, the scenic sense, of England that James evokes so affectingly, giving the story much of its richness. The story begins realistically, but at Lockely Park becomes partly a romance, complete with ghosts of the past and portraits that resemble Clement and Margaret Searle and have histories that complement theirs.

There is also a romance villain in the person of Richard Searle, Clement's English cousin, a diminutive gentleman with a "preternatural redness of his hair and beard," which surround his head "like a huge lurid nimbus" (p. 267). From a distance he has an appearance of innocence, but closer up seems aged and cunning; his eyes have a "vulpine keenness and redness" (p. 267). This fox-like man is seen with his back to the others, as he holds a Venetian hand-mirror in such a position that he can observe his sister's face when Clement Searle speaks to her. This indication of his sneakiness seems rather comic, like something out of a particularly bad melodrama. It is surprising that with such machinery James could have been able to endow his romance of Clement and Margaret with the degree of charm it has. He is able to do so partly because he has drawn them as fireside ghosts themselves, or as fairy-tale figures who enforce a willing suspension of disbelief. Clement kisses Margaret at one point, and at that moment she is the Belle au Bois Dormant, an ironically demure version of Sleeping Beauty awakened by her prince, even as Margaret's England has brought Clement to spiritual awakening.[6]

22

Their romance is platonic, and neither gains from it materially; yet it makes all the difference in their lives, which have hitherto been stifled by their circumstances, both American and English. Their lives are small and touching, and like the portrait ghosts they are exiles from the house, insofar as it stands for the heavy weight of material reality, or the idea of proprietorship only, as it does for Margaret's brother, who has kept her down. There is a primitiveness in James's depiction of Clement and Margaret Searle as characters who are "fine," and so are not destined to command, but to have a poignant moment of heightened awareness; yet they represent a theme James will explore later with authority.

James himself should not be identified with Clement Searle, for Searle sees England only as romance, and is described by James as a "vision-haunted knight of La Mancha" (p. 288). His pilgrimage at each stage is undercut by irony. At the beginning the London inn is beguilingly reminiscent of Dr. Johnson's eighteenth-century world, but it is here that the lawyer Simmons, an American who has successfully adjusted to England by enjoying roast beef and being sharp in business, tells Searle that his claim is visionary and that he does not know England or Englishmen. At Hampton Court, James evokes the poetry of the aristocratic past, but at the same time a tramp appears to beg a coin, and is a reminder of lower-class misery that exists side by side (as it had historically) with upper-class privilege. Lockely Park has the charm of the English country estate, but it also represents "the stern English fact of property" (p. 252) (the name *Lockely* implies that the estate is gated and closed to outsiders). Finally, Oxford is the most richly evoked of all, but these evocations are implied to be merely "a delightful lie . . . [a] sweet illusion" (p. 293), a veneer concealing a constriction of personal development in a class-regulated society. Rawson, one of Oxford's graduates and Searle's other self, is now a humble bath-chair attendant who longs to find opportunities in America. The romance of England, as seen through the eyes of Clement Searle, is continually called into question by a pervasive imagery of enclosure and a narrow confinement. By the end England seems a mirage of a perfect and realizable human fulfillment.

"A Passionate Pilgrim" is James's first important story, and Hawthorne's perception which inspired it is a reminder of the shared sensibility of Hawthorne and James, the tension felt in both writers between old-world richness and American austerity. And while Clement Searle is not James himself, he is a figure who suggests the alienation of the American writer in the nineteenth century. The atmosphere of an ethereal delicacy in the story is reminiscent of Hawthorne, too, particularly of the sense in Hawthorne of a spiritual reality, or spiritual ideal, that seems to stand above material reality. In this way Hawthorne has an affinity with the story that suggests a kinship between him and the youthful James. It is a kinship, however, that also involves a difference between them, for James emerges in the story as an accomplished ironist, concerned with symmetrical relationships of his characters and their differing points of view. James himself remains detached in "A Passionate Pilgrim," and his intelligence, somewhat dry or cold, works against romantic assumptions, creating a final sense of ambiguity. With this story James's critical scrutiny of a delicately spiritual ideal becomes an increasing preoccupation.

His next story, "The Madonna of the Future" (1873), is a variation on the same theme and has similar motifs—the pilgrimage idea, and the quixotism of an American solitary abroad.[7] Like "A Passionate Pilgrim," "The Madonna of the Future" occupies a middle ground between realism and romance. Its apparent source is Balzac's tale "Le Chef d'oeuvre inconnu," a *conte fantastique* which deals with the old artist Frenhofer, who has spent fourteen years working on a portrait, seeking perfection and "divine vision," and yet ends by producing only "confused masses of color and a multitude of fantastical lines." At the end, he awakens to the grotesqueness of his deception and within a few days dies of grief. Frenhofer, the admirer of Raphael and his madonnas, is James's model for Theobald, who also has not learned, as Balzac says, that "painters have no business to think except brush in hand."[8] But in adapting Balzac's tale James also transforms it, moving his setting from Paris at the turn of the seventeenth century to contemporary Florence, and making his story concern a group of Americans in Italy. His central figure, Theobald, is a version of Clement Searle, a gentle and pathetic Quixote who communes with the vanished past rather than present fact. He is an exile first from his American homeland ("our silent past, our deafening present, the constant pressure about us of unlovely circumstance, are . . . void of all that nourishes and prompts and inspires the artist" [p. 15]), and then is an exile in Florence.

In the opening scene the narrator encounters Theobald at night, a solitary figure in the moonlight, communing with the statues near the Palazzo Vecchio. He wears a medieval biretta (the cap of the clergy), but in his case it denotes his affiliation with the religion of art. They talk together while they look up at the statues, "seeing nothing but overwhelming greatness and dimness" (p. 13), an ironic comment on the inspiring presence yet irrecoverable remoteness of the more spiritual past. In another meeting, soon after the first, Theobald discourses on Raphael and his supremely spiritual painting, the *Madonna of the Chair*. But somewhat later the narrator visits *25* the American Mrs. Coventry, in whose salon the conversation is said to be not as good as the tea, and he notes that she wears a "huge" miniature copy of this painting on her bosom. Mrs. Coventry is a spurious, salon version of the Blessed Virgin; but when Theobald's model is introduced, the "Blessed Virgin" idea undergoes an even sharper devaluation. She is a figure ironic even in her name, Seraphina, associating her with the highest order of angels. The first meeting with her is sufficient to reveal that whatever spiritual grace she may once have possessed is now fled; she has grown heavy and "coarse." But it is the second meeting with her that is devastating. She is seated in a chair, holding in her lap a plate of smoking macaroni. "She had lifted high in air *[sic]* one of the pendulous filaments of this succulent compound," James remarks, "and was in the act of slipping it gently down her throat" (p. 39).

The "Madonna Seraphina" has allowed Theobald to visit her over the course of twenty years, to study the nuances of her spiritual beauty before committing her likeness to canvas. In return, he has been, as she says, her "benefactor." Her companion, and obviously her lover, is a man with "a sharp black eye" who also designates himself an artist. He greets the narrator with an amiable twisting of his mustache, since "he knew a money-spending *forestiere* when he saw one" (p. 40). He is a contriver of ingenious statuettes of monkeys and cats, arranged in bizarre and amorous conjunctions luridly suggestive of men and women. After Theobald's death, which follows his awakening at last to his delusion, the twenty years that passed while he was lost in contemplation of a virgin who grew old and soiled, the narrator walks by a shop and notices this man again, selling his humorous statuettes and repeating his earlier words: "Cats and monkeys, monkeys and cats; all human life is there!" (p. 52). He is the voice of the marketplace, the man who thrives, as Theobald so totally fails. The place assigned to him at the end, the way in which he acts as a concluding chorus, gives him a triumphant role as a mocker of innocence, certainly of Theobald's.

James's ending distinctly recalls Hawthorne, whose solitary and delicately organized idealists are mocked by skeptics and materialists. In "Rappaccini's Daughter," for example, Dr. Baglioni, the materialist, standing in a Gothic doorway, speaks the final words of vindication and triumph with the effect of a concluding chorus. Most of all, James's Theobald has a kinship with Hawthorne's artist-outcast Owen Warland in "The Artist of the Beautiful." Warland strives for spiritual perfection in his small, exquisite creations, which are wholly irrelevant to the other characters. His character opposite is Robert Danforth, the blacksmith who serves the community in a mundane way and is respected and rewarded. Warland is condescended to by his former employer, Peter Hovenden, and more subtly by Hovenden's daughter Annie; and it is the blacksmith, not the artist of the beautiful, whom she marries. Poor and alone, Warland labors for five years to create a mechanical butterfly, endowing it seemingly with a soul; but the butterfly is destroyed in a moment by the clutch of the blacksmith's infant—while Hovenden emits "a cold and scornful laugh." The mockery of Hawthorne's artist of the delicately spiritual is implicit in James's conception of Theobald in "The Madonna of the Future," which also deals with one of Hawthorne's most immediately recognizable themes, the shock of encounter between innocence and experience.

Yet James has also subjected his Hawthornesque conception of the

26

spiritually alienated artist to the scrutiny of his irony. In this tale poignancy is checked by intelligence, and it is intelligence that Theobald so disastrously lacks. His failure as an artist is due not merely to his having allowed too much time to pass without producing results; it is, more importantly, due to his inability to see what is immediately before him. Seraphina knows that she is not the ideal vision he contemplates, but allows him to go on for years being her "benefactor." Rather than typifying the spiritual in woman, she is a worldly exploiter, specifically of Theobald. Although having the form of a *conte fantastique*, "The Madonna of the Future" has more universal implications of real social experience in which discrimination plays a determining role. Theobald's experience of Europe, and his failed discrimination, will be refocused several years later in the frostily ironic and fully realistic story "Four Meetings."

In its mingling of romance and realism and its introduction of an American innocent in Italy, "The Last of the Valerii" (1874) is a companion story to "The Madonna of the Future." Its immediate source is Mérimée's tale "The Venus of Ille," which James had translated into English in his early twenties. In Mérimée's story a statue of Venus, unearthed in a French provincial village, appears all but living and gives the sense of a "terrible beauty" united with "an utter absence of goodness." Mérimée skillfully evokes the menace of the pagan statue, particularly of her jealousy, which would be fatal to anyone seeming to betray her love. He insinuates that her favor has fallen on young Alphonse de Peyrehorade, who on his wedding night is crushed to death by what appears, in the dimness of the bridal chamber, to be the statue. Although the plot of "The Venus of Ille" is implausible, the story is remarkable for its compelling atmosphere of brooding menace, an atmosphere made to seem believable by the coldness and objectivity of Mérimée's narration. In "The Last of the Valerii" James draws from Mérimée's plot and also uses his narrative procedure in which the sensational is chastened by objective realism.

But in reshaping Mérimée's material, James again affiliates himself with Hawthorne. James moves his setting from Mérimée's French provincial village to Rome, the setting of *The Marble Faun*, and, like

Hawthorne, evokes its ancient past in such a way that it seems capable of reentering the present. His young man, too, has a conceptual similarity to Hawthorne's Donatello, in the sense that he has a personal affinity with the pre-Christian past. Donatello and Count Valerii, or Camillo, are both the last of their line, extending far back into the ancient past, and are depicted in a double perspective of the present and of a not completely extinct antiquity.

Hawthorne plays upon Donatello's resemblance to the Faun of Praxiteles, particularly in the detail of the faun's ears, which Donatello's ample locks may possibly conceal; and James, more ominously, insinuates the period of the Roman Empire (and its cruel passions) through Camillo's physical appearance. He is handsome, with "a sunken depth of expression, and a grave, slow smile, suggesting . . . an . . . intensity of feeling" (p. 89). Having a head and throat seen in ancient busts, his figure is manly and powerful. Raised as a Catholic, he admits that the church is incomprehensible to him; even as a child, he could not learn his catechism, so that his old confessor pronounced him "a pagan." The narrator remarks that it is fortunate he is good-natured, because he has no natural moral sense to keep him in line. His pagan origins are the more pronounced because of his physical contrast with his fiancée, a pale American girl, a "princess" of the new world, who casts "dovelike glances" (p. 89) upon him. After their marriage Camillo and the innocent Martha settle at the Villa Valerio, which is gradually being reclaimed from its antique decay. The villa is described as being haunted with historic echoes. Its statues seem to brood in a perpetual twilight, to have strange secrets, and to whisper to their fellows below ground.

The central section of the story is set in the garden of the villa, where excavations are going on; and here James heightens the sense of the "evil germs" of the past lurking in Camillo through a muted use of Roman mythology. The individual in charge of the excavations, for example, is a grotesque little man who seems full of mockery, as if he knew that what lay beneath the garden boded ill. James calls him "an earthy gnome of the underworld" (p. 99), and as such he is a mythological being, one of the diminutive, subterranean crea-

28

tures of fable who guard mines and quarries. When a statue of Juno is unearthed, a German archaeologist, who has heard of the find, appears to ask about it. He is convinced the statue is a Proserpine (associated with darkness and the infernal regions). He is sent away, however, and told that there has been no discovery of a statue. Camillo hoards the figure to himself, locking her in the Casino, a deserted garden house, and paying her solitary visits. One evening the narrator finds him alone in the garden, staring at a statue of Hermes in a cluster of oleander (a poisonous shrub). Hermes has many associations. He was the god of treasure trove, and of magic and dreams, and has a connection with the erotic, particularly with Aphrodite. As the messenger of the gods he was qualified to control the souls of the dead and guide them to Hades, and so became known as the "Conductor of Souls." Communing under the starlight with the statue of Hermes, Camillo has begun to envision "the old feasts and the old worship" (p. 108). Thereafter, with his increasingly strange behavior—his appearance of worshipping at the Pantheon, his prostration before the statue of Juno, and, finally, the evidence that he has made a blood sacrifice to her—the narrator exclaims that Count Valerii "has crossed the Acheron" (p. 117). 29

Camillo's descent into the "underworld" of a pagan past (in Freudian terms, the "id") involves James's use of a gothic mode. He creates an atmosphere of supernatural agencies at work, and of an impending but nameless menace; it is intimated, in part, by the freeing of pagan sexual energy, associated with the statue goddess, who "possesses" Camillo's body and mind in the form of psychic enslavement. Camillo's "possession" is heightened in its effect by the presence of his American bride, whose "yellow locks" are a contrast to his "dusky" ones, and who "worships" Camillo innocently, with an unconsciousness of evil. The situation between them is a variation of a classic gothic situation—a strange and spooked Italian castle, a blonde maiden who has recently become a bride and is unwitting of the peril she may be in. In the end, of course, James creates a gothic nightmare only to dispel it. The old gods do not live; Camillo's infatuation is a "delusion" of which he is cured when the statue is once again buried; and his devotion returns to his pale

American bride. With consummate irony, James suggests that a subterranean darkness no longer exists in the modern world. "The Last of the Valerii" is not a reversion on the part of James to his early experiments in the gothic mode of the 1860s; it is the work of an urbane intelligence and is fully controlled in its ambiguity and power of suggestion. Part of its power of suggestion is the hint of an allegory that has not yet taken shape, one that has to do with American innocence as it comes into a dangerous proximity to deep Roman knowledge. Indeed, James's story takes place largely in a Roman garden that Hawthorne would have recognized as a ruined Eden.

But if Hawthorne's shadow looms over "The Last of the Valerii," the story is merely one of a group of tales James wrote at that time involving a character's psychic bondage to another. In "Professor Fargo" (1874) this theme has been given expression on American soil. A possible source for the tale is Turgenev's "A Strange Story," in which a narrator relates a disturbing experience he has witnessed. He encounters a weird, vagrant mesmerist who has, or seems to have, the power of communicating mystical experience. At the same time, he is introduced to the daughter of a wealthy and landed family, a girl with a "child-like face and soul impenetrable as stone." Later he meets the mesmerist–religious maniac elsewhere and finds that the girl now accompanies him, apparently revering him and humbling herself before him as his body servant. James may well have drawn from Turgenev's grotesque tale for his situation of an innocent girl's bondage to a strange, itinerant mesmerist; but in his handling of this situation he is influenced by Hawthorne and his conception of a mesmerist and passive maiden in New England in *The Blithedale Romance*.[9]

Professor Fargo is first seen in a small New England town, where in the town hall, adorned tellingly with a dingy and tattered American flag, he is preparing to perform. His posters announce: "A MESSAGE FROM THE SPIRIT WORLD . . . A NEW REVELATION! A NEW SCIENCE" (p. 260–61). Performing with him, through the necessity of his poverty, is the old-fashioned, gentle Colonel Gifford (described in the imagery of the knight of La Mancha), who does rapid mathematical calculations, and his daughter, "an exquisite creature of seventeen, who has all the childish grace and serenity of Mignon, in 'Wilhelm Meister,' as we see her grouped with the old harper" (p. 271). The narrator expresses his skepticism early, but out of curiosity attends a performance at which Fargo practices animal magnetism, which he calls "spiritual magnetism," and discourses on "the summer land" (as Mrs. Ada T. P. Foat will do later in *The Bostonians*). As a public performer whose "professor" title and spiritual claims are fraudulent, Professor Fargo is distinctly reminiscent of Hawthorne's Westervelt in *The Blithedale Romance*. The "new revelations" and "new science" they both speak of (their vocabulary is identical) are made to seem questionable even by their physical appearance, particularly in the impudence that shows na-kedly in their eyes. Westervelt is a wizard with a darkly unspecified past who belongs to a gothic convention; yet James has managed to imagine him in a more realistic form, to make him socially credible as a traveling charlatan, spawned by American social conditions at their imagined worst.

31

The story moves from the seedy New England village (which has the dilapidated vacancy of Hawthorne's village in "Ethan Brand") to New York City, and the grim, unprosperous misery of Excelsior Hall. In New York the act fails to pay the bills of the performers, but Fargo is undaunted and soon has a new scheme of performing, with the colonel's daughter as his mesmeric subject. He visits her alone, and by some means (there is a strong suggestion of sexual tampering) gains control over her volition, a turn of events that sends the colonel to an asylum, his mind shattered. His daughter is now left without a protector, a vulnerability made more striking by her infirmity, by the fact that she is deaf and dumb! All that is ex-quisite in her will now, presumably, be turned into the trash of pub-licity; and thus Fargo will in effect annihilate her soul. At the end the reader is left to imagine their future life together, but its cruel nature has already been intimated in an early allusion to Fargo as "cracking the ring-master's whip at the circus, while Mlle Josephine jumped through the hoops" (p. 261). The image is additionally un-savory since Fargo wears "fleshings," or flesh-colored tights, as he brandishes the whip, implying a sexual bondage. A gothic chill stands behind the conclusion of the story, but it is felt largely as a social shudder—at Fargo and the morally aimless and exploitative world that produced him. This world is, in fact, American democracy, and it is in the democratic conditions which account for Fargo that James gives his mesmeric sham a larger social relevance and typicality than Hawthorne had done with Professor Westervelt (a relevance that James will elaborate upon later in *The Bostonians*).

After producing a group of tales with closely related themes, James struck out in a new direction. In his next story, "Madame de Mauves" (1874), he orchestrated his international theme in a fully realistic context. "Madame de Mauves" is set in France and shows a French lucidity and an assured accuracy in its treatment of manners. The young American woman in the story, Madame de Mauves, née Euphemia Cleve, marries "an unclean Frenchman," acting on a romantic belief that "the best birth is the guaranty of an ideal delicacy of feeling" (p. 129). She is a precursor of Isabel Archer in *The Portrait of a Lady*, a daughter of the Transcendentalists' elevated mode of thought. James remarks that "even after experience had given her a hundred rude hints, she found it easier to believe in fables, when they had a certain nobleness of meaning, then in well-attested but sordid facts" (pp. 129–130). M. de Mauves disappoints her expectations, being a Frenchman who loves pleasure and keeps mistresses. His attitudes are easy and natural, hers morally idealistic and inflexible. Interposed between them is Longmore, an American strongly attracted to Madame de Mauves; at a certain point M. de Mauves actually encourages him to become his wife's lover, so that he will no longer have to answer to her moral superiority. Longmore, however, is scrupulous and hesitating; and in his inner conflict—his attraction to and yet recoil from the world and the flesh—he seems like one of Arthur Dimmesdale's descendants.

At the height of his conflict he visits the French countryside, where it comes over him that life is meant for pleasure, for enjoyment, not renunciation. His Victorian training has taught him the importance of self-denial, but he now dreams of "rebellion." He wanders into a woods and finding a shady spot lies down and has a disturbing dream. In the dream he catches sight of a woman and

32

hurries forward to meet her; but as he approaches, she is suddenly on the opposite side of the stream. She looks at him gravely, pityingly, and does not encourage him to cross. A boat appears and takes him to the opposite shore, but now the woman—Madame de Mauves—is on the other side. And as he recognizes the boatman as M. de Mauves, he awakens. The forest into which Longmore enters, and the dream he has there that is set in another forest, suggesting illicit passion, belong to the imagination of Hawthorne, and most particularly to his forest scenes in *The Scarlet Letter*. In that novel the forest beyond the community holds ambiguous meanings; it is natural and good, unperverted by man's artificial system, and yet it is also a moral wilderness inhabited by the Black Man of the forest. In the forest Dimmesdale meets Hester Prynne, who lets down her hair in the luxurious sunlight, and at this moment they seem in harmony with amoral nature. But they are also divided by a stream from Pearl, who will not cross over to join them, and is an admonitory voice. James uses Hawthorne's forest and stream imagery in a similar way to focus Longmore's inner conflict; and in doing so illustrates that his conflict is also New England's. If Hawthorne created the model of psychological conflict peculiar to New England, James illustrates it, in "Madame de Mauves," in a context of contemporary manners.

James's interpretive use of Hawthorne and the New England mind in "Madame de Mauves" is complemented by his use of Hawthorne in "Benvolio" (1875), written the following year, when James had returned from Europe and settled temporarily in New York. It is cast in the form of a modern fairy tale, with Benvolio as its prince charming. He has a dual nature, being torn between his attraction to solitude on the one hand, and to society on the other. One portion of his apartment is lined with paintings and books, tokens of his interest in the great world; but his sleeping room is as bare as a monk's cell. He falls in love with two young women—one a gently appealing although outwardly plain daughter of a blind old scholar, the other a countess who is the center of fashion and the arts. As the story progresses his attraction draws him first to one of these young women, and then to the other. The attractions are mu-

33

tually exclusive, and in the end he chooses the old scholar's daughter, Scholastica. In a sense Benvolio demonstrates the outward-inward conflict in normal human beings, the attraction to society and also to solitude, and is an allegory of general human duality. But beneath the surface, James deals with another theme.

The contrast he makes, through Scholastica and the Countess, is between America and Europe. The Countess is a titled member of an aristocratic society, is "the ripest fruit of a high civilization . . . the divine embodiment of all the amenities, the refinements, and complexities of life" (pp. 362, 364). In the Countess's circle Benvolio is able to express his poetic imagination and to win fame and popularity as the author of plays (one of James's own later ambitions). But what the Countess implies is made clearer when she goes to Italy and Benvolio joins her. James remarks at this point: "The world has nothing better to offer a man of sensibility than a first visit to Italy during those years of life when perception is at its keenest, when knowledge has arrived, and yet youth has not departed. . . . It seemed to him that his imagination, his intellect, his genius, expanded with every breath and rejoiced in every glance" (p. 391). The Countess, then, signifies Italy, and Italy signifies the "immense pictorial spectacle" (p. 392) of a high civilization—everything, in other words, that America is not.

Set off against Italy is an America that James has conceptualized, although it has gone unnoticed (as far as I know), through Hawthorne. Benvolio's room overlooks a garden, fragrant with plants and shrubs and suggesting a perfect solitude. In this garden, sometimes sitting under one of its trees, is Scholastica, who is dressed in black and has an unspoiled, "nun-like gentleness and demureness" (p. 366). He watches her from his window and finally gains admittance into the nearly inaccessible garden, which Scholastica finds "a paradise"; here she acts as a reader and secretary to her blind scholar father. Scholastica's own learning makes her "an anomaly," a "charming monstrosity." James comments that she had "imbibed the wine of science instead of her mother's milk" (p. 377). As the sheltered daughter of a "scientist" father, Scholastica is strikingly reminiscent of Beatrice in "Rappaccini's Daughter," who is observed by Giovanni from the window of his room which, like Benvolio's, looks down upon the secluded garden. Moreover, Scholastica's father, like Dr. Rappaccini, has introduced "poison" of a certain kind into his daughter's being, as James indicates: "Her mother had died in infancy. . . . Her father had been her nurse, her playmate, her teacher, her life-long companion, her only friend. He taught her the Greek alphabet before she knew her own, and fed her with the crumbs of his scholastic revels. She had taken submissively what was given her, and, without knowing it, she grew up a little handmaid of science" (p. 377).

Although the perfection of virtue, Scholastica is the product of her father's "unnatural system," of his extraordinary concern with mind, and there is thus a great oddness about her. There is also something about her, as there is about Beatrice, that is deadly. After Benvolio chooses her at last, the poetry he writes withers, is imaginatively starved and lifeless. If Scholastica is a version of America, she has been related by James even more particularly to the Puritan culture of New England. A contrasting figure to the richness of European art and society, she is a slender, demure little maiden, dressed in black, appealing in her innocence but at times also forbidding (when Benvolio goes to Italy, she wears a disapproving frown). The house in which she lives is "an ancient grizzled, sad-faced structure" (p. 367) which looks like a convent or a prison. Her father has shaggy white brows that seem like patches of a "pale winter sky" (p. 375). In his presence Benvolio writes a little poem in the style of Milton's *Il Penseroso*, a reminder of the moral seriousness, gloom, and preference for solitude of the Puritan tradition. (It might also be noted that while Scholastica's father is preoccupied by idealistic abstractions, his brother, the real *owner* of the property, is obsessed by the accumulation of money, and is hostile to art.)

James has drawn Scholastica's garden, furthermore, in such a way as to imply a later-day New England as well, and the Transcendentalists in particular. Scholastica's father, for example, is described as being "serene and frigid, impartial and transcendental." He lives in a cloistered simplicity, essentially sheltered from the world, in an atmosphere of "transcendent abstractions" until he has become "un-

35

conscious of all concrete things" (pp. 391, 375). It is significant that the Countess, who represents the great world, is described as being "brilliantly concrete"; and that James, early in the tale, remarks that dullness is "at the end of everything that [does] not multiply our relations with life" (p. 356). Thus, on a subterranean level, "Benvolio" is an ironic fairy tale about the death of the artist in America, a story complementing *Roderick Hudson*, published in the same year, in which James treats at far greater length the subject of the artist's death in Italy.

If we regard 1875, and the publication of *Roderick Hudson*, as a dividing line, "Benvolio" is the last of the apprenticeship stories. When we examine these stories it is impossible not to be struck by the number of times James refers to Hawthorne in the conception of his characters and situations. In at least twelve of the twenty-seven tales, there is some discernible evidence of the Hawthorne background. This frequent incidence alone is sufficient to render very questionable both Leon Edel's assertion that the sum of Hawthorne's influence on James's earliest work consisted of two stories and the even stranger claim of T. S. Eliot, in "The Hawthorne Aspect," that there was no influence at all. "No more in the case of Hawthorne than any of the other figures of the background," Eliot noted with crisp certitude, "is there any consideration of influence. James owes little, very little, to anyone; there are certain writers, whom he consciously studied, of whom Hawthorne was not one."[10] No pronouncement of Eliot's is less well founded. In his apprenticeship period James was frequently and repeatedly guided by Hawthorne in the conception of his stories. The best and most characteristic stories of James's apprenticeship are all indebted to him.

But more is revealed by the apprenticeship stories than the frequency of James's referring to Hawthorne. In this period one sees James in his first years as a creative writer attempting, with some uncertainty, to find his direction, drawing upon French realism but also at times upon Hawthorne. By the 1870s he enters a stage of growth and development, and as he begins to achieve his first mastery in the short story form, his preoccupations and themes show a quite definite affinity with Hawthorne's. His international theme,

36

his placing of American innocence in a context of European corruption, his concern with situations of bondage in which helpless purity is traduced, or threatens to be, by worldliness, are all affected by Hawthorne's art, despite James's distinctive handling. If Hawthorne had not existed, James's earliest fiction might have had a different orientation than it does.

Moreover, in certain of the stories of the 1870s, James transforms Hawthorne's conceptions into realism. This is a most interesting development to note, since it becomes the early part of a pattern. Charlotte Evans is a realistically redrawn version of Hilda; Professor Fargo a modern, democratically outlined specimen from the mold of Westervelt; Count Valerii a variation on the ambiguously modern and yet ancient Roman Donatello. These transformations suggest both temperamental affinity and the beginnings of an adversary relationship, insofar as James has reproduced Hawthorne's conceptions in the "superior" mode of realism. In "The Madonna of the Future" James both evokes Hawthorne, in his conception of the alienated artist of the delicately spiritual, and subjects his model to critical scrutiny and urbane irony. In other stories James's different handling of a common subject comments on his own difference as an artist from Hawthorne. In "Benvolio" particularly James implies that Hawthorne's New England enclosure cannot sustain his imagination as an artist absorbed by manners, social differences, and the many-sided spectacle of the great world. "Benvolio" embodies the tensions of the Hawthorne-James relationship, with its shared sensibility and emerging conflict. *Roderick Hudson*, of the same year, brings the apprenticeship to a close, for in that novel James asserts a new authority, challenging Hawthorne directly.

3 *Roderick Hudson:*

The Merging of

Opposite Traditions

Roderick Hudson comes out of James's nearly two-year residence in Italy, particularly the winter of 1873–1874, when he lived in Rome and had an opportunity to observe Roman society and its colony of American artists. When he began work on the novel during that winter, he would necessarily have had to be conscious of Hawthorne. *The Marble Faun* was by then firmly established as a classic work about Americans in Rome; it was as much a part of the American traveler's equipment in Rome, James noted, as his *Murray*. Moreover, James came to meet a number of people Hawthorne had known in Rome fifteen years earlier. He was entertained by the American sculptor William Wetmore Story at his immense apartment in the Palazzo Barberini, where he saw the Guido Reni portrait of Beatrice Cenci that had fascinated Hawthorne and appears in *The Marble Faun;* and he visited Story's studio in the Via San Nicolo di Tolentino, which Hawthorne had described in his novel as Kenyon's. He was on friendly terms with a group of others, too, from the earlier circle—the Bootts; Mrs. Terry, widow of the American sculptor Thomas Crawford; and Harriet Hosmer, who had shown Hawthorne her statue of Zenobia. There must have been many times when James felt as if he were retracing Hawthorne's footsteps.

But if reminded of Hawthorne by the surviving members of his circle, James judged that circle more critically than Hawthorne had done. Hawthorne, for example, had taken it for granted that Story was a sculptor of deserved eminence, whereas James recognized at once that he lacked stature. In a letter of 1873 to Charles Eliot Norton, he remarked that "I have rarely seen such a case of *prosperous* pretension as Story."[1] The difference in their perceptions is suggested by James's review in *The Nation*, in the spring of 1872, of Hawthorne's *French and Italian Notebooks.* James refers to the charm and "impression of moral integrity" which the notebooks convey; but he also criticizes Hawthorne for his "*leisure* of attention," amounting to a "blessed intellectual irresponsibility." At the heart of his criticism was Hawthorne's relative failure to respond to the continent. James describes him as being "excessively detached . . . from Continental life, touching it . . . distrustfully, shrinkingly." He gives the impression of being "uninformed, incurious." He attempts to appreciate European art, but prefers "Mr. Brown, the American landscapist, to Claude," and is unreconciled to nudity in sculpture. James concludes that part of the interest of the book is the "fascination of seeing so potent a sovereign in his own fair kingdom of fantasy so busily writing himself simple . . . as to the dense realities of the world. . . . Exposed late in life to European influences, Mr. Hawthorne was but superficially affected by them—far less than would be the case with a mind of the same temper growing up among us today."[2] In this passage James seems to affiliate himself "in temper" with Hawthorne, but to distinguish himself from him by his own concern with social descriminations and the "dense realities" of European life. As a novel dealing with the colony of American artists in Rome, *Roderick Hudson* begins where *The Marble Faun* left off; but at the same time James subjects Hawthorne to the correction and refocusing of a cosmopolitan understanding.

James's allegiance to the cosmopolitan attitude was strengthened during this period by his discovery of Turgenev, who represented a different tradition than Hawthorne's nationally conscious one.[3] A personal friend of James, senior, Turgenev was the leading figure in the Parisian literary circle that included Flaubert, Daudet, the Goncourts, and Zola. James was before long to know the members of this circle personally, and he shared their concern with precise observation and experimentation in technique; but the French naturalists were to seem to him "cynical" and preoccupied by the "base" and the "unclean." Turgenev, on the other hand, had a larger outlook and a greater respect for his characters. No other novelist, James remarked, "has mingled so much ideal beauty with so much unsparing reality."[4] The importance of sensibility and cosmopolitan culture in Turgenev made him the "French" writer James most respected and admired.

In 1874 James read through much of Turgenev's fiction and published an essay (the most ambitious he had yet written) on Turgenev which reveals his attitudes toward him. He describes him as belonging to a "limited class of very careful writers," and as being a "searching realist," an "attentive observer." "The result of his temper," he continues, "is to make him take a view of the great spectacle of human life more general, more impartial, more unreservedly intelligent, than any novelist we know." Turgenev, moreover, always strikes for the significant, the "*morally* interesting" in an incident, situation, or character, and so provides "absolutely a greater amount of information about the human mind." He is an "analyst," distinguished by his "moral curiosity," sympathetic to his characters and yet detached from them. He does not intrude onto his narration, presenting a situation and its outcome so that its effect is "dramatic" rather than being commented upon or explained. Interestingly, practically all of these comments apply equally well to James himself. Furthermore, a personal identification with Turgenev is implied at certain points in the essay, as when James points to the similarity in Turgenev's situation, as a Russian expatriate living in Europe, with the American expatriate experience. "M. Turgéniéff," he writes, "gives us a peculiar sense of being out of harmony with his native land—of his having what one may call a poet's quarrel with it. He loves the old, and he is unable to see where the new is drifting. American readers will peculiarly appreciate this state of mind; if they had a native novelist of a large pattern, it would probably be, in a degree, his own."[5] In this passage James implies his own kinship with Turgenev; for surely *he* is the American writer "of a large pattern" who feels out of harmony with America.

By the mid-1870s Turgenev's influence on James had become quite discernible. One has only to observe the ending of *The American* (1876), where Christopher Newman walks past the convent in which Claire de Cintré is confined, to see how James is indebted to the gently melancholic ending of *A House of Gentlefolk*, in which Lavrentsky takes a last look at the convent where Lisa is closed up for life. In some of the short stories, too, one finds adaptations of one kind or another from Turgenev. "Four Meetings" (1877), for example, employs the method of Turgenev's "Three Meetings" to convey briefly an observer's sense of another character's life; and two other stories, "A Bundle of Letters" (1879) and "The Point of View" (1881), use the device of Turgenev's story "A Correspondence," in which the narrator acts as the "editor" of a bundle of letters written by a number of different people. "Eugene Pickering" (1874) is set in Germany, among the sophisticated upper class, a setting familiar from some of Turgenev's stories and novels, and in it James appears to derive his conception of Madame Blumenthal from a character type in Turgenev. The narrator describes her as belonging to a class of people who are "sincere attitudinizers," who "cultivate fictitious emotions in perfect good faith."[6] She is conceptually similar to Turgenev's worldly women with an inner contradiction, who reduce men to puppets; she has in particular an affinity with Irina in *Smoke*.

Passionate and willful, Irina marries General Ratmirov in order to occupy a place in high society, even though she realizes that society is fundamentally stupid and empty, and feels stifled by it. She is a deeply divided personality who cannot commit herself to sincere emotion. Mme Blumenthal has this complication in her psychology; but she in turn is merely James's preliminary sketch for Christina Light in *Roderick Hudson*. The peculiar psychology of Irina, the morbid melancholy of the lady of fashion who is sick and weary of the world, but can't live outside its circle, is reproduced by James in Christina—and with a similar result for the young man who falls in

41

love with her. In *Smoke,* Litvinov is described as being "afraid of falling into [Irina's] clutches" (p. 164),[7] and asks himself questions about her—Is she sincere? Is she capricious? Is she an actress?—but his questions are beside the point, because he has no will. Neither has Roderick Hudson, who becomes the pawn of Christina Light.

Irina is set off by contrast with Turgenev's "pure" girl, Tatyana, Litvinov's fiancée. Tatyana arrives in Baden-Baden to meet Litvinov, but she comes too late. He has already fallen under Irina's spell, and for her sake will dishonor himself and Tatyana too. Deeply deceptive, because so self-deceived, Irina persists until Litvinov breaks his engagement with Tatyana, his "guardian angel." A man in a "false position," he becomes a "moral failure." This situation, this study in moral failure, is explored by James in *Roderick Hudson*. James's novel follows the situation in *Smoke* in many essentials—the antithetical contrast between Christina, the worldly woman, and Mary Garland, Hudson's unspoiled fiancée; Mary's arrival in Rome too late to "save" Hudson from Christina's influence; the recognition scene which takes place between the two women shortly after Mary's arrival; Roderick's "false position" and moral failure. Hudson's moral failure, indeed, had already begun during his vacation at Baden-Baden which, not coincidentally, is the setting of *Smoke*. Turgenev's Baden-Baden is a continental watering place conspicuous for its fashionable gambling houses, its collection of effete foreigners, its women in costly but somewhat tasteless costumes who are consumed by boredom; and it is this same world which first drains Roderick Hudson of his will to create.

James's inspiration for Hudson may also have come from Turgenev. Turgenev's young sculptor Shubin in *On the Eve* provides interesting clues for Hudson, since Shubin feels stifled by his life in the Russian provinces, and dreams of being a sculptor in Rome; he thinks of love in the most personal way, as a thirst for happiness, and is absorbed by his own egotism. In *Roderick Hudson* James creates an American equivalent for the antithetical characters of Irina and Tatyana, with a version of Shubin the sculptor interposed between them. But in dealing with this situation, James is also affected by Turgenev in a philosophic way, in the attitude toward life his characters reveal. Late in *Smoke*, Litvinov exclaims that "there's no escaping one's fate" (p. 190), and in *Roderick Hudson* James refers to Roderick as standing passive "in the clutch of his temperament" (p. 152).[8] There is a very strong sense in Turgenev of temperament as placing unavoidable constraints upon his characters, as being a determining factor in their destinies. His characters are all hemmed in in some way temperamentally, and Turgenev observes attentively how their natures are acted upon by circumstances. Frequently, in a number of different ways, his characters are losers in life, or have only a small amount of free will. One of the questions that is asked in *Roderick Hudson* is whether there is free will, and judging by James's cast of characters in the novel, one is apt to conclude that there is not a great deal. In *Roderick Hudson*, *The American,* and again in *The Portrait of a Lady,* temperament plays a decisive role in the fate of James's characters. There is a stronger sense of a future that is "open" in James than in Turgenev, but it is an openness that is strongly qualified by a sense of innate limitations.

George Moore once remarked that James went to Europe and studied Turgenev, and that Howells stayed at home and studied James,[9] an observation that is amusing but much oversimplified. But it is certainly true that James admired Turgenev and learned much from him about the art of fiction. As *Roderick Hudson* reveals, James uses Turgenev's detached, "dramatic" method in his novel and shares his interest in sensibility. But *Roderick Hudson* also has a different texture than one finds in Turgenev, partly because Turgenev was more genuinely worldly than James. In contrast with Turgenev's extraordinary naturalness, one finds in *Roderick Hudson* an upper-class Anglo-American stiffness and consciousness of vulgarity. Turgenev's characters seem to live from their souls, while many of James's characters in *Roderick Hudson* live merely from the surface of their minds. When Turgenev died in 1884, James published a reminiscent essay about him in which he remarked that he believed Turgenev did not find his own fiction to have "the air of reality," or to be "quite meat for men," [10] a comment that underscores the different quality of their responses to experience. James's world in *Roderick Hudson* has a mentalized cast and is suffused with a sense of Christian

43

myth and allegory. It is in this respect that James approaches Hawthorne.

As has sometimes been noted, *Roderick Hudson* is similar to *The Marble Faun* in that both novels treat a close group of four characters who inhabit the American artist colony in Rome. Hawthorne's Kenyon is a sculptor (as well as marginal participant and observer), and both Miriam and Hilda are painters, strongly contrasted in type— Miriam a "dark lady" with a worldly past, and Hilda a sainted innocent who inhabits a dove tower high above the corruption of the Roman streets. In *Roderick Hudson* James has in effect used Hawthorne's characters as counters, arranged so that his sculptor stands between his worldly woman, Christina Light, and his American innocent, Mary Garland. If this design comes from Turgenev, James nevertheless uses it to illustrate typically American experience outlined by Hawthorne. And Mary Garland in particular seems a more fleshed-out and psychologically plausible version of the Hilda figure. The daughter, granddaughter, and sister of ministers, Miss Garland is firmly rooted in a theological tradition; she comes, indeed, from the small community of West Nazareth. "I shall be," she affirms at one point, "what I was made, what I am now—a young woman from the very heart of New England" (p. 220). She is touched by proxy with Rome's corruption, but she herself remains faithful to the stern truths in which she has been bred. There is even a hint of Hilda's doves in Christina's description of her. "I told her," she says, "I liked her immensely, and she glared. . . . She looks magnificent when she glares—like a Medusa crowned . . . with a tremor of doves' wings" (p. 246).

Just as James makes Hawthorne's New England virgin credible, so he does also the expatriate colony in Rome. In Hawthorne, the American artist colony is so shadowy and unsubstantiated that it seems to include hardly more than four people. In James, however, there is a larger elaboration, and a precise notation of the social and psychological types who make up the American circle. Included in this circle is Miss Blanchard, a painter who "did backs very well, but was a little weak in faces" (p. 84); she reads Mr. Willis and Mrs. Sigourney and is the product of an American consciousness of Europe

chiefly at second hand. Sam Singleton is a watercolorist from Buffalo, New York, who, with much industry, has developed a small
gift. Included in this circle, too, is the Italian Gloriani, who "now
drove an active trade in sculpture of the ingenious or sophisticated
school" (p. 82). Artist and tradesman in one, he inhabits a halfway
house between art and worldliness; "at his lodging he introduced
you to a lady without art of utterance whom he called Madame
Gloriani—which she was not" (p. 83). The most personally
touching member of this group, and an instance of James's gift for
catching sharp profiles with an economy of means, is Madame Grandoni. "I was not always so ugly as this," she says; "as a young girl I
had beautiful golden hair, very much the colour of my wig." James
relates humorously the background of this widow of a German archaeologist:

Her acuteness had failed her but on a single occasion, that of her second   *45*
marriage. . . . A couple of years after her first husband's death she accepted the hand and the name of a Neopolitan music-master ten years
younger than herself and with no fortune but his fiddle-bow. The union
had proved a union of exasperated opposites and the Maestro Grandoni
was suspected of using the fiddle-bow as an instrument of conjugal correction. He had finally run off with a *prima donna assoluta*, who, it was
commonly hoped, had given him a taste of the quality implied in her
title. (P. 86)

Nothing could be further from the vagueness of Hawthorne's artist
colony in *The Marble Faun* than this passage, with its sophisticated
humor and tone and its sharply delineated notation of manners.

More important still, the situation explored in *The Marble Faun*,
the ensnarement of American innocence in old-world corruption, is
brought into a more sharply particularized focus by James. Hawthorne creates a pervasive atmosphere of the dense Roman past and
implicates his Americans in its historic sin, but he does so by the
most implausible means—a gothic phantom from the St. Calixtus
catacombs who pursues Miriam until Donatello hurls him over the
edge of the Tarpeian Rock. Hawthorne continually evokes the at-

mosphere of Rome's ancient corruption, but he seems unable to demonstrate how this corruption operates in specific cases. The melodramatic murder for which Miriam is responsible cheapens Hawthorne's theme of man's fall from grace and for the same reason makes Donatello's subsequent moral growth seem not entirely authentic. In contrast, *Roderick Hudson* is lucid in its conception, and James's theme is demonstrated convincingly with an intense particularization.

But in drawing his characters as distinct individuals, James has also learned from Hawthorne how to endow them with an underlay of rich suggestiveness. Roderick and Christina Light have a sharp individuality, and yet they seem to suggest something more than themselves, to give the sense of a larger experience than their own; at times they seem even to have the quality of characters in a morality. Roderick's "American-ness" is implied in his name, Hudson, and as the "American" he believes confidently in the self and ingenuously in "happiness" and the possibility of its fulfillment in this world. Christina's grandfather had been an American, but her parentage is oddly mixed, and she has been perfected, in the course of twenty years, by Europe. In fact, it is not too much to say that Christina *is* Europe. She is "the greatest beauty in Europe" (p. 140) and is thus the standard bearer both of Europe's spiritual heritage and esthetic richness and of its corruption. Christina seems to appear at times in a dazzling burst of light and has a religiously connotative name. More than once she is shown in church, and it might be noted that her maid's name is Assunta, which in Italian means "Assumption," linking Christina with the Blessed Virgin. At Mrs. Light's reception for Roman society, she appears dressed in white, the color of purity. "Dressed simply in vaporous white relieved with half a dozen white roses," James remarks, "the perfection of her features and of her person, and the mysterious depth of her expression, seemed to glow with the white light of a splendid pearl" (p. 139). The image of the radiant pearl is a traditional symbol of the soul, but the reception at which Christina appears is Mrs. Light's way of offering her daughter for sale, in the European style. It is here that Prince Casamassima, the unimpressive scion of an ancient house, first makes his appearance; and it is he to whom she will consent to sell herself. Radiantly beautiful, yet destined for a cynical marriage of advancement with an ancient aristocratic house, Christina stands for Europe as much as Hudson suggests America.

The sense of a large pattern and contour in Roderick Hudson's experience in Europe is reinforced also by James's subtle use of a knighthood motif, involving a reversal of the knighthood promise. When Hudson is about to leave for Italy, he is seen strolling in the pathway of a moonlit garden at Northampton, speaking lines of verse: "The splendor falls on castle walls / And snowy summits old in story." The lines are from Tennyson's poem *The Princess* and are used to introduce its knighthood theme, the idea of gallantry and successful exploits. But they are ironic, because Hudson will later die amid the "snowy summits" of the Alps, his quest ended in failure. Even his first name has knightly, but unfortunate, associations, since Roderick, the famous knight of history, and the subject of Walter Scott's poem "The Vision of Don Roderick," is defeated in a decisive battle, failing the Christian cause in its most critical hour.

The knighthood motif is insinuated, furthermore, through the name of Roderick's *doppelgänger*, Rowland Mallet. James refers to "Burd Helen in the ballad" (p. 302), an allusion to the old Scottish ballad in which Childe Rowland (or Roland), the son of King Arthur, rescues his sister, "the fair Burd Ellen," from an enchanted castle. He appears again in Browning's poem "Childe Roland to the Dark Tower Came" as a brave knight who succeeds in a perilous exploit in which others have failed. But the actual knight appearing in *Roderick Hudson,* as opposed to the fabled knights of the old ballads, is a dismal figure, soiled by the world, the Cavaliere Giacosa. His curious title, *cavaliere,* means knight or chevalier, and his surname Giacosa, from the Italian word *giaco* (a coat of mail), reinforces the knighthood idea ironically. He follows humbly in the train of "Madama Light" and her daughter, attending them as a servitor with what is left of his broken manhood. James describes him as giving an impression of an "elaborate waxen image adjusted to perform certain gestures and emit certain sounds" (p. 120). He is knighthood in ruins, and one among a group of other men in the work whose man-

47

hood has been maimed by the women they loved or married. *Roderick Hudson,* in fact, resounds with an extreme masculine vulnerability, which the character of Christina Light emphasizes. The dangerous female who destroys the men susceptible to her beauty, Christina anticipates by fifty years Hemingway's Lady Brett Ashley in *The Sun Also Rises.*

But the knighthood motif is also seen, revealingly, in James's allusions to Ariosto, whom Hudson reads when he is disintegrating as an artist. In Ariosto's *Orlando Furioso* (Orlando Mad), Orlando, the Italian form of Roland, forsakes his responsibility to his uncle, Charlemagne, when he falls in love with Angelica, and in breaking faith enables the Islamic forces to invest Paris. Only after his reason has been restored can the victory of Christianity be possible. Ariosto distinguishes between profane and sacred love, *eros* and *agape,* and it is Orlando's fate to confuse one with the other, finding in "Angelica the bright" a vision of celestial beauty which she does not represent. A succession of men fall in love with her, and she hears their lamentations of lovesickness with cool calculation, wondering what advantage she can derive from their devotion. Orlando's jealous passion for her has particularly unfortunate consequences, since it impairs his right reason, and he fails in a great cause. In his allusions to Ariosto, James clearly implies a similarity in Roderick's situation, and in his sacrifice unworthily of himself and his high calling. If Christina is a "divinity," as Roderick calls her, she is so in the way Angelica is; and it is Christina who judges herself best when she declares: "I'm corrupt, corrupting, corruption!" (p. 262).

The motif of corruption in *Roderick Hudson* is accompanied by a motif of damnation. A drama is acted out behind the drama in which Roderick's soul is wagered and lost. When Roderick first sees Christina, she is strolling with a party that includes her mother and the Cavaliere Giacosa. She leads on a leash her poodle, her "toy," named Stenterello, from the Italian word *stento* (stunted), which implies what her effect will be upon Roderick as an artist. The poodle she leads is compared to a male sheep to be sacrificed upon her altar; it is "combed and decked like a ram for sacrifice" (p. 76). Later she is called a "creature who might easily draw down a too confiding spirit into some underworld of unworthy sacrifice, not unfurnished with traces of others of the lost" (p. 130). A snare for Hudson's soul, she has specifically Faustian associations. When Christina first appears, her poodle is compared to "the black dog in *Faust*" (p. 77), a reminder of Mephistopheles's first appearance in *Faust* in the guise of a poodle. The cynical Mephistopheles tempts Faust with a vision of "happiness," a fulfillment of earthly desire, but with the motive of deranging his moral sense and thwarting his will to aspire; and Christina has a similar role of luring Hudson to his ruin, both as man and artist. Off at the side of this drama, looking shrewdly on, is Christina's fellow Roman, the worldly artist Gloriani, "a genial Mephistopheles" (p. 92). By the end of the novel, Roderick Hudson actually exclaims that he is "damned."

The large play of suggestion surrounding Christina also includes James's insinuation into the novel of Christian myth and the concept of the Fall—a motif that is relevant to Hawthorne. In *The Marble Faun* it is the darkly sensuous Miriam, in some shadowy way contaminated by worldliness, who reenacts the Fall and has an association with Eve. In *Roderick Hudson* Christina has the Eve role, and Roderick becomes a version of Adam. Edenic imagery appears at various points in the novel and is intimated at the beginning in Northampton, where a series of scenes take place in gardens, in one of which Hudson pledges himself to Mary Garland. It is also at this time that Rowland Mallet first sees Hudson's work, a statuette entitled *Thirst*—of a naked youth drinking from a gourd. The nakedness of the youth suggests his unselfconscious relation to nature, but the cup from which he drinks, Hudson explains, is "knowledge, pleasure, experience" (p. 36). In rural New England the Fall has not as yet occurred, but it is anticipated.

Rome is a very different world from Northampton, but it too has its gardens, both real and metaphoric. Later in the novel, Rowland Mallet guides Miss Garland through a spot reminiscent of the Edenic ruins of Hawthorne's gardens in *The Marble Faun*: "There came a morning that they spent among the ruins of the Palatine, that sunny chaos of rich decay and irrelevant renewal, of scattered and overtangled fragments, half excavated and half identified, known as the Palace of the Caesars. Nothing in Rome is more interesting than this confused and crumbling garden, where you stumble at every step on the disinterred bones of the past." (pp. 227–28). The garden, ambiguously, holds both life and death, is a "sunny chaos." The imagery James uses—"scattered and overtangled," "confused and crumbling" —suggests a ruin beyond repair because embedded so deeply in time, a garden "rich" but with the sense of death and undoing. Earlier, when the scene shifts from New England to Rome, another garden is emphasized, the garden of the Villa Ludovisi, and it is here that Roderick first sees Christina Light and is awed by her beauty. Soon after, he creates a life-size figure which he calls *Adam,* and then begins his *Eve,* which is to be both the high point of his career and the beginning of his steady decline. By the end, his "knowledge" has become the source of his wretchedness, and he is an exile from his former, simpler existence. Knowing all that he does, he can no longer be content to return to his austere New England village, and yet Europe is also a misery to him because it has destroyed his ability to create. That is his metaphorical Fall, his expulsion from the garden, which ends with his suicide.

Roderick's association with Adam is intimated even in the profession he abandoned, the law, which his nature is too unruly to accommodate. It is the rich life of the senses that is primary with him. In New England he still has some degree of discipline, since external conditions keep him in check. But in Italy, the garden of the world, his discipline disintegrates; he indulges his strongly egocentric nature and is shaken by inner turbulence of elation and despondency. After an interval of dissipation in Baden-Baden, Roderick meets Mallet in Geneva, and they hold a conversation by the statue of Rousseau. The statue of Rousseau, of course, underscores Roderick's allegiances as a romantic artist—the priority of impulse over discipline; freedom above constituted authority; the individual rather than mankind. Roderick is all "self" and so is much like Christina, whose inner nature is characterized by pride and unruliness. She spent part of her girlhood in a convent, where she had devoutly read Thomas à Kempis, whose *Imitation of Christ* teaches that the only peace comes from the submission of the self to God's will.

But in keeping with her Eve role, she has since tasted "knowledge" and beguiles Roderick to follow her. She ruins him to prove that she can, but because of her restlessness and vanity she finds no happiness. The greater unhappiness, however, is Roderick's, because he is deep enough to know what, for her sake, he has lost. Late in the work he exclaims:

> "If I hadn't come to Rome I shouldn't have risen, and if I hadn't risen I shouldn't have fallen."
> "Fallen—fallen!" sighed Mrs. Hudson. "Just hear him!"
> . . . And Roderick, who had hardly removed his eyes from the exhibition of his work, got up again and went back to the great figure in which . . . he had embodied his idea of the primal Adam. (P. 280)

Through his use of the Fall, James creates an underlay of archetypal suggestion in Roderick's experience, endowing the novel with a sense of cultural fable. But his use of the Fall is unlike Hawthorne's use of it in *The Marble Faun*, written in the Protestant tradition of the "fortunate fall," in which man falls only that he may rise. In James's novel the hero rises only to fall—without redemption. The difference in the use of the Fall in Hawthorne and James is, in part, the difference of a generation's time in America. Hawthorne writes with a sense of a personal closeness to religious emotion, whereas James gives the impression of religious emotion felt at a greater distance, and become a form of esthetic contemplation. It is perhaps significant that Roderick's paradise forfeited is the loss of the creative artist's life, which for a writer of James's allegiances was damnation indeed, a terrible fate.

There is something terrible, too, about the world James imagines in the novel. There is little love in it, and what there is is chiefly a form that proves to be fatal. His characters are all so limited temperamentally that there seems no possibility of transcendence for anyone. The widow-mother and the jilted fiancée return to their New England village to wait patiently for death; Sam Singleton returns to the *large* village of Buffalo, to remain on the dim sidelines of life and art; Augusta Blanchard makes an uninspiring, sensible, second-choice marriage with the Unitarian Mr. Leavenworth. If the new world is chilled by austerity, the old world is a poisoned garden, beautiful and dangerous, like the woman at Baden-Baden who attaches herself to Roderick Hudson "as with a horrible sincerity to her prey" (p. 101). She is a version of Christina Light, who preys "on the faith of her victims," and is called a "vampire" (pp. 130, 154). In a different way, Rowland Mallet, who derives in type from Hawthorne's Coverdale, is also vampiric. He remarks, "I shall be at any rate an observer" (p. 65), and lives by prying into the lives of others, touching creative energy and passion vicariously through Hudson while secretly coveting his fiancée. Like Coverdale, who confesses at the end of *The Blithedale Romance* that he was "in love with Priscilla," Mallet lusts meekly for a New England virgin, in this case the immaculate Mary from West Nazareth. She will not have him, but no matter, he will wait—and "observe." Antithetical to Hudson, as renunciation is to passion, Mallet illustrates how little human fulfillment there is in this novel which explores the possibility of happiness.

Yet the world James envisions is neither extremely gloomy nor very personal; James himself is detached from it, an observer who looks on and makes an objective report. *Roderick Hudson* is flawed in some respects; it is too plotted and cerebral, and its passionate male character is too stiff. Yet it is a very impressive and mature first novel which grips its theme firmly. It is James's first "international" novel, one which shows how he drew from Hawthorne but moved beyond him to formulate his own world. *The Marble Faun* is essential to James's conception of *Roderick Hudson*—in its subject matter of American artists in Rome; its theme of American innocence implicated in old-world corruption; its highly suggestive patterning of a Fall. But James has improved upon Hawthorne by providing plausible and realistic specification that makes his conception socially lucid. Hawthorne's fable of the Fall is still discernible in *Roderick Hudson*, but it has receded into the background as poetic and moral suggestion, while the foreground is occupied by James's precise notation of manners. In his apprenticeship stories James sometimes referred to Hawthorne for insights into the nature of American ex-

52

perience; in certain cases, he shaped his realistic characters from Hawthorne's romance models. But in *Roderick Hudson* James takes leave of his old master and arrives as a novelist in full possession of his own world. James will refer to Hawthorne again in the future, but he will do so as a master realist, and from the standpoint of a cosmopolitan understanding. Hawthorne's "heir" in the American novel, he will now have come into his inheritance, and will describe his predecessor's genius as beautiful and "provincial."

53

4 *The Europeans* and *Daisy Miller:* Motifs Transfigured

The waning of Hawthorne's influence during the several years following *Roderick Hudson* can be noticed in such works as *The American* and *Confidence*, novels of courtship which enjoyed a relatively popular success and are set abroad. Having introduced his international theme in *Roderick Hudson*, James continues to expand upon it in works that have the scenic form, and suggest the comic conventions, of the stage. But although Hawthorne no longer preoccupies James as he had earlier, he is not wholly absent from this period of international satire and observation.

After James finished *The American* he began *The Europeans* and the two works are, despite their obvious formal differences, companion pieces, comparative studies in manners and points of view. In each an ambassador (Newman from America in *The American,* and Eugenia, together with Felix, from France in *The Europeans*) crosses the Atlantic to take possession of an unfamiliar world, and by the end arrives at a cul-de-sac. For Newman, Claire de Cintré provides a large new vision, of which he had formerly been in ignorance, and he comes close to possessing her without actually being able to do so. Eugenia arrives in New England seeking to possess herself of a new home, and at the beginning at least she has glimpses of an "enlargement of opportunity which had been born of her arrival in the

New World" (p. 285).[1] Robert Acton takes her for a drive in the country, and on the hillside they can see "half the hill-tops in Massachusetts" (p. 285). The moment captures the opportunities she is conscious of but will somehow miss. Her frustration is not given the dramatic projection of Newman's, but in its way it is as final. "Her irritation came, at bottom," James remarks near the end of the novel,

from the sense, which, always present, had suddenly grown acute, that the social soil on this big, vague continent was somehow not adapted for growing those plants whose fragrance she especially inclined to inhale. . . . She found the chief happiness in the sense of exerting a certain power and making a certain impression; and now she felt the annoyance of a rather wearied swimmer who, on nearing the shore, to land, finds a smooth straight wall of rock when he had counted on a clean firm beach. Her power, in the American air, seemed to have lost its prehensile attributes; the smooth wall of rock was insurmountable. (Pp. 337-38)

55

At the opening of *The Europeans*, James sharpens his impression of place through dramatic foreshortening. The window of the hotel where Eugenia and Felix are staying looks out upon a "narrow grave-yard in the heart of a bustling, indifferent city" (p. 207); and the accompanying imagery—"mouldy tombstones," "funereal umbrage"—indicates a pall of gloom. Near the graveyard is a church, whose white spire rises high "into the vagueness of the snow-flakes" (p. 209). A horsecar appears and **stops** by the graveyard, and people scramble aboard it as if it were a lifeboat at sea. All of the elements of New England's culture are present in this scene—its Puritan past, its democratic foreground, the "vagueness" of abstraction peculiar to the New England imagination in the early nineteenth century—and they form the smooth wall of rock that is to be insurmountable for Eugenia.

In the opening pages James has also insinuated an exoticism in the landscape. His depiction of the horsecar, for example, suggests a vehicle the like of which has hardly been witnessed before in the world. To Felix, the visual effect of this unfamiliar scene is reminiscent of the East, of Arab countries and Mahometan decoration, an impression which, in the fairy-tale motif of *The Europeans,* intimates a fabulous meeting between East and West. The fairy-tale quality is not as predominate as it is in *The American,* but it is nevertheless present and can be noticed particularly at the beginning when Felix appears at the Wentworth house while Gertrude is reading the *Arabian Nights*:

> She possessed herself of a very obvious volume—one of the series of the Arabian Nights—and she brought it out into the portico and sat down with it in her lap. There, for a quarter of an hour, she read the history of the loves of the Prince Camaralzaman and the Princess Badoura. At last, looking up, she beheld as it seemed to her, the Prince Camaralzaman standing before her. A beautiful young man was making her a very low bow—a magnificent bow, such as she had never seen before. He appeared to have dropped from the clouds: he was wonderfully handsome; he smiled—smiled as if he were smiling on purpose. (Pp. 227–28)

56

The story of Camaralzaman and Badoura in the *Arabian Nights* concerns a handsome young prince and a beautiful young princess who live at opposite ends of the world, China and Persia. They are in fact twins, physical counterparts of one another; and they appear before each other first in dreams. After Prince Camaralzaman has seen Princess Badoura in a vision while he sleeps, he sets off for the East to find her, which he miraculously does, and after many adventures, and a separation for a time, brings her with him to Persia as his bride. The tale provides a romantic frame for the experience of Gertrude and Felix, who belong to the different cultures of East and West, but are able to make the discovery of one another, and are united finally in marriage. When Felix appears before Gertrude in a quasi-magical materialization, she has been "dreaming" over the *Arabian Nights*, and he is a realization of what she has been dreaming about. Although they may not seem so at first, they are, like Prince Camaralzaman and Princess Badoura, spiritual twins. Felix's vocation is "to enjoy," and it is this capacity which lies dormant in Gertrude; he comes like a fairy-tale prince to "awaken" her to life.[2]

But there is a romantic implication of a kind in Eugenia also, since she has an old-world history out of a storybook. She is the Baroness of Munchen, of the principality of Silberstadt-Schreckenstein, and her appearance in New England is made to seem like an adventurous arrival in Arcadia. The Wentworths' house, indeed, has an Arcadian setting and, with its wooden pilasters and classic pediment, suggests the idea of a Greek temple and an age of classical simplicity. "The front door of the big, unguarded house stood open," James writes, "with the trustfulness of the golden age"; and after his first visit Felix reports back to Eugenia that the Wentworths' style of life has "the *ton* of the golden age" (pp. 227, 236). James's treatment of this pastoral scene, with its suggestions of Arcadia and the golden age, is reminiscent of Hawthorne's use of an Arcadian motif in *The Blithedale Romance*. And like Hawthorne's novel, *The Europeans* begins in Boston during a snowstrom in May, an ominous prelude to an experiment in pastoral simplicity.

In *The Blithedale Romance* the Arcadian supposition is contrasted with the worldly passions that the colonists bring with them to their new home in the country. There is further irony in that the pastoral setting is associated even with "paradise." Coverdale goes to Blithedale to begin "the life of Paradise anew" (p. 8), and while there he and the others enact a Fall, with Zenobia a version of Eve.[3] At the end they are cast out again into the world. James uses the Arcadian motif in a witty way, but in the general way Hawthorne had, as a new beginning, an attempted reordering of life on a less complicated basis. In Europe Eugenia has suffered from the highly formalized conventions of an older society. Her morganatic marriage to the younger brother of a prince has brought her only a meager pension, and even that will be cancelled if she does not agree soon to an annulment; in her old-world marriage, she has been merely a pawn in a game of statecraft. She comes to America for gain, for what is "golden" in a material sense, but she comes also in a Utopian attempt to "belong" to a new scheme of things.

The imagery of Arcadia and paradise can be noticed particularly in the early section of *The Europeans*. By the Wentworth house is a garden, and beyond it an orchard of apple trees, a pond, and a cottage, all of which make Felix feel that he has never known anything so "pastoral." Even dining with the Wentworths has an Arcadian quality. "There was," James comments, "a kind of fresh-looking abundance about it which made him think that people must have lived so in the mythological era, when they spread their tables upon the grass, replenished them from cornucopias, and had no particular need of kitchen stoves" (p. 259). When Felix strolls in the garden with Gertrude, he says that he has seen wrongs overseas, but "this is a paradise." Shortly afterwards it is said that "Boston is a paradise, and we are in the suburbs of Paradise" (pp. 272, 281). But it proves to be an unrealizable paradise for Eugenia, partly because she has brought her worldly nature with her, and partly because New England is a paradise of blandness. In the end she can only withdraw, defeated, her Blithedale adventure in classless living a failure.

But if *The Europeans,* as a satirical pastoral, is a witty variation on a theme in Hawthorne, its style and form suggest the well-made plays of the French. Oscar Cargill has remarked upon the probable influence of writers such as Dumas *fils,* Augier, Feuillet, and Cherbuliez;[4] and I would think Cherbuliez, the great creator of the coquette type, particularly likely. *The Europeans,* however, also has an affinity (which has not been noted previously) with Howells's novel *Private Theatricals,* published serially in the *Atlantic Monthly* shortly before *The Europeans* was written.[5] The principal character in *Private Theatricals* is Belle Farrell, a coquette from Boston who spends a summer at a New England country house that takes seasonal boarders. She proves a disturbing element at the resort since, as a flirt, she comes between two old friends, Easton and Gilbert; and by the end she is virtually banished to Boston, where, with her actresslike nature and need to make an effect, she finds her proper sphere as an entertainer in private theatricals.

But whether or not James reflected on *Private Theatricals* while he was writing *The Europeans,* the two works form an interesting transition—from regional realism to an international satire of manners. That Belle Farrell of Boston should represent worldliness might well have seemed to James a contradiction in terms. James's Boston in *The Europeans* is a provincial town, where Eugenia and Felix stay at a "gloomy-looking inn" that is revealed, a few sentences later, to be the best hotel in the city. To heighten his effect, James has placed the time of the novel approximately thirty years earlier, near the end of the 1840s, a golden age in New England of plain living, high thinking, and classic old-fashioned integrity. It is also the period in France of the beginning of the Second Empire, over which Louis Napoleon was to preside as Napoleon III, with his Empress Eugenia, whose name James's heroine shares. Her name alone evokes the period of the so-called Gaudy Empire. The historian Albert Guerard describes the Second Empire as a triumph of materialism in all of its forms: morose realism in the arts (Flaubert and Baudelaire are examples), material power, material pleasure. It was the period of Haussmann's new boulevards, Offenbach's operas, the stage door and the Bourse. The contrast between this elegantly showy, cynically pleasure-loving Paris and the Puritan capital of Boston is extraordinary, and reinforces the sense of an almost wondrous strangeness in Eugenia's first impressions of Boston.

59

Eugenia's culture shock at the beginning involves the irony that the old world should suggest youth, while the new world should stand for sobriety and advanced age. Felix's surname is Young, and the smile that is so usual with him implies that his attitude toward life will always be youthful, that he will regard his circumstances in terms of fortunate opportunity. Eugenia is somewhat older and has an older head than Felix, but she also has essential associations with youth. She is compared to Hebe, the Roman goddess of youth, and cupbearer to the gods. She carries "her three and thirty years as a light-wristed Hebe might have carried a brimming winecup" (p. 209). The Wentworths, on the other hand, are all described as being "pale," and Mr. Wentworth in particular has "semi-mortuary manifestations" (p. 239). His face is "high-featured," and Felix describes him to his sister as a "tremendously high-toned old fellow; he looks as if he were undergoing martyrdom, not be fire, but by freezing" (p. 237). His eyes are "frigid organs of vision," and when Felix and Eugenia arrive at his doorstep, his reception of them is not so much a pleasure as an extension of "duty." When he learns that Eugenia has been morganatically married, he ponders to himself: "Was it right, was it just, was it acceptable? . . . It reminded him of a certain Mrs. Morgan, whom he had once known and who had been a bold, unpleasant woman" (p. 240).

When Felix first appears at the Wentworth house, Gertrude unlocks the cupboard and offers him wine, a contrast to the cake which is the habitual refreshment of Mr. Brand, the Unitarian minister. Mr. Brand believes that he is in love with Gertrude, but his love is expressed largely in the form of paternalism. He often speaks "impressively," and smiles down upon Gertrude "from his great height" (p. 224). Perhaps he is in love most of all with the idea of duty and self-sacrifice, in which he resembles Charlotte, who is in love with him but sacrifices herself for the sake of her sister, until Mr. Brand and Charlotte are married at last, and he has the satisfaction of sacrificing himself for Gertrude's happiness.

Mr. Brand is symptomatic of the New England men in the novel, all of whom appear sexually inhibited. Young Clifford Wentworth "is rather afraid of ladies" (p. 241) and when Eugenia is introduced is seen "slowly sidling" about the room. He has been rusticated from Harvard for drinking, but his marginal drinking seems merely an effort to overcome his shyness, or to relieve the burden of conscience he shares with his father, in whom it has produced symptoms of "physical faintness." James remarks of Clifford that he "was apt to have an averted, uncomfortable glance, and to edge away from you at times, in the manner of a person with a bad conscience" (p. 260). The man of the world in the Wentworth circle is Robert Acton, who has made a large fortune in trade and has been to China; but he, too, is on guard. When Eugenia first arrives and Charlotte embraces her, in a gesture of acceptance, Acton turns away, "his hands stealing into his pockets" (p. 248). He is shown more than once with his hands in his pockets, and what is noticeable about him is his avoidance of passion. The most important woman in his life is his mother, who is dying in the upstairs of their immaculate house, where she reads Emerson's essays. Her dying is Transcendental—elevated, serene, colorless, and strangely unreal.

In his courtship of Eugenia, Acton seems like a version of what D. H. Lawrence called "the American homunculus," a disembodied head. "From the first," James observes, following Acton's thoughts, "she had been personally fascinating; but the fascination now had become intellectual as well. He was constantly pondering her words and motions; they were as interesting as the factors in an algebraic problem. This is saying a good deal, for Acton was extremely fond of mathematics" (p. 322). At one point, he can imagine himself going off with Eugenia to Newport, where she would make a brilliant social effect, and his own attachment might blossom into an "amatory passion"; but in the suburbs of "paradise," he cannot forget the need for prudence. Decidedly, Eugenia is not "safe," and Acton seems even to revel in catching her out as one who cannot be trusted. With his hands in his pockets, he meditates upon Eugenia as "a woman who will lie." " 'She is not honest, she is not honest,' he kept murmuring to himself" (pp. 357–58).

What he cannot deal with is her European complexity, the fact that she can be good and bad at once, can be physically unattractive and yet "beautiful." In a scene occurring late in the work, Acton *61* calls on Eugenia at night, and while he is present Clifford appears unexpectedly from Felix's studio, off the parlor. The scene has the makings of a boudoir comedy in which a young lover tumbles inopportunely out of a closet, with the difference that its effect is anticlimactic. Neither Clifford nor Acton has the reflexes of a jealous lover; they merely sidle awkwardly and shamefacedly away. Soon afterward Eugenia packs her things, recognizing that, with her actress nature, she cannot function in this world. In the last paragraph of the novel James reveals that Acton later married "a particularly nice young girl"—an almost mathematically safe choice.

One of the pivotal ironies of *The Europeans* is that the characters who live close to nature are unable to be "natural" or spontaneous; that the "natural" should be possible only in a highly formalized society. The ending of *The Europeans* is genial and involves nearly as many marriages as *Pride and Prejudice;* yet it leaves an impression of a certain distaste for New England, an impression that "the Europeans" are fortunate to be returning to the other side of the Atlantic where, in a world of forms, they can be "natural." As a novelist of manners James undoubtedly sympathized with their situation. Only later, in *The Bostonians,* did he return to New England as the setting of another of his novels; and it is a feature of that work, too, that New England poses the threat of suffocation.

In *The Europeans* James introduced Hawthorne's Blithedale motif playfully, in the idea of a failed adventure in Arcadian simplicity. But the figure of Zenobia this motif brings to mind is also a reminder of the exile in the New England countryside of the fully sexual woman. Distinctly worldly, and with an actresslike nature, Zenobia suffers the fate of a radical estrangement in the countryside beyond Boston; it could hardly be otherwise, for she is too vivid to belong there. Howells's Belle Farrell is not nearly as vivid as Zenobia, but she is still too many-sided, too oppressed by simplicity, to be accepted by the local people in rural New England. In order to "exist" she must return to the city, taking with her the sexuality she embodies and all that it implies about a direct exposure to life. The fate of James's Eugenia is similar, but with the important difference that in order to come back into relation to life she must cross the Atlantic.

But if James has introduced Hawthorne's motif as underscoring, *The Europeans* has also been written in a different spirit, and from a different point of view, than *The Blithedale Romance,* in which Hawthorne's somber ordering of experience leads to the renunciation of all his characters. Hawthorne contemplates a golden age of sensuous pleasure in the physical world, only to reject it as illusion. In *The Europeans,* on the other hand, James rehabilitates the idea of pleasure in the actual world, or "enjoyment" as an alternative to renunciation. The artist Felix is the most fortunate character in the novel— his name itself means "fortunate"—and he characterizes New England by its failure to "enjoy" (p. 272), a characterization repeated only a short time later in *Hawthorne.* In *Hawthorne,* commenting on Hawthorne's world at the time when *The Europeans* is set, James remarks: "I imagine there was no appreciable group of people in New England at that time proposing to itself to enjoy life; this was not an undertaking for which any provision had been made, or to which any encouragement was offered" (p. 24). In *The Europeans* the words of the artist Felix comment indirectly on *The Blithedale Romance,* in which Hawthorne contemplates the idea of "enjoyment," but has frozen his characters in attitudes of separateness and isolation from one another.

If James proposed an openness to experience in *The Europeans,* elsewhere, during the same period, he commented with considerable irony on the hazards of such a response. "Four Meetings," in which Miss Caroline Spencer suffers the grotesque consequences of reaching out with an openness of heart to Europe, has a frosty perfection. But *Daisy Miller,* which also deals with innocence abroad, made a deeper impression on the reading public, becoming something like an international event. The story begins in Switzerland, at Vevey, a neutral setting, as a resort frequented by Americans, and an easy transition from Newport. The relaxation of formalities at Vevey enables Winterbourne to meet Daisy casually, and she is seen thereafter through his eyes. Winterbourne is, at this point in James's fiction, a not entirely unfamiliar figure. He has a kinship with Rowland Mallet, Longmore in "Madame de Mauves," and Robert Acton, since he is more careful than ardent. Although an American by birth, he has been educated abroad and is uncertain how to respond to Daisy, an American "original" who flouts the rules of conduct laid down for young women in Europe. He is charmed and a little frightened. Had he been more willing to take risks, Daisy's fate might have been different, for she would not have turned to Giovanelli as an escort in Rome. 63

Her fate might have been different, too, if she had had a different mother. The Millers are well-to-do people from Schenectady, but Mrs. Miller seems unacquainted with "society." She misses obvious social clues, including digs at her daughter's behavior at Mrs. Walker's party, and there is a quality about her that seems vague and wandering. Her absent husband is absorbed by business in America, and abroad she suffers from headaches and allows her children to do as they like. The other American women in the story, Mrs. Costello (Winterbourne's aunt) and Mrs. Walker, are dowager figures, and strict observers of form; their dissociating themselves from Daisy has the effect of pushing her further toward defying social rules. In a sense, she is "sacrificed" by them before she is sacrificed more callously by Giovanelli. She is quintessentially alone, and the poignancy of her situation has much to do with the reader's sense of her spiritual isolation, her naive confidence in the adequacy of the self to deal with all the complications of experience.

Daisy Miller has been drawn with a small but distinct individuality, and yet there is a broadly representative norm in her experience in Rome. It is in fact Hawthorne's Rome, in *The Marble Faun,* that stands in the background of James's conception—that of a vast, inescapable Roman past that reaches out to claim American innocence. Daisy may be the "new" American girl, but her ancestry can be traced to the unspotted, white-dressed Hilda who goes alone and unchaperoned through the cynical streets of Rome—"an exquisite conception," as James calls her in *Hawthorne.* Moreover, Daisy's experience is defined suggestively in a series of stages by gardens, which come to have a Hawthornesque quality by the time she takes up residence in Rome.

Daisy first appears in the story on a spring morning, wearing a white dress, in the garden of the Vevey hotel; it is here that she meets Winterbourne and enters immediately into a relationship of trust. Her second appearance in the garden occurs at night, when Winterbourne finds her "wandering about in the warm starlight" (p. 158). She looks out from a parapet of the garden toward the lake and the Alps and impulsively asks Winterbourne to take her rowing, revealing her naiveté, since their rowing together at night would be taken locally as meaning that she had abandoned herself openly to a sexual involvement. In this nocturnal scene she makes her initial gesture toward ruin, which is to occur in Italy, where Daisy is depicted in a series of Roman gardens.

Gardens appear in literature elsewhere than in Hawthorne, but it is Hawthorne who is brought to mind by the Roman gardens of *Daisy Miller,* where American innocence is placed in a delicate juxtaposition with ancient European corruption. In *The Marble Faun,* moreover, Hawthorne has depicted his Roman gardens as versions of a fatally deceptive Eden. The Campagna, for example gives the impression of a vast garden which, in the nocturnal beauty of its lawns and woodlands, resembles "Paradise"; and yet, Hawthorne adds, "what the flaming sword was to the first Eden, such is the malaria to these sweet gardens and groves" (p. 778).[6] He dwells particularly upon the grounds of the Villa Borghese, of which he remarks:

The final charm is bestowed by the malaria. There is a piercing, thrilling, delicious kind of regret in the idea of so much beauty thrown away, or only enjoyable at its half-development, in winter and early spring, and never to be dwelt amongst, as the home scenery of any human being. For it you come thither in summer, and stray through the glades in the golden sunset, fever walks arm in arm with you, and death awaits you at the end of the dim vista. Thus the scene is like Eden in its loveliness; like Eden, too, in the fatal spell that removes it beyond the scope of man's actual possessions. (Pp. 631–32)

In *Daisy Miller* James gives a realistic focus to Hawthorne's conception of a malarial Rome that is a piercingly beautiful but poisoned garden.

65

There are three Roman gardens in which Daisy is seen. The first is "the beautiful garden at the other end of the Pincian Hill" (p. 178), where Daisy makes a first rendezvous with Giovanelli. The second scene is not quite so innocent, or at least is ambiguous; it occurs at the gardens of the Villa Borghese, where, disquieting to Winterbourne, Daisy and Giovanelli are observed with their heads screened by a parasol. The final garden scene occurs at the ruins of the Palace of the Caesars, and is ominous in its reminders of ancient undoing: "A few days after his brief interview with her mother, he encountered her in that beautiful abode of flowering desolation known as the Palace of the Caesars. The early Roman spring had filled the air with bloom and perfume, and the rugged surface of the Palatine was muffled with tender verdure. Daisy was strolling along the top of one of those great mounds of ruin that are embanked with mossy marble and paved with monumental inscriptions. It seemed to him that Rome had never been so lovely as just then" (p. 198). The intermixture of a delicate spring freshness and beauty with the evidence of so much ancient ruin and undoing gives the suggestion not merely of a garden, but of a moral garden that embraces both youth and age, innocence and deep knowledge. Shortly afterward Winterbourne finds Daisy at the Coliseum at night with Giovanelli, a romantic gesture that soon after results in her death from malaria. With an effect almost of symbol, she is buried in a little Protestant cemetery by the "wall of imperial Rome" (p. 205).

But if Hawthorne's Rome stands in the background of Daisy's experience, the tale itself is distinctly realistic. Its full title, indeed, is *Daisy Miller: A Study.* Despite its lyrical quality, the work is controlled by an objectivity that enables James to comment on his characters without direct statement. Giovanelli, for example, is captured in his negativity in James's allusions to him as "the brilliant Giovanelli," "the handsome native," "the subtle Roman," and so on; in the coldness of these references James also implies a lack of deep feeling in Giovanelli. Skillfully, James does not bring out the full extent of his callousness until the end, when he stands by Daisy's graveside and admits that he allowed her to go to the Coliseum at night because he had nothing to lose himself, since she would not have married him anyway. How ironic Daisy's words, "the beautiful Giovanelli," seem at this moment, and how much they comment critically on Daisy, and her sense of life.

In his critical biography of James, F. W. Dupee has remarked intelligently on Daisy Miller as being not altogether a tribute to the American girl. "As a social being," he comments,

she is without a form and without a frame. She has no sense of the inevitable—which was what traditions and taboos, conventions and manners finally signified to James when we discount his merely temperamental conservatism—and without this feeling for the limits of life she can scarcely be said to be fully alive. . . . Extremely imprudent and somewhat callow, even on occasion rude by any standard, she has within her a strange little will, which, when it is thwarted by Winterbourne's defection, turns rather easily into a will to die. . . . Daisy inhabits a human vacuum created equally by a large fortune and no commitments, much freedom and little use for it.[7]

Dupee's judgment of Daisy is harsh, but it is not entirely unwarranted. A disciplined awareness of the world, which Daisy so fatally lacks, is exactly the quality in the story that checks and restrains its poignancy, making it a spare and meticulous study in realism.

During the several years following the publication of *Roderick Hudson,* Hawthorne's influence visibly wanes. Motifs from Hawthorne appear in *The Europeans* and *Daisy Miller,* but they are transfigured in a literature of social observation. James has by now come into possession of his art and has begun to expand upon it. Unlike Hawthorne's vision, which leads to tragic recognition or renunciation, James's vision embraces the relativity of reality. The great world holds both the potential for expansion and "enjoyment," and for frustration and defeat, with discrimination one's only guide. The relativity of his perspectives reveals James as a spokesman for a different generation than Hawthorne's; he moves further outward into actual experience, where there is only uncertainty and the necessity for accurate observation. In the next book he writes, his critical biography of Hawthorne, he will even seem to regard Hawthorne, in his romantic allegiances and in the comparatively "closed" nature of his world, as his adversary. Like *Roderick Hudson, Hawthorne* is an important stage of James's assertion of his own art, as against Hawthorne's. In it he seems practically to repudiate his predecessor. Yet Hawthorne was like a tar baby, from which, once touched, James could never completely free himself. In the biography, James points to Hawthorne's failure as an "observer," and yet, as he knew, Hawthorne was one of literature's great observers—of the human mind. The depth and power of his observations, the moral weight and allegorical shading he brought to his conceptions of American experience, will continue to haunt James. In its assertions and also its telling omissions, *Hawthorne* is a document that reveals James's ambivalent relationship to Hawthorne, involving more than a simple conflict of romantic and realistic traditions. It was also a relationship of struggle and entanglement.

5 James's *Hawthorne:*

Criticism as Self-Definition

The decision to write a critical biography of Hawthorne did not come about on James's own initiative, having been proposed by John Morley, editor of the English Men of Letters series. Hawthorne was the only American author included in the series, and James was approached as the most eligible author to write the book, as an American writer who was then also becoming well known in England. One of the striking features of the book is its tone, its frequently dwelled-upon condescension toward Hawthorne as a provincial. In 1870 James had written to his brother William, boasting, perhaps somewhat insecurely, that he hoped someday to write a novel as good as *The House of the Seven Gables*—which William had just read and recommended to him;[1] but James's attitude toward Hawthorne by the time of the biography had altered considerably. In his study he sometimes refers to him as "poor Hawthorne," and there is an oddly ambiguous note in his use of the word "almost" in the final sentence of the book, when he concludes that the peculiar nature of Hawthorne's art gives him "an interest, and, as I may almost say, an importance."

James had not yet arrived as Hawthorne's peer, but he had arrived sufficiently to challenge Hawthorne, and the romantic tradition in which he wrote, and to imply a "superior" perspective in his own realism. When James wrote *Hawthorne* he had some reason to feel confident of the direction in which his career was moving. The publication of *Daisy Miller* had recently established his reputation and given him a popularity he had not enjoyed before. He was consolidating his reputation in England, moreover, by bringing out editions which had appeared earlier in America. Leon Edel has noted that "in the history of authorship few novelists have seen through the press in a single year so many volumes."[2] In February 1879 *Daisy Miller* appeared in a two-volume edition with "An International Episode" and "Four Meetings"; in March a revised edition of *The American* appeared, and in May a revised edition of *Roderick Hudson;* in August *Confidence* began to come out in serialized form; and in October *The Madonna of the Future & Other Tales* was published. Appearing in December, *Hawthorne* completed James's "conquest" of London in 1879.

James's patronizing tone toward Hawthorne was not entirely new, since he had patronized Hawthorne the traveler in his 1872 review of Hawthorne's *French and Italian Notebooks;* what is new is his patronizing of Hawthorne's whole career. If James at this point felt ready to challenge Hawthorne, his attitude was no doubt sharpened by his reading of *A Study of Hawthorne* (1876) by George Parsons Lathrop, Hawthorne's son-in-law.[3] James drew his factual information from Lathrop's book and in *Hawthorne* acknowledged his indebtedness, adding, however, that "his tone is not to my sense the truly critical one" (p. 4); and in a letter of 1879 to Thomas Sergeant Perry he characterized Lathrop's book in even more unflattering terms.[4] In his biography Lathrop had enshrined Hawthorne for his moral elevation and purity of spirit, making his career a compliment to the culture of Boston. The thrust of the book is intensely nationalistic; Lathrop actually says at the end that Boston's moral tone not only is to be recommended over the European one, but will in time be recognized as authoritative. Partly, no doubt, in reaction to Lathrop's Boston orientation and his rejection of European standards in art, James emphasized Hawthorne's limitations, as well as those of his New England environment. He asserts that this environment was not centrist, as Lathrop claimed, but actually parochial.

James's book is a portrait not only of Hawthorne but also of his time and place, and James is often wittiest when he is describing the look of America during that time, or drawing inferences from what Hawthorne has written in his *American Notebooks* and elsewhere. He calls attention, for example, to Hawthorne's dedicatory letter to Horatio Bridge at the beginning of *The Snow Image,* in which he refers to his college days in Maine, particularly those times when he and Bridge skipped classes to pick blueberries in the woods or to watch logs tumbling along the Androscoggin River. "This is a very pretty picture," James remarks, "but it is a picture of happy urchins at school. . . . Poor Hawthorne was indeed thousands of miles from Oxford and Cambridge; that touch about the blueberries and the logs on the Androscoggin tells the whole story, and strikes the note, as it were, of his circumstances" (p. 16).

Hawthorne's circumstances were not less limited after he left college, since he lived for years in seclusion in Salem. The "society" into which he was introduced was hardly a society at all, as James has pictured it. He depicts Hawthorne's being invited out for an evening's visit, with the Misses Hawthorne, at the home of Elizabeth Peabody, and upon their arrival Miss Peabody's bringing out Flaxman's designs from Dante, over which they made an evening's "entertainment." The austerity of this "entertainment" (James has also added the touch of winter snow against the window pane of the "barren" parlor) is striking, and it reappears in James's account of Hawthorne's contemporaries, particularly Margaret Fuller. James refers to Margaret Fuller's memoirs (which had been published posthumously by Emerson, Channing, and J. F. Clarke), and pictures her as an "apostle of culture" at the Boston Athenaeum, poring over engravings of European art with passionate emotion. He remarks that she "could hardly have been more [enthralled] had she been prostrate with contemplation in the Sistine Chapel or in one of the chambers of the Pitti Palace" (p. 56). And how pitiful her opportunities for culture seem at that moment—how meager the uncolored outlines and engravings of the Athenaeum seem compared to European art encountered at first hand. James dwells upon Margaret Fuller because her life deepens his impression of Hawthorne's situation. Artist and culture apostle, they both seem spiritually starved by their conditions and substantiate James's view of New England as provincial.

In treating the thinness of American society in Hawthorne's time, James frequently cites Hawthorne's own *American Notebooks*, which are "characterized by an extraordinary blankness—a curious absence of color and paucity of detail" (p. 33). It is in this section that he enumerates his famous list of the items of a high civilization that were missing in American life:

No sovereign, no court, no personal locality, no aristocracy, no church, no clergy, no army, no diplomatic service, no country gentlemen, no palaces, no castles, nor manors, nor old country houses, nor parsonages, nor thatched cottages, nor ivied ruins; no cathedrals, nor abbeys, nor little Norman churches; no great Universities nor public schools—no Oxford, nor Eton, nor Harrow; no literature, no novels, no museums, no pictures, no political society, no sporting class—no Epsom nor Ascot! (P. 34)

James's starting point for the enumeration of these "items" was, of course, Hawthorne's own statement, in his preface to *The Marble Faun*, that no one could imagine the difficulty of writing a romance about a country where there is only broad and simple daylight, where there are no shadows, antiquity, or mystery. But the effect of James's enumeration is somewhat different, since it gives the impression not of a picturesque gloom but of brightness, of a multitudinous and variegated social life, the material of the novelist of manners.

The contrast between Hawthorne and himself, implied in his enumeration of a high civilization, is no less present in the section dealing with Hawthorne abroad. The picture James draws of Hawthorne here comes largely from Hawthorne's own words, in his *French and Italian Notebooks*. He is the last of the old-fashioned Americans, slightly troubled by representations of the nude in sculpture, preferring the pictures of his countryman, Mr. Thompson, to those of most of the old masters, and sometimes even admiring paintings according to the brightness of their frames. What makes him provincial to James, however, is not merely his inexperience, but his disinclination to enter into the life of the places he visits—"his constant mistrust and suspicion of the society that surrounded him, his exaggerated, painful, morbid national consciousness" (p. 121). This picture is completed by the implicit comparison James makes between Hawthorne and himself. "What I mean," he writes, "is that an American of equal value with Hawthorne, an American of equal genius, imagination, and, as our forefathers said, sensibility, would at present inevitably accommodate himself more easily to the idiosyncrasies of foreign lands. An American as cultivated as Hawthorne, is now almost inevitably more cultivated, and as a matter of course, more Europeanized in advance, more cosmopolitan" (p. 128). Can there be any doubt whom James has in mind by the younger, more cosmopolitan American artist of "equal genius" to Hawthorne? The boldness of this implied comparison is part of James's skill as a portraitist in the book. His portrait has the vitality of confrontation, and quite apart from his criticism of Hawthorne's work, James has "created" Hawthorne as a man.

As a critic of Hawthorne's work, James seems continually reluctant in his admiration. He says that Hawthorne is a master of expression, but on a "limited scale," and a consciousness of Hawthorne's limitations is present throughout the book. In 1884 James published his well-known essay "The Art of Fiction," in which he defended organic form in art and the integrity of each artist's vision, regardless of its orientation, as against a prescriptive standard to which a work of art must adhere. But in *Hawthorne* James's criticism tends to be prescriptive and gives the impression that the romance form in which Hawthorne wrote was intrinsically inferior to realism. "Hawthorne," he remarks, "to say it again, was not in the least a realist—he was not to my mind enough of one" (p. 52). In commenting on *The Blithedale Romance* he emphasizes what the novel does *not* concern itself with—close social observation. He is critical of the book for the satire that does *not* appear in it. Its human background is indistinct. The character he praises chiefly is Zenobia, who is "the nearest approach that Hawthorne has made to the complete creation of a *person*" (p. 106). She has been drawn in part from a real person (Margaret Fuller), and the greater variation in her moods and states, the greater elaboration of detail in her characterization, bring her to the threshold of the novel of manners.

James's reservations about *The Scarlet Letter* are rather similar. Hawthorne's characters strike him less as real people than as picturesquely arranged representations of a single state of mind. He finds in Hawthorne's conception "a want of reality" (p. 90) and an over-ingenuity in the use of symbolism. Such a merely fanciful use of symbolism is seen in Hawthorne's representations of the letter A, which manifests itself in the sky above the scaffold, and even imprints itself mysteriously on Dimmesdale's breast. Such uses of the letter A, James remarks, have nothing to do with "real psychology." In Hawthorne's historical coloring, too, there is "little elaboration of detail, of the modern realism of research." Furthermore, in its cold moral delicacy, the novel is "passionless" (pp. 90, 91). To illustrate what he means, James compares *The Scarlet Letter* to John Gibson Lockhart's *Adam Blair* (1822), which also deals with a minister's act of adultery in a rigidly theological society, and has a much more strongly communicated human warmth. "Lockhart," James comments, "was a dense, substantial Briton, with a taste for the concrete, and Hawthorne was a thin New Englander, with a miasmatic conscience" (p. 92).

In making this comparison, James tends to slight Hawthorne's novel and to make Lockhart's seem greater than it is. He calls *Adam Blair* an excellent novel of the second rank, but in fact its interest today is almost entirely historical. There is too strong an element of melodramatic predictability in the series of events culminating in the adulterous act, which takes place during a violent thunderstorm and is indicated by omission with a hundred asterisks. The "passion" of *Adam Blair* may convey more warmth, but it does not reveal as serious a mind, or compare with the somber depth of emotion that grips *The Scarlet Letter*. James remarks that "Lockhart, by means much more crude, produces at moments a greater illusion, and satisfies our inevitable desire for something, in the people [it deals with] that shall be [at] the same pitch and continuity with ourselves" (p. 92). What he is really saying is that Lockhart, whom he calls "concrete," was a pioneering realist. The Reverend Adam Blair is the product of a special set of social conditions, and he is studied steadily in the light of those conditions. He is examined in his relation to his special society in rural Scotland, and it is a wholly natural, rather than supernatural, world in which he "falls" and is later redeemed and accepted back into the fellowship of his former parishioners. His experience illustrates not only his own psychology but also that of the other inhabitants of his district; and as regional realism, the novel is a precursor of George Eliot's studies in rural English life, a quite different direction in fiction than Hawthorne's.

An element of distortion sometimes appears in James's diminishment of Hawthorne as an exemplar of the "wrong" tradition; and, generally, James does not enter far into Hawthorne's world. At one point he remarks that Hawthorne's notebooks give the impression that he did not have any "general views that were in the least uncomfortable" (p. 22), which surely credits Hawthorne with more serenity than his tales of tormented outcasts suggest. Stranger still, he goes on to say that Hawthorne's fiction does not seem to him to be particularly tragic:

74

Nothing is more curious and interesting than this almost exclusively *imported* character of the sense of sin in Hawthorne's mind; it seems to exist there merely for an artistic purpose or literary purpose. He had ample cognizance of the Puritan conscience; it was his natural heritage; it was reproduced in him; looking into his soul, he found it there. But his relation to it was only, as one may say, intellectual; it was not moral or theological. He played with it, and used it as a pigment; he treated it, as the metaphysicians say, objectively.

. . . What pleased him in such subjects was their picturesqueness, their rich duskiness of colour, their chiaroscuro; but they were not the expression of a hopeless, or even of a predominately melancholy, feeling about the human soul. Such at least is my own impression. He is to a considerable degree ironical—that is part of his charm—part even, one might say, of his brightness; but he is neither bitter nor cynical—he is rarely even what I should call tragical. (Pp. 46–47)

James's sense of a nontragical Hawthorne has been remarked upon by Lionel Trilling in his essay "Our Hawthorne," one of the few articles to give attention to James's *Hawthorne*. Trilling writes that James "denies the darkness of Hawthorne's mind and in the course of doing so actually seems to deny that it is a serious mind. For he tells us that we must understand Hawthorne's concern with conscience to be largely 'ironical'." Trilling wonders why and how James came to this conclusion, and if he could be right, after all; but decides, finally, that his version of Hawthorne *must* be mistaken. "No doubt James's ironical entertainer makes a graceful and charming figure as he amuses himself with the toys strewn over the playground of a disused morality. But how can any member of the literary community fail to conclude that there is an intrinsic superiority in the grave, complex, and difficult Hawthorne we have learned to possess, the Hawthorne who represents 'man's dark odyssey in an alien world'?"[5] For Trilling, Hawthorne's modulation of what he sees, his qualification through ambiguity, make him less fully committed to a "chthonian" vision than Kafka, but he is nevertheless a different figure than James's Hawthorne, and more nearly the one I am able to recognize.

Although James was an extremely perceptive critic, his criticism was often affected by his biases as a creative writer. He was a great admirer of Stendhal, and *The Charterhouse of Parma* was one of his favorite European novels, but he dismissed *The Red and the Black* as being "unreadable." He described Jane Austen's novels as having sprung into being without meditation or any formed process of art. He never responded with any interest to the work of his great contemporaries Tolstoy and Dostoyevsky, whose large, sprawling novels seemed to him, as he said, like "loose fluid puddings." He could find no sense of evil in Baudelaire,[6] and he dismissed Whitman early in his career as a poet who had no ideas. In *Hawthorne* he describes Thoreau as a provincial who wrote less originally than Longfellow, Lowell, or even Motley! His remark that Thoreau wrote less originally than Motley is revealing, suggesting as it does how much he wishes to put Thoreau "down," how much he feels a distaste for him and the socially formless, morally enclosed world of the New England Transcendentalists he represented.

James's characterization of Hawthorne as an ironist with no general views that were in the least uncomfortable has a degree of plausibility on the basis of Hawthorne's notebooks alone; but even in the notebooks, Hawthorne's entries show so much reserve that they suggest large chasms of thought that have not been committed to paper. James seems determined to emphasize Hawthorne's "simplicity," and in doing so does not pursue clues that were available to him. There are some clues to Hawthorne's interior life in Lathrop's biography, for example, that James did not inquire into. Lathrop refers to Hawthorne's friendship with Melville and even quotes at length from Melville's letter about *The House of the Seven Gables*, including the following brief passage:

> There is a certain tragic phase of humanity, which, in our opinion, was never more powerfully embodied than by Hawthorne; we mean the tragicalness of human thought in its own unbiased, native, and profound workings. We think that into no recorded mind has the intense feeling of the whole truth ever entered more deeply than into this man's. By whole truth, we mean the apprehension of the absolute condition of present things as they strike the eye of the man who fears them not, though they do their worst to him.[7]

In reading Lathrop's book James had to have read both this reference to the Hawthorne-Melville friendship and the extracts from Melville's letters, but he apparently made no effort to learn who Melville was, if he did not already know, or to read his books, as any modern biographer or critic would have done. Had he done so, he might have had to qualify his view of Hawthorne as a nontragical ironist, produced by an uncomplicated age.

Throughout the biography James stresses that Hawthorne's world was uncomplicated and makes it seem as if a dialectic of affirmation and denial did not exist in that period of emergent American genius. The Transcendentalist period in New England seemed to him "a dawn without a noon" (p. 66) which had produced only two figures of consequence, Emerson and Hawthorne, whose work in terms of volume alone was slight or fragmentary. The whole thrust of the book is to diminish the achievement of New England in Hawthorne's time, to make it seem meager, particularly in comparison with the culture of England. It was not, obviously, a world to which James could readily relate, or against which he could define himself, except in terms of a fortunate escape. Early in the biography James remarks that it was possibly a blessing for Hawthorne that he was not "expansive and inquisitive" and lived much to himself; for "if he had been exacting and ambitious, if his appetite had been large and his knowledge various, he would probably have found the bounds of Salem intolerably narrow" (p. 23). James leaves the impression that he has imagined what it would have been like for him if he had been placed in Hawthorne's world, and the sense of "threat" this poses gives the book part of its tension.

77

For James, Hawthorne's world was not only uncomplicated, but was an era of a virtually uniform innocence, a golden age of uncritical confidence in America's future, a prelapsarian garden; and James sometimes uses the imagery of flowers and fragrant blooms to evoke the age and its pastoral nature. It was the age, of course, of Henry James, senior, a mystical democrat with whom James also seems in conflict in *Hawthorne*. When James refers to "poor Hawthorne" in the book, one is reminded of his references to "poor father" in his letters to his brother William. The elder James had been a close friend of Emerson's (one of the bedrooms of the James house was always known as "Mr. Emerson's room"), and Emerson and his friends were strikingly unworldly. In discussing the Transcendentalists and their founding of Brook Farm, James recalls his own childhood memories of some of these representative men, who were friends and colleagues of his father. He remarks that they "appeared unstained by the world, unfamiliar with worldly desires and standards, and with those various forms of human depravity which flourish in some high phases of civilization." They possessed a "certain noble credulity and faith in the perfectability of man" (pp. 65,

66). This description particularly suggests that it is not so much the whole country as his father and his associates whom James has in mind when he speaks of an earlier age of innocence.

Tocqueville's picture of America in the 1830s is more credible than James's in *Hawthorne,* in the consciousness he shows of conflict, underlying tensions, and uncertainty about the future. New England experienced a Utopian craze during that time, but its life was more complicated than the uniform innocence James claims. In the years that preceded the Civil War the country was torn by sectional differences which, as time went on, deepened and became irreconcilable; and there were sharp differences of attitude and opinion in New England itself. Yet James characterizes the spirit of the country at that time as "simple and uncritical," enlivened by a "genial optimism" (p. 112) that a special providence watched over the country. He quotes Hawthorne's remark, in his campaign biography of Franklin Pierce, that the slavery issue was "a misty philanthropic theory," and seems to suggest that Hawthorne's attitude was held generally by his contemporaries, which it was not. At such moments James gives the impression of being too remote from America, of touching it, as it were, with his fingertips.

A slightly jarring note of self-congratulation appears, too, in James's picture of the two generations the Civil War divided. The war, he observes, "introduced into the national consciousness a certain sense of proportion and relation, of the world being a more complicated place than it had hitherto seemed, the future more treacherous, success more difficult. . . . the good American, in days to come, will be a more critical person than his complacent and confident grandfather. He has eaten of the tree of knowledge. He will not, I think, be a sceptic, and still less, of course, a cynic; but he will be, without discredit to his well-known capacity for action, an observer" (p. 114). The Civil War had at least the beneficial effect of producing a Jamesian observer!

But if James seems determined to present himself in an adversary relationship to Hawthorne and his age, he nevertheless reveals an identification with Hawthorne on a certain level, in his moral consciousness. His tales, James remarks, "are glimpses of a great field, of the whole deep mystery of man's soul and conscience. They are moral, and their interest is moral; they deal with something more than the mere accidents and conventionalities, the surface occurrences of life. The fine thing in Hawthorne is that he cared for the deeper psychology, and that, in his way, he tried to become familiar with it. This natural, yet fanciful, familiarity with it; this air, on the author's part, of being a confirmed *habitué* of a region of mysteries and subtleties, constitutes the originality of his tales" (p. 51). But Hawthorne still remains for James an esthetic observer with tragic perspectives although not necessarily a tragic vision; and he does so quite possibly because what James found most admirable in Hawthorne was what he also found in himself. James was not at this point in his career committed to a tragic art; like that part of Hawthorne with which he seems to affiliate himself, he was an ironist and morally interested observer of "mysteries and subtleties."

In his introduction to a 1967 edition of *Hawthorne*, Tony Tanner has compared James's assessment of Hawthorne in the biography with his later assessments and noticed James's change of attitude with time.[8] In his essay on Hawthorne in 1897, the condescension of *Hawthorne* is no longer present. James still refers to the earlier American society as having a greater simplicity than the age that followed, but he is now conscious of "a life of the spirit more complex than anything that met the mere eye of sense," and of Hawthorne as an artist whose imagination was capable of grasping all the subterranean clues of the common life. And in the section on Hawthorne's European experience, he no longer patronizes Hawthorne's failure of response. He speaks of the way in which Hawthorne "surrendered himself to the charm of Italy" and is aware of "the mixture of sensibility and reluctance, of response and dissent, the strife between his sense of beauty and his sense of banishment." Tanner calls attention to James's own situation in the late 1890s, to his sense of the artist's exile, which he has incorporated into his later vision of Hawthorne. Instead of picturing Hawthorne as a provincial outsider in Europe, he has treated him more sympathetically, as a universally alienated writer. James's final sentence—"His collection of moral mysteries is the cabinet of a dilettante"—suggests that he has not altered his view of Hawthorne as an esthetic observer and ironist; but there is, at least, a more positive valuation of Hawthorne, a different way of defining himself against him.[9] James's disillusionment in novels of this period suggests a more chastened attitude toward Europe, against which he had, rather loftily, measured Hawthorne earlier. His own alienation seems to have given him a new fellowship with Hawthorne, the earlier American artist who is "outside of everything."

In a still later article on Hawthorne, written in 1904 on the observance of the centenary of his birth, James emphasized not the disadvantages to Hawthorne of his "national consciousness," but what he gained by belonging so much to his region. "Salem had the good fortune," James writes, "to assist him betimes, to this charming discrimination—that of looking for romance near at hand, and where it grows thick and true, rather than on the other side of the globe." It might be claimed, in view of the fact that his article was addressed to the town fathers of Salem, that his words were merely an expected compliment.[10] But James was by then, as Edel's biography shows, very conscious of what he had lost as well as gained by his expatriate life abroad, and I think that he was more genuinely ready to concede to Hawthorne the positive benefits of his American milieu.

But his last, and best, word about Hawthorne in the article is that he was an innovator.

What was admirable and instinctive in Hawthorne was that he saw the quaintness or the weirdness, the interest *behind* the interest, of things, as continuous with the very life we are leading . . . round about him and under his eyes; saw it as something deeply within us, not as something infinitely disconnected from us; saw it in short in the very application of the spectator's, the poet's mood, in the kind of reflection the things we know best and see oftenest make in our minds. So it is that such things as *The Seven Gables, The Blithedale Romance, The Marble Faun*, are singularly fruitful examples of the real as distinguished from the artificial romantic note.[11]

James was to comment on Hawthorne, however, one further time, near the end of his life, in *Notes of a Son and Brother* (1914). He relates how, at the age of twenty-one, at the very hour of Hawthorne's death, he came belatedly to recognize Hawthorne's genius, an experience that actually caused him to break down with emotion and sob. In a phrase surprisingly similar to Melville's "shock of recognition," he speaks of his "joy of recognition," that was "like the uplifting of a wave." But here is the passage in full:

There associates itself with my cherished chamber of application the fact that of a sudden, and while we were always and as much as ever awaiting him, Hawthorne was dead. What I have called the fusion strikes me as indeed beyond my rendering when I think of the peculiar assault on my private consciousness of *that* news: I sit once more, half-dressed, late of a summer morning and in a bedimmed light which is somehow at once that of dear old green American shutters drawn to against openest windows and that of a moral shadow projected as with violence—I sit on my belated bed, I say, and yield to the pang that made me positively and loyally cry.

. . . I fondly felt in those days invaluable that I had during certain last and otherwise rather blank months at Newport taken in for the first time and at one straight draught the full sweet sense of our one fine romancer's work—for sweet it then above all seemed to me; and I remember well how, while the process day after day drew itself admirably out, I found the actual exquisite taste of it, the strain of the revelation, justify up to the notch whatever had been weak in my delay.[12]

81

James goes on to speak of the "moral" of Hawthorne's career: "For the moral was that an American could be an artist, one of the finest, without 'going outside' about it, as I liked to say; quite in fact as if Hawthorne had become one by being American *enough*, by the felicity of how the artist in him missed nothing, suspected nothing, that the ambient air didn't affect him as containing."[13] The statement suggests another kind of identification with Hawthorne, as the predecessor who showed that an American could be an artist, "one of the finest," as one on whom, as James sometimes says of his imaginative characters, "nothing is lost."

On each occasion that James wrote on Hawthorne, he defined himself against him with a somewhat different perspective, and for that reason it would be rash to take James's appraisal of him in his biography as a final word. *Hawthorne* reveals where James was in his career when he wrote the book: becoming established as a realist with an international outlook, and needing to challenge Hawthorne and his "little" world. In his critical biography he "corrects" Hawthorne, as he had corrected Hawthorne previously in his fiction. The dominant metaphor James uses in *Hawthorne*, that of a "fall" from innocence into knowledge, reveals that James has used Hawthorne's own archetype against him and his generation, depicting their time as a "blissful" innocence.

Hawthorne is a very deceptive book, however, not only because there is an element of caricature in it, but also because it gives no indication of how deeply James's own earlier career was influenced by Hawthorne. He speaks of the structural failure of *The Marble Faun* without acknowledging that it lays the foundation for his own international theme. He is critical of *The Blithedale Romance*, but does not mention how important the character of Miles Coverdale had been in his conception of Rowland Mallet (one of the earliest in a long series of disengaged observers in James's work). The distinctions he makes seem to be absolute—the superiority of realism to romance, of a cosmopolitan attitude to a national consciousness—and yet James is not wholly a realist, nor wholly without national consciousness. In his formulation of American experience he gravitates repeatedly to Hawthorne—and quite as important, will do so again in the future. Lyall Powers has concluded of this deceptive book that "James's biography *Hawthorne* is clearly a hail and farewell to that influence,"[14] yet, in fact, Hawthorne's influence will continue well beyond *Hawthorne*. It would be more accurate to say that *Hawthorne* opens a new phase of James's relation to Hawthorne. In the biography James announces the superiority of his fiction of social awareness and discrimination to Hawthorne's socially indistinct conceptions. In the 1880s he will go on to make good his claims.

6 Washington Square: Romance Shadows in the Drawing Room

In a letter of 1880 to Howells, James called *Washington Square* "a tale purely American"; yet Buitenhuis, in *The Grasping Imagination*, is unable to account for the novel under his classification of James's "American" writing. "The conflict," he says, "does not depend much on the national identity of the characters." Nor does James gain anything, he thinks, in setting the novel in New York City: "Since the action is practically confined to drawing-rooms, it can be divorced almost completely from local physical conditions." He concludes that lacking "formed schemata for the setting of the novel, James was forced to resort to familiar conventions in writing it. . . . in this novel, if anywhere, it can be claimed that James was a kind of male Jane Austen."[1] In his account of the novel, Buitenhuis finds himself quite unable to explain why James referred to *Washington Square* as a tale peculiarly American. An explanation is possible, but first one ought to notice how *Washington Square* came into being.

The *donnée* of the novel, furnished by James's friend, the actress Frances Kemble, is recorded in his notebook entry of February 21, 1879.[2] Mrs. Kemble had related the story of her brother's engagement many years before to a "dull, plain, common-place girl" who stood to inherit a fortune from her father. Young Kemble was an exceptionally handsome ensign in a marching regiment; selfish and "luxurious," he was interested in the girl only for her money. The girl's father (the master of King's College, Cambridge—"the old Doctor") disapproved of the engagement and threatened to disinherit his daughter if she should marry Kemble. Convinced that the father meant to keep his word, Kemble jilted her. Later the father died, and the girl came into her inheritance. Perhaps ten years after the engagement, Kemble returned to England from knocking about in the world (still a handsome, selfish, and impecunious soldier), and once again sought to pay his addresses to her. She turned him away, even though she cared for no other man. "H. K.'s selfishness had over-reached itself and this was the retribution of time."

Mrs. Kemble's account would not, in itself, seem especially promising as the basis for a novel. What gives *Washington Square* its interest is James's superior treatment of his material. His treatment was almost certainly indebted to Balzac, as Cornelia Kelley has argued in *The Early Development of Henry James*.[3] In "The Lesson of Balzac" (1905), James described Balzac as "the man who is really the father of us all." "I speak of him," he declares "and can only speak, as a man of his own craft, an emulous fellow-worker, who has learned from him more of the lessons of the engaging mystery of fiction than from anyone else."[4] "The Lesson of Balzac" was written late in James's career, but he had read and admired Balzac while he was still a young man, as can be seen in his references to him in the second literary review he published. In this review of Harriet Prescott's *Azarian, An Episode* (1865), James criticized Prescott's florid style and held up Balzac's *Eugénie Grandet* to her as a model to be studied:

Balzac does not *paint*, does not copy, objects; his chosen instrument being a pen, he is content to *write* them. He is literally real; he presents objects as they are. The scenes and persons of his drama are minutely described. Grandet's house, his sitting-room, his habits, his appearance, his dress, are all reproduced with the fidelity of a photograph. The same with Madame Grandet and Eugénie. . . . We almost see the musty little sitting-room in which so much of the action goes forward. We are familiar with the gray *boiserie*, the faded curtains, the rickety card-tables, the framed samplers on the walls, Madame Grandet's footwarmer, and the table set for the meager dinner. And yet our sense of the human interest of the story is never lost. Why is this? It is because these things are described *only in so far as they bear upon the action,* and not in the least for themselves.[5]

In *The Early Development of Henry James,* Kelley contends that Balzac's *Eugénie Grandet* intervened between James's source, outlined in his notebook entry, and the completed version of *Washington Square.* The plots of these two novels, of approximately the same length, are similar in many ways. "Both girls," Kelley points out, "are fundamentally good; both are somewhat plain physically, but not unattractive to people who place the radiance which comes from their nobility of soul above mere prettiness; both have reached their twenties (Eugénie is twenty-three) without knowing the meaning of love except as it is a feeling for parents. . . . Each [story] is the account of what a cruel father and a false suitor between them can do to a sensitive nature."[6] Her criticism considers similarities not only of plot but also of form and technique, in regard to which, she feels, *Washington Square* has a close relation to *Eugénie Grandet:*

[James] abjured all use of a narrator or an interpreter or a perceiving consciousness in favor of a straightforward narrative such as Balzac used. . . . James opened his novel with an account of setting and antecedent action; he carefully explained everything which would help the reader to understand the relation of father and daughter and thus the ensuing action, before he began the main story; and then at the end he detailed quickly but completely subsequent events. *Eugénie Grandet* begins and ends the same way; the story is in between.[7]

The formal similarities Kelley points out are quite convincing; indeed, even more might be said of Balzac's presence in *Washington Square.*[8] In "The Lesson of Balzac," James praised especially Balzac's intense "saturation with his idea," his ability to grasp in a flash of intuition "the complicated human creature or human condition." Whatever his faults, he does not fail to possess his image, to fix and hold his characters and their conditions. "What immediately strikes us," James writes, "is the part assigned by him, in any picture, to the *conditions* of the creature with whom he is concerned. Contrasted with him other prose painters of life scarcely seem to see the conditions at all."⁹ Perhaps the deepest affinity *Washington Square* has with *Eugénie Grandet* is its exceptional consciousness of conditions as they act on the temperaments of the novels' principal characters. (In *Eugénie Grandet*, the nature of provincial life, the obsession of old Grandet, the condition of women at the time, all conspire to determine the outcome of the novel; in *Washington Square*, the action proceeds from Dr. Sloper's psychological history and fixation as they act, in the austerity of his social world, upon Catherine's unaggressive nature.) The consciousness of conditions is so pronounced that in both works the characters seem denied very much freedom of movement. In *Washington Square,* to put it another way, one sees James using the method of the social "study" and the procedures of critical realism employed by Balzac. One might even say that James has consciously translated Balzac's study of provincial life to an earlier-day New York City.

86

Yet James did not admire Balzac without reservation, and in this connection it is worth noting his essay entitled "Honoré De Balzac," which appeared in periodical form in 1875 and was later included in his collection of critical essays, *French Poets and Novelists* (1878). Here James placed himself on record, granting to Balzac the greatest gift for portraiture in fiction and yet finding him incomparable but not *fine*. What placed James himself in a different tradition, after all, was that Balzac, for all his vitality and power, did not have a moral imagination, or "any natural sense of morality." "When we approach Thackeray and George Eliot, George Sand and Turgénieff," James remarks, "it is into the conscience and mind that we enter, and we think of these writers primarily as great consciences and great minds. When we approach Balzac we seem to enter into a great temperament—a prodigious nature." Balzac was obsessed by picture, not truth; when virtue appealed to his imagination, it was not because it was true but because it was picturesque! "What he represents best is extremely simple virtue, and vice simple or complex, as you please. In superior virtue, intellectual virtue, he fails."

Washington Square

The essay reveals that while James admired Balzac's highly developed skills of representation, he did not include him in the tradition of George Eliot and Hawthorne, who "care for moral questions" and "are haunted by a moral idea."[10]

It is because of James's more moral imagination that he improves in certain respects upon Balzac, bringing to his novel, if not necessarily greater projective power, at least more impressive refinements of perception. Dr. Sloper is a more complicated human being than Balzac's "humor" character Grandet, and his relationship to his daughter reveals a psychological sophistication that is not found in Balzac. Similarly, James's conception of Catherine improves in an important respect upon Balzac's of Eugénie. Eugénie is idealized in her innate purity, nobility, and naive generosity. Balzac informs the reader that a painter would find in the shape of her eye, the way she moved her eyelids, "a hint of the divine." By the end of the novel, she has "the nobility of suffering, the saintliness of a person whose soul has never been contaminated by this world." The modern reader, especially, is apt to find Balzac's depiction of Eugénie's transcendence of the world, through the nobility of her soul, to be more picturesque than true—to find it, on its deepest level, to lack sincerity. With greater moral realism, James does not allow Catherine such transcendence. But most of all, he surpasses Balzac in his study of his characters' consciousness. He examines the moral interiors of his characters, and this examination is the center and focus of the novel.

James has placed Catherine at the moral center of *Washington Square*, and certain critics, notably R. P. Blackmur, have felt that she is too simple or inconsequential to bear the weight of the entire work. Blackmur describes her in the following way: "In her emptiness she grows to understand that the emotions that are bent on her have nothing to do with fondness and in the end there is no violence in her, and no room for any, except the violence of her heartbeat, to which she chooses to listen in the increasing vacuum and halting circulation. She has given up everything for the lover who has deceived her and has now deserted her; but at the same time she has given nothing to anybody, any time, least of all to herself"[11] But in fact

87

Catherine has given all of her love—to her father first, and then to Morris Townsend; by the end, against formidable odds and at large cost, she has managed to achieve a personal integrity.

A more searching reading of *Washington Square* than Blackmur's may be seen in Richard Poirier's chapter on the novel in *The Comic Sense of Henry James*. Poirier sees Catherine growing almost unpredictably from an obedient daughter, with an undeveloped self, into a person, and in doing so thwarting the deepest certainties of Dr. Sloper as to her nature; that she has "freedom" rather than "fixity" calls Sloper's whole ordering of reality into question. He has spent his life measuring surfaces and gauging symptoms, dividing people into types, and predicting their behavior. He measures Morris Townsend correctly because he knows his "type," as well as the social and economic conditions in which he is placed. Catherine's refusal to conform to type ("poor old Catherine," as he calls his presumed nullity of a daughter) pushes Sloper toward an increasing frustration; his imagination begins to move in the direction of desperation, and his irony becomes self-torturing. "The development of his character," Poirier notes, "is from scientist to melodramatist."[12]

Poirier seems to me to be right when he says that the victimizer himself becomes a victim, and that Dr. Sloper, who prides himself upon intellect, does not, by the end, know his daughter at all. Yet his more encompassing thesis that James was dealing with "comic" strategies, with reversals of expectations as his central concern, leads him to some curious conclusions. It leads him to deny that there is any injury in *Washington Square,* or any melodrama either, except insofar as it is entertained only to be declined. Poirier remarks that lacking native material with which to work, James turned to the conventions of the melodramatic fairy tale (the Cruel Father, Motherless Daughter, Handsome Lover, and Fairy Godmother), and then presented ironic reversals to the stock responses of its archetypes. While it is true that melodrama has often been used by James in what Poirier calls a "contemplative" way, it is *not* true that melodrama has always been strictly declined. An element of melodrama is certainly present and its presence is related, moreover, to the American sources Poirier believes were unavailable to James. In a letter to

Howells, James does complain of the lack of "paraphernalia" which his new-world setting imposed.[13] But there is reason to believe that James found American sources from which to draw, and that he found them in Hawthorne.

James had reread Hawthorne's fiction and written his biography of Hawthorne just before writing *Washington Square;* and his description of Hawthorne in the biography as a regular dweller "in the moral, psychological realm" suggests his value to James, who followed Balzac only to a certain point in his conception of *Washington Square.* In exploring the relationships of his characters, James introduced Hawthorne's psychological themes into his novel, and more particularly the situation and theme of "Rappaccini's Daughter." In *Hawthorne* James describes certain of Hawthorne's tales of fantasy and allegory as "little masterpieces," and of these singles out two as representing "the highest point that Hawthorne reached in this direction"—"Young Goodman Brown" and "Rappaccini's Daughter" (p. 44).[14] James had made an ingenious interpretive use of "Rappaccini's Daughter" earlier in "Benvolio," but in *Washington Square* Hawthorne's story plays an even more important role.

In "Rappaccini's Daughter" and *Washington Square,* an innocent young girl is torn between her father and her would-be lover (in both of whom she has placed an implicit trust), who each fail her in her greatest need of them. Catherine Sloper does not duplicate Beatrice, who embodies spiritual truth in a fallen world; yet a correspondence of a certain kind exists. Catherine is not imposing, is not "quick with her book, nor, indeed, with anything else" (p. 167),[15] but her offer of love (which is pure) is mocked, and her inmost being is violated. This situation appears in "Rappaccini's Daughter," in which the figures who surround Beatrice deny her "soul." Beatrice is betrayed by her father, who returns her love by using her for the purpose of a psychological experiment, and failed by Giovanni, the "beautiful," vain young man who can believe only in outward appearances. Beatrice is the victim of her guardian; and similarly, Catherine is encircled by characters, including most particularly her father, who ought to protect her but instead lacerate her innocence.

The imagery James employs (frequently of knives and killing) makes it clear that all of the principal characters in *Washington Square* are implicated in Catherine's victimization. After he has broken off with her, Catherine writes appealingly to Townsend: "Morris, you are killing me" (p. 273), and Dr. Sloper concedes that he is doing the young man a favor by providing Catherine with the improving advantages of a European trip: "We have fattened the sheep for him before he kills it" (p. 252). Mrs. Penniman asks the doctor: "Don't you wish also by chance to murder your child? . . . You will kill her" (p. 232). And she, in turn, is described as bearing the knife. "If Morris had been her son, she would certainly have sacrificed Catherine to a superior conception of his future; and to be ready to do so, as the case stood, was therefore even a finer degree of devotion. Nevertheless, it checked her breath a little to have the sacrificial knife, as it were, suddenly thrust into her hand" (p. 264). Catherine does not perish like Beatrice, but after the others have dealt with her, her life faces in death's direction.

90

Critics have sometimes regarded Catherine as merely a "simpleton" daughter, but it should be remembered that this description comes from Dr. Sloper. By the time she returns from Europe, she has begun to establish her own identity, and she preserves the sincerity of her emotions in the face of a world that is deeply compromised. She may be slow and unimposing, but she is not superficial; yet it is on the level of surfaces that she is judged by the others. Like Beatrice, she finds that it is her fate to suffer the judgment of the worldly. Mrs. Penniman (whose name suggests a coin of small price) is not a woman of great perspicacity, and she is much less impressed by Catherine, who has integrity, than by the handsome Morris Townsend, who does not. Mrs. Penniman "uses" Catherine to indulge in a vicarious romance with Townsend, an act of moral obtuseness which pushes Catherine toward what will be her torment. At an important point, furthermore, she sells Catherine out. For she knows by then that Townsend is interested in Catherine for her money, and sides with him when it has become clear that he would rather leave the field clear to advance his fortunes elsewhere than accept Catherine without her full inheritance. In this betrayal Mrs.

Penniman reveals that she sees Catherine as the others do—as marketplace commodity.

Dr. Sloper and Morris Townsend are more "conscious" than Mrs. Penniman, but they too deny Catherine a selfhood that they need respect. Dr. Sloper sees Catherine first in terms of the credit she would be to him if, like her mother, she were beautiful and clever (would have worldly "value"). Since she is neither, and does not redound to his credit, he treats her patronizingly, often with a cuttingly ironic form of address. He has even come to feel that by being as she is "she had played him a trick." "He had moments of irritation at having produced a commonplace child," James observes, "and he even went so far at times as to take a certain satisfaction in the thought that his wife had not lived to find her out" (p. 168). Despite their differences, the doctor and Townsend are in many ways alike, including the way in which they regard Catherine. On several occasions Dr. Sloper describes Townsend as "intelligent," as he thinks of himself as being. Townsend's frequently referred to smile is "satiric," much like the satiric irony of Dr. Sloper, expressed in his glance and smile. And there are times when Townsend's smile, like the doctor's, is directed, with an implication of mockery, at Catherine—as when he courts her with a "smile of respectful devotion" (p. 182) in his eyes. When he is invited to dinner at the Slopers', Townsend samples the doctor's claret with approval, and "while he sipped it . . . reflected that a cellarful of good liquor . . . would be a most attractive idiosyncracy in a father-in-law" (p. 187). At this moment he has the frosty wit of Dr. Sloper. Later, when the doctor and Catherine are away in Europe, Townsend makes himself at ease, smoking many cigars (like Sloper) in the doctor's study, and the two men are made to suggest one another. They are like character doubles, and each sees Catherine not for herself, but as an adjunct of his own self-concern.

Sloper himself had made an advantageous (although honorable) marriage, and he understands the way Townsend thinks because he too knows the value of property. Catherine, also, is property; he calculates her "worth" in money terms—in the amount she stands to inherit. There is no other reason a young man would be interested in her, and this estimation of his child even gives him a peculiar satisfaction; he is pleased to deny that she has any "worth" he cannot know and measure. At an early point in the novel when Dr. Sloper reflects upon his daughter, his thinking is expressed in the language of commerce. "Besides, he was a philosopher; he smoked a good many cigars over his disappointment, and in the fulness of time he got used to it. He satisfied himself that he had expected nothing, though, indeed, with a certain oddity of reasoning. 'I expect nothing,' he said to himself; 'so that, if she gives me a surprise, it will be all clear gain. If she doesn't, it will be no loss'" (pp. 168–69). When Lavinia Penniman, attempting to defend Catherine, asks him if it is not better to be good than to be clever, Sloper replies that "you are good for nothing unless you are clever" (p. 166). That he is concerned not with whether a thing is good, but with what it is good for, is a comment on Sloper as a "philosopher."

92

In their relations to their daughters, there is more than a slight resemblance between Dr. Sloper and Dr. Rappaccini. Both are doctors and men of science (Sloper is even described at the beginning as a "scholarly doctor") whose pride of intellect has replaced their capacity for love; and their daughters' "hearts" become for them the occasion of an experiment. Dr. Rappaccini sacrifices his daughter's life in the course of his using her in a psychological experiment that gratifies his overweening egotism. In a sense, Dr. Sloper enacts the same role and has a similar relation to his daughter. Father-daughter relationships, including those in which there is a degree of cruelty, have been treated elsewhere in nineteenth-century fiction; there are instances of this not only in Balzac but also in Dickens and George Eliot.[16] But the situation treated in "Rappaccini's Daughter" and *Washington Square* is so special that the two works have a unique relation to each other.

There is no question that James associates Sloper, the "scholarly doctor," with intellect, and indeed with intellect that has developed at the expense of emotions. Sloper is described early in the novel as an "observer" (p. 163), Mrs. Penniman has occasion to speak of his "hard, intellectual nature" (p. 220), and Townsend is not wholly wrong in calling him a "heartless scoffer" (p. 198). His intellectual nature manifests itself frequently in his habit of irony, which is almost always sharp and lacerating. His irony is noticed at the beginning, when Catherine appears in new clothes that are rather ill-chosen. Dr. Sloper turns to her with his "little smile" and remarks: "Is it possible that this magnificent person is my child?" (p. 176). This incident occurs before Catherine meets Morris Townsend; after their affair begins, his smile and irony are like torture instruments, as in the scene in which she announces to him her "engagement" to Townsend:

> "And who is the happy mortal whom you have honoured with your choice?"
> "Mr. Morris Townsend." And as she pronounced her lover's name, Catherine looked at him. What she saw was her father's still grey eye and his clear-cut, definite smile. She contemplated these objects for a moment, and then she looked back at the fire; it was much warmer. (P. 201)

These are not isolated incidents; James remarks that "it is a literal fact that he almost never addressed his daughter save in the ironical form" (p. 176). Perhaps the cruelest moment occurs when Catherine is seen standing in the window of the house on Washington Square after having been jilted by Townsend, and her father, entering below, tips his hat to her. He cannot know that Townsend has just abandoned her, but he must know that she is suffering, and his courtly addresses can be nothing other than a mockery of her maiden's heart.

In contrast particularly with the doctor, James has made Catherine remarkably selfless. In an early passage he comments that "in spite of her taste for fine clothes, she had not a grain of coquetry, and her anxiety when she put them on was as to whether they, and not she, would look well" (p. 170). In this section Catherine looks to her father almost as Providence; she assures Townsend that he is "full of goodness" (p. 196). The way in which she regards her father is worth noting:

93

To her mind there was nothing of the infinite about Mrs. Penniman; Catherine saw her all at once, as it were, and was not dazzled by the apparition; whereas her father's great faculties seemed, as they stretched away, to lose themselves in a sort of luminous vagueness, which indicated, not that they stopped, but that Catherine's own mind ceased to follow them. (P. 168)

In Catherine's impression of his infinite faculties, Dr. Sloper appears almost as God, an impression borne out in other references. "She had an immense respect for her father," James writes, "and she felt that to displease him would be a misdemeanor analogous to an act of profanity in a great temple" (p. 227). In playing God, as it were, with his daughter's spirit, Dr. Sloper has a close kinship with Dr. Rappaccini.

Dr. Sloper is like Dr. Rappaccini, certainly, in his speculative manipulation of the lives of the young couple: "It is immense," he comments, "there will be a great deal to observe" (p. 238). During a conversation with Mrs. Penniman, he reports on the progress of his "experiment" in the language of a clinician:

> "Say it amuses you outright. I don't see why it should be such a joke that your daughter adores you."
> "It is the point where the adoration stops that I find it interesting to fix."
> "It stops where the other sentiment begins."
> "Not at all—that would be simple enough. The two things are extremely mixed up, and the mixture is extremely odd. It will produce some third element, and that's what I am waiting to see. I wait with suspense—with positive excitement; and that is a sort of emotion that I didn't suppose Catherine would ever provide for me. I am really very much obliged to her." (P. 238)

Dr. Sloper refers to his psychological experiment, furthermore, as an "entertainment," and it is said at one point that he had "hoped for a little more resistance for the sake of a little more entertainment" (p. 216). His manipulation is noticed in the scene where he warns

Catherine of the grief she will cause him if she sees Townsend again, after which he listens at the door he has just closed behind him to see what effect his words will have:

> The Doctor took several turns round his study, with his hands in his pockets, and a thin sparkle, possibly of irritation, but partly also of something like humor, in his eye. "By Jove," he said to himself, "I believe she will stick—I believe she will stick!" And this idea of Catherine "sticking" appeared to have a comical side, and to offer a prospect of entertainment. (P. 231)

In the end, however, Dr. Sloper's manipulation of Catherine's life leads to no positive good for anyone, including the doctor himself. His ingenuity, like Dr. Rappaccini's, proves futile. He continues to mock Catherine, but his mockery is hollow and insecure, since he is no longer sure that he understands her. In his loss of control over her, in his sense of not knowing and being powerless, Dr. Sloper is himself thwarted and mocked.

95

But if James incorporates Hawthorne's doctor-and-daughter archetype into *Washington Square,* he also transforms it into psychological realism. Dr. Sloper is not a "fiend," but a vulnerable human being, a character with a psychological fixation whose actions have been convincingly motivated. In the scene in the Alps, one sees the rage his detachment and irony turn into; and this is but one instance, given stronger emphasis, of the life of the emotions with which he cannot cope, and from which he has tried to shield himself by attempting to control life intellectually. There is a very strong suggestion that he feels responsible for the death of his wife and infant son; yet it is not himself he punishes but his daughter. His treatment of Catherine is a neurotic denial of guilt. This more plausible motivation is part of the difference in mode between "Rappaccini's Daughter" and *Washington Square,* which together show the movement from the American romance to the modern social study. Hawthorne's fable of the doctor's sacrilege of his daughter's inmost being, through intellectual presumption, informs *Washington Square* and enriches its power of suggestion. Yet James has chastened Hawthorne's conception, placing it in a fully specified social context (the drawing rooms in which much of the action takes place contrast sharply with Hawthorne's fabled setting), and treated it with an observant irony.

At the same time, *Washington Square* suggests the ambivalence of the relationship of Hawthorne and James; for if James surpasses his predecessor in realistic representation, he is also dependent on him for the archetype of psychological obsession he treats. *Washington Square* reveals the close bond between them in their shared psychological interests and in their sense of the sanctity of the individual's being. This sense of the individual's importance is part of the American democratic vision, allying James with Hawthorne despite James's allegiances to realism, and despite his criticism of democracy. With this continuation of sensibility in mind, and treatment of a common subject, it cannot be claimed that James lacked any American sources from which to draw in his conception of *Washington Square.*

96

These sources were not of New York, where the novel is set, but of New England and the imagination of Hawthorne. Moreover, "Rappaccini's Daughter" provides a clue, indirectly, to *Washington Square* as a tale peculiarly American. Beatrice is sacrificed in a vacuum, but with his greater social awareness James has located Catherine's experience within the city of New York. The New York background of *Washington Square* has been lightly sketched, but it is not quite nonexistent, as critics have sometimes claimed. There is a remarkable thinness in the texture of social life in New York as James has presented it, but its very thinness, its austerity, is significant. In "An International Episode," written shortly before *Washington Square,* James viewed New York satirically as a hotel culture, with a continual expansion uptown. The men in the story are all overworked in their business pursuits and spend most of their lives at their offices. One of the men, Mr. Westgate, is described as having "a thin, sharp, familiar face . . . with a business-like, a quick, intelligent eye."[17] His "sharp" face is a reminder of the practical and utilitarian nature of New York, of which Dr. Sloper and Morris Townsend are both representative. It is a world in which money may also be a metaphor of mind. The men in "An International Episode" are obsessed by business, and the women have as their only fulfillment marriage and the raising of families, lacking which they have virtually no life at all. Catherine Sloper is one of these, one whom life has passed by while the city, with its commercial activity, moves continually northward. Critics have been puzzled by James's reference to *Washington Square* as a peculiarly American tale, but there is, after all, something characteristic of her place in Catherine's fate. James did not need either Balzac's bleak provinces or Hawthorne's haunted, postlapsarian gardens for his image of spiritual austerity. He has envisioned it very memorably in the concluding view of Catherine, in the house on Washington Square that does not move with the city, that belongs with the quaintness of the past rather than the renewing energies of the future, as she picks up her morsel of fancywork, "for life, as it were."

97

7   *The Portrait of a Lady:*
The Great Dramatic Chiaroscuro

98   In *The Portrait of a Lady* a number of characters can be seen to have evolved from earlier characters in James's fiction (Ralph Touchett from Roger Lawrence in *Watch and Ward,* Isabel Archer from Madame de Mauves and Bessie Alden, Lord Warburton from Lord Lambeth in "An International Episode"); and yet the novel's conception was also importantly affected by other writers, most notably by George Eliot.[1] James wrote critical articles on George Eliot on no fewer than nine separate occasions, beginning with his essay "The Novels of George Eliot" in the *Atlantic Monthly* in 1866, in which he considered her work up through the publication of *Felix Holt* and revealed his admiration of her fiction, together with certain reservations about it. He speaks of the "comparative feebleness of her dramatic movement" in early novels like *Adam Bede* and of the fragmented quality of *Felix Holt,* which leaves "no single impression" upon the mind. *Romola,* the most impressive of her novels up to that time, is a failure in a dramatic sense: "Its dramatic construction is feeble, the story drags and halts, the setting is too large for the picture."[2] In his review of *Middlemarch* (1873), James seems, as he conceded to his brother William, rather too stingy in his praise. He comments that *Middlemarch* "sets a limit, we think, to the development of the old-fashioned English novel," by which he meant that discursiveness in the novel (the tendency of Eliot's work to which he most objected) could hardly be carried further. In a letter of the same year to Grace Norton, James noted, in regard to *Middlemarch,* that his own ambition was to produce stories with more form, "little exemplary works of art."[3] At this time James was publishing his Hawthornesque tales "The Madonna of the Future" and "The Last of the Valerii," and it is revealing that in his review he should remark, as a final reservation, that *Middlemarch* lacked "the great dramatic *chiaroscuro.*"[4]

James's comments on *Daniel Deronda* (1876), when it first appeared, seem at times contradictory. To William James he wrote that the novel seems "a great failure compared with her other books. Gwendolen, to me, *lives* a little; but not the others." Yet to Alice James, he remarks: "I enjoyed it more than anything of hers—or any other novelist's almost—I have ever read. . . . The English richness of George Eliot beggars everything else, everywhere, that one might compare with her."[5] That James was of different minds about *Daniel Deronda* is suggested further by his review of the novel, which takes the form of a "conversation" among three imaginary people of differing views—Pulcheria, Theodora, and Constantius—the last of whom speaks most nearly for James himself. Pulcheria argues that *Daniel Deronda* lacks "current," that its ponderousness is more German than English, and that the Jewish burden of the novel fails to produce an illusion of life. Constantius-James is inclined to agree, and compares George Eliot with Turgenev. "Turgéniéff," he says, "is a magician, which I don't think I should call George Eliot. One is a poet, the other a philosopher. One cares for the aspect of thinks and the other cares for the reason of things." Yet Theodora, who defends George Eliot, is "right" too, and Constantius is willing to make concessions. "The intellectual brilliancy of *Daniel Deronda,*" he says, "strikes me as very great, in excess of anything the author has done. . . . I delighted in its deep, rich English tone." Where Pulcheria and Constantius agree—the thrust of the review—is in their admiration of the character of Gwendolen Harleth, which Constantius calls a "masterpiece." "The fact remains," he observes, "that Gwendolen's whole history is vividly told. And see how the girl is known, inside out, how thoroughly she is felt and understood. It is the most *intelligent* thing in all George Eliot's writing, and that is saying much. It is so deep, so true, so complete, it holds such a wealth of psychological detail, it is more than masterly."[6]

In his discussion of George Eliot in *The Great Tradition*, F. R. Leavis has remarked that without *Daniel Deronda* James could not have written *The Portrait of a Lady*—a statement that is rather sweeping and yet partially correct, at least in the sense that Gwendolen Harleth provided the inspiration for Isabel Archer.[7] *Daniel Deronda* establishes the psychological model of the spirited, self-centered girl who learns, in the course of a deeply scarring marriage, that her self-assertion is powerless before the world. George Eliot's unhurried revelation of Gwendolen Harleth's mind, the depth of psychological probing in her characterization, stand behind James's treatment of Isabel Archer, a study far more ambitious than any James had undertaken until that time. In their attention to the consciousness of their characters, *Middlemarch* and *Daniel Deronda* move to the outer limits of the Victorian novel without ever quite leaving the Victorian world. In *The Portrait of a Lady*, James begins where George Eliot left off.

Dorothea Brooke and Gwendolen Harleth, the young heroines of *Middlemarch* and *Daniel Deronda*, have important features in common. They both aspire toward personal enlargement, make disastrous marriages, and find not an enhancing expansion, but baffling constriction and frustration. Dorothea Brooke, in particular, precipitates her own disaster by choosing to marry too early, acting from motives so elevated as to be unreal. There is, as Eliot observes, a puritan strain in her psychology. "Her mind," she comments, "was theoretic. . . . She was enamoured of intensity and greatness, and rash in embracing whatever seemed to her to have those aspects; likely to seek martyrdom, to make retractions, and then to incur martyrdom after all in a quarter where she had not sought it."[8] From high-minded motives, she marries Mr. Casaubon, much her senior in years, a lifeless embalmment of erudition. As time goes on she comes to recognize the sterility of his nature and her own irremediable mistake. Instead of fresh pulsing life, she finds only chill, colorless, ever narrowing landscapes, and moral imprisonment. Her experience is an earlier version of Gwendolen Harleth's—and, one might add, of Isabel Archer's.

It is Gwendolen Harleth's situation, however, that touches closest to Isabel's. Gwendolen and Isabel have a youthfully presumptuous, egotistic orientation toward life. More than once, as she is seen early in *Daniel Deronda*, Gwendolen is described as "a princess in exile," a phrase also applicable to Isabel in Albany before she voyages out into the world. Both are endowed, too, with the qualities of the goddess Diana. Early in the novels, like the chaste huntress Diana, they both reject a suitor; and Isabel experiences a vision almost of nightmare at the end when Goodwood kisses her. Gwendolen is described by Sir Hugo Grandcourt as "an uncommonly fine girl, a perfect Diana", and elsewhere it is said that she objected, even to the point of physical repulsion, to being made love to. "With all her imaginative delight in being adored," Eliot remarks, "there was a certain fierceness of maidenhood in her."[9] Their sexual coldness is connected, in turn, to their tendency to be unyielding. And yet, despite all their pristine self-containment, they have within them an unadmitted component of self-doubt, of quick, blind impulse, and are haunted by romantic phantoms.

At the beginning of *Daniel Deronda*, Gwendolen feels ready to "manage her own destiny." She declares that she is determined to be happy, to enjoy a more ardent sense of living than those whom she sees around her who have merely muddled through their lives. The world seems to lie all before her; but she really knows little of it. She knows little, for example, of the power of money, and of what her family's suddenly reduced circumstances will do to her conception of a large personal freedom. Moreover, it is only when she meets and measures herself against Herr Klesmer that she begins to have any really defined idea of her limitations as a performing artist. She had been catered to previously by her sisters and her widowed mother: "No one had disputed her power or her general superiority."[10] Isabel Archer's situation at the beginning of *The Portrait of a Lady* is rather similar. Isabel's sister considers her a "genius" because she reads books, but the word is meaningless because it is undefined, does not

101

refer to anything specific. Even more pointedly, there is irony in the comment of Isabel's paternal aunt, Mrs. Varian, when she considers Isabel "a prodigy of learning, a creature reported to have read the classic authors—in translations" (I, 66).[11] Mrs. Varian can hardly be considered an authority on prodigies of learning, since she has no books in her home and reads only the *New York Interviewer,* a publication she herself deplores. James's description of Isabel in this section is strikingly similar to George Eliot's depiction of Gwendolen Harleth:

> She had no talent for expression and too little of the consciousness of genius; she only had a general idea that people were right when they treated her as if she were rather superior. Whether or no she were superior, people were right in admiring her if they thought her so; for it seemed to her often that her mind moved more quickly than theirs, and this encouraged an impatience that might easily be confounded with superiority. It may be affirmed without delay that Isabel was probably very liable to the sin of self-esteem; she often surveyed with complacency the field of her own nature; she was in the habit of taking for granted, on scanty evidence, that she was right; she treated herself to occasions of homage. . . . Her thoughts were a tangle of vague outlines which had never been corrected by the judgement of people speaking with authority. . . . She had an unquenchable desire to think well of herself. (I, 67)

But Isabel's resemblance to Gwendolen consists of more than this. Gwendolen marries Henleigh Mallinger Grandcourt to secure the benefits of his considerably higher social rank; her marriage, she believes, will be "the gate into a larger freedom." Isabel's circumstances are different, and it is *she* who elevates Osmond in their marriage, but her choice of Osmond has much to do with her sense of a future in which there will be the largest amount of personal freedom. Gwendolen and Isabel are both deceived; ironically, their husbands turn out to embody the same egotistic impulse they have in themselves—but in a way that is psychologically cruel and stifling. A memorable study in perversity, Grandcourt recognizes no one's selfhood but his own. He is attracted to Gwendolen for the spirit and pride she possesses, but for the unpleasant reason that it would please him to master her, to force her to "kneel down like a horse under training for the arena, though she might have an objection to it all the while." He regards her as an object upon which to apply his will and finds it gratifying to have her admired by others while remaining his own creature. She may do nothing Grandcourt considers "vulgar," that is, nothing that does not conform to the stately, processional life he has dictated: "Grandcourt had an intense satisfaction in leading his wife captive after this fashion: it gave their life on a small scale a royal representation and publicity in which everything familiar was got rid of, and everybody must do what was expected of them whatever might be their private protest—the protest (kept strictly private) adding to the piquancy of despotism."[12]

In this way Grandcourt provides the initial model for James's Gilbert Osmond. After they are married, Osmond subjects Isabel Archer to a very similar psychological despotism, converting her into an object to be admired by others while being strictly controlled by him. She must do nothing "vulgar," by which is meant that she must have no spontaneous life or instincts, no individuality. That the perversity of Grandcourt and Osmond is associated with the darker side of human nature is suggested by their comparison to reptiles and snakes (Grandcourt's will is compared, in a chilling image, to a "boa-constrictor which goes on pinching or crushing without alarm at thunder");[13] they have a similar kind of bored lassitude, together with the power to inflict intense psychological suffering. They not only rule the heroines' outward behavior but also invade their inner lives and consciousness, causing them to feel imprisoned and in torture.

In the studied arrangement of their marital lives, Grandcourt and Osmond have the same attitude toward the world without, which exists for them so that they may cast a disinterested glance upon it. In reality, Grandcourt's attitude is not quite so indifferent as it seems. "It is true," Eliot observes, "that Grandcourt went about with the sense that he did not care a languid curse for any one's admiration; but this state of not-caring, just as much as desire, required its related object—namely, a world of admiring or envying spectators."[14] There is irony also in Osmond's ostensible indifference to the world's opinion, since he is ever conscious of it. Indeed, it pleases him to pique the world's envy and curiosity, so that he may decline to satisfy it. But in this world without there is, for Grandcourt and Osmond, one man whose relationship to the heroines is an irritation. For Grandcourt it is Daniel Deronda, whose large, humane imagination draws Gwendolen to him in her suffering. Undervalued and slighted by Gwendolen at first, Deronda comes to educate her consciousness, to awaken in her an awareness of what is larger in life than herself alone. Ralph Touchett comes to have a similar relation to Isabel, since he stands for a humane set of values that are opposed to Osmond's; and in her distress she later gravitates toward him. (Significantly, however, Touchett does not, like Deronda, awaken the heroine to a Victorian altruism; he comes to stand for the individual whose responses to life have the large, fine disinterestedness of art.)

In the ways that have just been sketched, *Daniel Deronda* provided James with his *donnée,* his given situation and starting point for *The Portrait of a Lady.* James's indebtedness to George Eliot was obviously large—extraordinarily large in fact—and yet *The Portrait of a Lady* achieves a life and integrity and distinctness of its own. In refashioning Eliot's material, James strips away her massive sense of social actuality to produce a more attenuated reality, but also a more sharply focused dramatic movement. Sacrificing expanse for form and intensity, he invests his novel—in a way that makes Hawthorne relevant to it—with "the great dramatic chiaroscuro."

The resonant suggestiveness of *The Portrait of a Lady* has been achieved, in part, through James's use of the fairy tale. The appearance of Isabel's aunt Touchett at the Albany house is a fairy-tale visitation, a more wondrous materialization than that of Felix Young before Gertrude Wentworth in *The Europeans.* Like Gertrude, Isabel has been poring over a book, in this case in a secluded room called "the office" where her inner life is lived. Previously a "princess" in an imaginary way, in the small room of a provincial house, she is now called into the great world as Lydia Touchett takes her up, transporting her to a handsome and historic country estate in England. Upon her arrival Gardencourt seems to her, as she says, like something out of a novel; Lockleigh, the neighboring estate of Lord Warburton, impresses her, too, as "a noble picture . . . a castle in a legend" (I, 108). With an effect that seems larger than life, this eligible lord proposes to her on their third meeting; and more extraordinary still, she refuses him. Her aunt Touchett then takes her to live with her in a habitation becoming a princess—an old-world palace —and later she comes into a great bequest, enabling her to meet the requirements of her imagination. But she marries unwisely, and is held in a kind of durance by a husband whose world, unlike her own, is closed. Other characters in the novel attempt to rescue Isabel— Ralph Touchett, who dies uttering his love for her, and the persistent Goodwood, a modern knight whose eyes seem "to shine through the vizard of a helmet" (I, 218). But like the knights in *Roderick Hudson,* Goodwood fails in his mission, and Isabel is condemned to a fate which reverses a fairy-tale expectation.

    James's use of the fairy tale contributes to a romance largeness that is felt in the novel, but romance is evoked in another way by his use of settings, particularly gardens, which come to seem eventually like Hawthorne's romance gardens reimagined in a plausible and yet highly suggestive realism. The novel begins at Gardencourt, a name which intimates both nature (with its associations of instinct, emotion, and expression) and civilization (with its received standards, restraints, and limitations imposed on the individual). At Gardencourt nature and civilization are brought into close relation; the shady lawn, for example, seems like an extension of the luxurious interior of the house, and is "furnished" with richly colored rugs, cushioned seats, books, and writing paper. The opening impression intimates a poised, and as it were, ideal world, and a number of phrases James uses suggest even a paradise—"the perfect middle of a splendid summer afternoon" that seems "an eternity of pleasure" (I, 1). This tea-time occasion, however, does not belong to an eternal world, but to a temporal one. Shadows have already begun to lengthen on the lawn, time passes, and before long it will be dark.

Furthermore, the house is intimately connected with history, and therefore with time, and the disappointment in man's experience; the brickwork of the house looks "weary" (I, 3). At the center of this "perfect" scene is invalidism and approaching death. Both Touchetts, father and son, are seriously ill, and neither has known any large fulfillment. Their presence makes the impression of an ideal consummation seem elusive and ambiguous. It is in this setting, with its resonant ambiguities, that Isabel Archer is first seen—an apostle of freedom and brightness, who yet wears a black dress and has hair that is dark "even to blackness" (I, 61).

Shortly afterward, the garden image expands into a metaphor of Isabel Archer's inner life. "She was always planning out her development," James writes,

> desiring her perfection, observing her progress. Her nature had, in her conceit, a certain garden-like quality, a suggestion of perfume and murmuring boughs, of shady bowers and lengthening vistas, which made her feel that introspection was, after all, an exercise in the open air, and that a visit to the recesses of one's spirit was harmless when one returned from it with a lapful of roses. But she was often reminded that there were other gardens in the world than those of her remarkable soul, and that there were moreover a great many other places which were not gardens at all—only dusky pestiferous tracts, planted thick with ugliness. (I, 72)

This garden image (which, in its play of sunlight and shadow, is reminiscent of Milton's picturing of Eden) implies an inviolable innocence, a "paradise" that is somehow precarious, or even illusory. In fact, Isabel's introspection is not as harmless as she thinks. She herself even wonders at times if she does not have a morbid tendency, and James has hinted at something more than innocence in her inner life—hidden, complicated fears, that are like dark, unexamined corridors.

The garden image is soon after elaborated in a series of scenes, set in gardens, which emphasize the essentially inward nature of Isabel's experience. It is in the garden at Lockleigh that Lord Warburton first speaks to her as a suitor, and that she draws back from him "from a certain fear" (I, 113). And it is in the park garden at Gardencourt, seated on a bench amid sunlight and "flickering shadows," that she reads Goodwood's letter, announcing that he has followed her to England, and that she looks up to hear Lord Warburton propose to her. His words, furthermore, are described as being "uttered with a breadth of candour that was like the embrace of strong arms—that was like the fragrance straight in her face . . . of she knew not what strange gardens" (I, 152). It is on the same grounds at the end of the novel, Isabel again wearing a black dress, that Goodwood kisses her, with the effect of white lightning—following which she returns to Osmond. James's placement of this scene at the climax of the novel emphasizes its finality—in what it reveals about Isabel's "remarkable soul."

The lawn and garden settings of the English country houses also serve to prepare for the gardens of Italy, described by Byron in a famous phrase as "the garden of the world." When Isabel first arrives Italy seems to stretch "before her as a land of promise, a land in which the love of the beautiful might be comforted by endless knowledge" (I, 320), and is thus a greater Gardencourt, uniting, or apparently uniting, nature and civilization. The enlargement of Isabel's experience begins at Mrs. Touchett's residence outside Florence, the Palazzo Crescentini (from the Italian *crescente*, meaning growing or increasing); and before long she visits Gilbert Osmond at his hilltop villa, with its "tangled garden" (I, 326). Osmond's "narrow garden" that is somewhat like a terrace looks out upon the Arno valley below. The view has evocations of ideality: "The air was almost solemnly still, and the large expanse of the landscape, with its garden-like culture and nobleness of outline, its teeming valley of delicately-fretted hills, its peculiarly human-looking touches of habitation, lay there in splendid harmony and classic grace" (I, 380).

This aloof hilltop view, however, also intimates Osmond's inmost nature; it suggests an aloofness in him that, in a different form, is also in Isabel. Even on her initial visit she begins to take a heroic view of Osmond and his hilltop life. It seems to her that she "had never

met a person of so fine a grain" (I, 376), and she envisions him as a
sensitive, distinguished man strolling in this garden and holding the
hand of his little girl, who makes a cameo impression of innocence.

The picture [of his life] had no flourishes, but she liked its lowness of
tone and the atmosphere of summer twilight that pervaded it. It spoke
of the kind of personal issue that touched her most nearly; of the choice
between objects, subjects, contacts—what might she call them?—of a
thin and those of a rich association; of a lonely, studious life in a lovely
land; of an old sorrow that sometimes ached to-day; of a feeling of pride
that was perhaps exaggerated, but that had an element of nobleness; of a
care for beauty and perfection so natural and so cultivated together that
the career appeared to stretch beneath it in the disposed vistas . . . of a
formal Italian garden. (I, 399–400)

108   There are a number of ironies in Isabel's impression—her failure to
grasp the meaning of Osmond's "formal" garden, her conception of
an ideal life as being studious, lonely, and sorrowful.

   Osmond's garden is merely the first of a series of gardens in Italy
that James depicts. When Isabel spends a first spring in Rome, for
example, she visits the Forum (the garden grown from ruins that
Daisy Miller had visited earlier), and its ambiguous implications are
projected by the qualities of light which play over it: "The sun had
begun to sink, the air was a golden haze, and the long shadows of
broken column and vague pedestal leaned across the field of ruin"
(I, 414). There are moments when Isabel feels the "sense of the terrible human past" (I, 413) in Rome, but her spirits are generally
buoyant, particularly when she thinks of the future. In Rome Osmond begins to pay court to her, and Warburton reappears, only to
be shunted aside, as in the scene where Isabel and Osmond sit together in a box at the opera, while Warburton is seated somewhat
behind them—in the dark.

   When Lord Warburton first appears in Rome, in the sculpture
gallery of the Capitol, he stands by the statue of the Dying Gladiator, the vanquished figure that intimates his own defeat in his love

for Isabel. But the statue suggests more than Warburton's own personal fate. In *Childe Harold's Pilgrimage*, Byron had immortalized the gladiator as the type of man's lonely suffering and defeat, and Hawthorne later implied the same in *The Marble Faun*, which begins in the Capitol gallery with Kenyon, Miriam, Hilda, and Donatello grouped significantly about the statue of the Dying Gladiator. Near the statue, too, is the Faun of Praxiteles, with whom Donatello is compared in the innocence of his pre-fallen state. As Isabel speaks to Warburton she is said to glance at the Faun, which brings to mind Hawthorne's novel, and its conception of the Fall.

After Isabel's visit to Rome, the pleasantest experience of her life, the novel moves ahead a year to a spring in Florence, an interval of time which has been taken up for Isabel in travel with Madame Merle and ended in her engagement, on her return, to Osmond. She relives the year in her memory as she stands by a window, where "the bright air of the garden had come in through a broad interstice and filled the room with warmth and perfume" (II, 31). James remarks that she "had ranged, she would have said, through space and surveyed much of mankind" (II, 32), words which echo lines in *Paradise Lost*, in the passage where Adam and Eve must leave Eden to enter the world. In the garden of the palazzo, Ralph Touchett sits in dejection by a statue of a dancing nymph. There is a noontime sunlight (in *Paradise Lost*, it is at noon that the Fall occurs), but there are also patches of shade that make "bowers like spacious caves" as he sits in "a clear gloom" (II, 63). When Isabel meets Ralph in the garden, and they discuss her engagement, he tells her that "it hurts me as if I had fallen myself" (II, 70).

After their marriage the Osmonds live at the Palazzo Roccanera in Rome, and Rome now reflects Isabel's own inner state. In *The Marble Faun* Hawthorne speaks of the dweller in Rome who "should learn to bear patiently his individual griefs, that endure only for one little lifetime, when here are the tokens of such infinite misfortune on an imperial scale, and when so many far landmarks of time, all around him, are bringing the remoteness of a thousand years ago into the sphere of yesterday" (p. 826). And it is the same lesson of history, become a brooding presence, that Isabel now learns when she visits ancient ruins where she meditates alone and enters into Rome's own tragic past:

> She had long before this taken old Rome into her confidence, for in a world of ruins, the ruin of her happiness seemed a less unnatural catastrophe. She rested her weariness upon things that had crumbled for centuries and yet were still upright; she dropped her secret sadness into the silence of lonely places, where its very modern quality detached itself and grew objective, so that as she sat in a sun-warmed angle on a winter's day, or stood in a mouldy church to which no one came, she could almost smile at it and think of its smallness. Small it was, in the large Roman record; and her haunting sense of the continuity of the human lot easily carried her from the less to the greater. She had been deeply, tenderly acquainted with Rome; it interfused and moderated her passion. But she had grown to think of it chiefly as the place where people had suffered. This was what came to her in the starved churches, where the marble columns, transferred from pagan ruins, seemed to offer a companionship in endurance and the musty incense to be a compound of long-unanswered prayers. (II, 327–28).

James uses Rome here in much the way that Hawthorne had before him, as a symbolic tableau, giving dimension to his heroine's inner experience and developing awareness.

The idea of a Fall suggested by James's Rome is also implied in his conception of Osmond, who is compared specifically to a serpent in the garden. In chapter 42, when the reality of Isabel's married life is revealed in the course of a long reverie, James observes that under "all his culture, his cleverness, his amenity, under his good-nature, his facility, his knowledge of life, his egotism lay hidden like a serpent in a bank of flowers" (II, 196). Grandcourt is a figure of perversity similar to Osmond (he, too, is compared to a snake), and James's conception of Osmond begins with him. But there is an important difference between them, for Grandcourt belongs strictly to a world of social fact, while Osmond belongs partly to fable and romance, to a world—like that of *The Marble Faun*—conditioned by the Christian parable of the Fall.

James's modeling of Osmond, furthermore, is specifically indebted to Hawthorne's romance conception of the egotist Dr. Rappaccini. Osmond is guilty of the same kind of intellectual pride as Rappaccini; and, like him, he plays God with "the delicate organism of his daughter" (II, 348). Osmond's daughter has been conceived in the Beatrice mold; with her purity of instinct and feeling, she is remarkably unassertive, and virtually as helpless as Beatrice in her father's garden. Indeed, Pansy belongs peculiarly to a garden world, and has the name of a small flower. She is first seen with her father in the garden of the Osmond villa and is shown finally in the garden of a convent, where she has been placed by her father until he finds a suitable "use" for her. Osmond rejects Rosier as a possible husband for Pansy—even though she is in love with him, and he with her—because the financial security he offers is adequate rather than large. *111* The marriage Osmond contemplates for her would have to have a certain grandeur that would reflect upon himself.

In giving Pansy a flower name, James increases her likeness to Beatrice, who, in the mind of Dr. Rappaccini, is both "a rich flower and a beautiful girl." She is another flower that he cultivates perversely. Hawthorne speaks of an "evil mockery" in Rappaccini's cultivation of these flowers: "Several [blooms] also would have shocked a delicate instinct by an appearance of artificialness indicating that there had been such commixture, and, as it were, adultery, of various vegetable species, that the production was no longer of God's making, but the monstrous offspring of man's depraved fancy, glowing with only an evil mockery of beauty." It should be recalled, furthermore, that Dr. Rappaccini is not only a scientist; he has also been depicted as an artist of a kind—of an obsessed egotism. "As he drew near," Hawthorne writes, "the pale man of science seemed to gaze with a triumphant expression at the beautiful youth and maiden, as might an artist who should spend his life in achieving a picture or a group of statuary and finally be satisfied with his success." [15]

With this passage in mind, compare James's depiction of Osmond after he has converted his daughter into "a convent-flower." The garden of the convent where Pansy is shut up produces an unpleasant impression on Isabel; the convent itself "affronts" and frightens her, giving the effect of a well-appointed prison. Osmond's decision to send Pansy back to this convent is a stroke he particularly prides himself upon; "unexpected and refined" (II, 349), it places the finishing touches upon Pansy as his completed work of art. What is innocently "living" is converted into an artifact having only a mocking semblance of life, an artifact esthetically "placed" and arranged in his gallery. At the moment when Osmond announces to Isabel that he is sending Pansy to live in the convent, he is seen, artistlike, arranging a basket of flowers, after which he stands back and admires his work; and it is cruelly clear that Pansy's soul has become another of his studied floral arrangements. At this "triumphant" moment, Osmond's resemblance to Rappaccini, the presumptuous artificer, is striking.

112

Osmond's relationship to Isabel, after their marriage, is an extension of his relationship to Pansy, except that it is complicated by Isabel's being less malleable. Earlier James had compared her consciousness to a garden; now Isabel comes to recognize her situation in garden imagery. "The real offence," James observes, "as she ultimately perceived, was her having a mind of her own at all. Her mind was to be his—attached to his like a small garden-plot to a deer-park" (II, 200). He will be the "gardener," she the little garden plot that must reflect only his own tastes and preferences. Osmond's conversion of "life" into a lifeless mockery of life is captured gothically in James's reference to "his faculty for making everything wither that he touched" (II, 188). The replacement of the spiritual in his nature by sterile, self-regarding intellect is intimated even in his family history and hobbies. His mother, who called herself "the American Corinne," had come to Italy to hold communion with her soul; but Osmond's sister, the Countess Gemini, who is altogether worldly, says of the family presently that "we're dreadfully fallen" (II, 87). It is said of the Countess Gemini that she has "no soul" (II, 225); and the sterility of Osmond's soul is suggested in the scene in which he is shown reproducing in watercolor, from a plate, a copy of a small gold coin from the period of the Roman Empire.

But if Osmond is a refinement upon a romance archetype in Hawthorne, there are also gothic, indeed infernal, associations in his marital relation to Isabel. The dark shading of their relationship is intimated in James's allusion to Proserpine who, closely identified with gardens, was snatched away to the Plutonian shades; and it is implicit in the residence Osmond adopts in Rome, the Palazzo Roccanera. James's description of the front of the dwelling brings together the imagery of light and darkness, the diminutive and the massively overshadowing. The palazzo is "a high house in the very heart of Rome; a dark and massive structure overlooking a sunny piazzetta" (II, 100). There is a gothic quality in James's description of the building as a "domestic fortress, a pile which bore a stern old Roman name, which smelt of historic deeds, of crime and craft and violence, which was mentioned in 'Murray' and visited by tourists who looked, on a vague survey, disappointed and depressed, and which had frescoes by Caravaggio in the *piano nobile* and a row of mutilated statues and dusty urns in the wide, nobly-arched loggia overhanging the damp court where a fountain gushed out of a mossy niche" (II, 100).[16]

113

Early in the work Isabel had expressed a determination to regard the world as a place of brightness; but in her long reverie, as she stands in the living room of the palazzo by the flickering light of the fireplace, the images which form in her mind are dominated by darkness. She thinks back upon her experience of finding "the infinite vista of a multiplied life to be a dark, narrow alley with a dead wall at the end" (II, 189). Her developing awareness of what lies beneath Osmond's cultured surface has "darkened the world." Ralph Touchett's brief visit has been "a lamp in the darkness" (II, 203). Osmond has led her "into the mansion of his own habitation," where it seems to her that she is "shut up with the odour of mould and decay" (II, 199); and where, with a mounting sense of terror, she takes the measurement of its narrow walls, the discovers that this habitation is "the house of darkness, the house of dumbness, the house of suffocation" (II, 196).

The Hawthorne aspect of *The Portrait of a Lady* can be noticed in James's poetically suggestive use of Rome as the setting of Isabel's "fall" from innocence and in his adaptation of the Rappaccini archetype in his conception of Osmond, a figure of sterile intellectual pride. But Hawthorne is also relevant to *The Portrait of a Lady* in James's tendency to invest external phenomena with symbolic contours. In the Roman world of *The Marble Faun,* art objects almost always have a symbolic connotation, or are reflectors of the spiritual experience of Hawthorne's characters. Guido's painting of Beatrice Cenci, who seems an angel fallen, even though sinless, comes to embrace Hilda's own experience. Many other art works in the novel have a similar metaphoric function—the Faun; the figure of the child holding a dove while being attacked by a snake; the Laocoön; the painting of the Archangel Michael setting his foot upon the demon. In *The Portrait of a Lady* James refines upon Hawthorne's correspondences, muting their effect.

When Isabel, after her unhappy marriage, visits the Coliseum, she wanders alone, along desolate ledges where wild flowers bloom in deep crevices. The presence of the flowers suggests with the effect of symbol the idea of spiritual awareness growing out of defeat and suffering and is related to Ralph Touchett's serenity that "was but the array of wild flowers niched in his ruin" (I, 54). Similarly, Osmond's residences—his villa with its duplicitous, masklike facade and the Palazzo Roccanera with its cruel associations—seem like symbols of his inmost nature. The sitting room of the hotel in Rome where Isabel stays on her first visit is garish like "lying talk," and it is here that Osmond declares his love. This room, furthermore, with its sham splendor and "wilderness of yellow upholstery" (II, 13), is recalled later in the "yellow *salottino*" (II, 112) of the Palazzo Roccanera, a room designed by Osmond himself, in an apparent identification with Napoleon. A cold, oversized Empire clock dominates the room, and by it Rosier and Pansy acknowledge their love, which Osmond's egotism will check. Moreover, in one instance at least, a character tends to expand into moral parable, like Hawthorne's characters in *The Marble Faun.* When she first appears, Madame Merle is described as being like a perfect piece of porcelain; but later in the work, when she and Osmond are together at Osmond's villa, and Madame Merle has grasped the futility of her life, she absently picks up a delicate, mantleshelf coffe cup which reveals the existence of a crack, and as she does so asks herself: "Have I been so vile all for nothing?" (II, 338).

The image of the apparently perfect yet flawed cup is an anticipation of *The Golden Bowl,* and a reminder of how James, in his late period, brought Hawthorne's romance even more fully into the novel of manners. In *The Wings of the Dove* James built his work around an inclusive symbol, contained in its title, as Hawthorne had done in *The Marble Faun,* and reimagined Hawthorne's theme of the education of the inner life. *The Wings of the Dove,* however, has a weakness at its center, since Milly Theale hardly exists humanly. In *The Portrait of a Lady* romance has been assimilated into the novel of manners without a loss of the sense of reality. Hawthorne's romance, which reaches toward abstraction and symbolic statement, informs *The Portrait of a Lady;* but it is James's social intelligence, the equipment of the novelist of manners, that controls and dominates the work. James never fails to perceive Isabel Archer as a young American girl from Albany who exists in her closely specified relationship with others. Henrietta Stackpole, in this respect, is more than a foil for Isabel; she helps to measure her and is a continual reminder of the world to which she most deeply belongs. Osmond is a serpent in the garden, but even more he is Osmond the social being, the expatriate American dilettante who has made a cunning marriage. In the last chapter of the novel, pleading with Isabel to begin a new life with him, Goodwood calls Osmond a "fiend," and at this moment, one is aware of exaggeration in his assertion. There is a romance, even at times a gothic, quality in James's drawing of Osmond, particularly in the way he is *felt* by Isabel after their marriage; but he does not belong to a romance darkness that makes his nature inexplicable. Osmond's motives are absolutely clear, and he has been socially placed in a world inhabited also by the Countess Gemini, who could not be more defined, more "known."

Although James makes use of Hawthorne's romance theme of American innocence confronted with knowledge in an Italian garden setting, *The Portrait of a Lady* belongs essentially to "the great world," as *The Marble Faun* belongs essentially to the lonely study of the romantic artist. The polished surfaces and formal perfection of *The Portrait of a Lady* make *The Marble Faun* seem primitive by comparison. Compare for a moment the almost infinitely greater sophistication of James's treatment of art as encompassing metaphor with Hawthorne's more static use of works of art, particularly his rather embarrassingly wooden conception of the statue of Pope Julius, in the square of Perugia, which seems to bless Hilda and her group. James's novel, like Hawthorne's, draws its title from a work of art; but it is significant that James chooses the painter's portrait for his title, for his interest in the novel is in the delineation of character as it evolves through social experience. How different from Hawthorne, whose characters have only a vague social identity, and do not expand, is James's portrait of Isabel Archer, which requires hundreds of pages to execute, and is not completed until, on the last page, her final gesture is made.

8 The Blithedale Romance and The Bostonians: From Rural Tragedy to Urban Satire

The Portrait of a Lady is usually considered the concluding work of James's first period, dominated by the international theme. The next novels he writes, *The Bostonians* and *The Princess Casamassima,* both published in 1886, show a stronger concern with the texture and density of a particular society, its proletarian as well as its upper-class life. They address themselves to the political and reforming questions of the time in America and England and enter into the mainstream of nineteenth-century realism exemplified by Dickens and Zola. And although written with his characteristic detachment, they suggest that James has something personally at stake, that he has assumed a cultural, if not a public, role.

In 1884 James revisited Paris and renewed his earlier acquaintance with Edmond Goncourt, Zola, and Daudet; and many statements he made at that time, in letters and conversation, indicate that he was reappraising their approach to the novel. He felt that they were "not getting hold of that larger humanity which is alone eternally interesting"; they were "incomparable," but only "in a very narrow way." Nevertheless, remarks in his letters show that he had begun to regard them more favorably. At this time he wrote to Howells: "I have been seeing something of Daudet, Goncourt, and Zola; and there is nothing more interesting to me now than the effort and experiment of this little group, with its truly infernal intelligence of art, form, manner—its intense artistic life. They do the only kind of work, today, that I respect . . . in spite of their ferocious pessimism and their handling of unclean things."[1]

In *The Bostonians* and *The Princess Casamassima*, James was clearly influenced by their method, writing as a naturalist himself, although with a difference, as a "poetic" naturalist. While preparing to write *The Princess Casamassima*, James visited Milbank Prison with notebook in hand, rather like Zola; but he did not need to take notes for *The Bostonians*, having taken them mentally for years. James's characters in *The Bostonians* have some relation to actual reforming personalities of the period, and in the case of Miss Birdseye, it was felt in Boston that James had drawn his character from Elizabeth Peabody, the sister-in-law of Hawthorne. When Mrs. Fields, wife of the Boston publisher James T. Fields, read *The Bostonians*, she said that Miss Birdseye was Elizabeth Peabody "to the life," and many others, including Lowell, shared her impression. James's brother William wrote to him objecting to his use of an actual person, a letter which drew a firm denial:

118

I am quite appalled by your note . . . in which you assault me on the subject of my having painted a "portrait from life" of Miss Peabody! I was in some measure prepared for it by Lowell's . . . taking it for granted that she had been my model. . . . I should be very sorry—in fact deadly sick, or fatally ill—if I thought Miss Peabody *herself* supposed I intended to represent her. I absolutely had no shadow of such an intention. I never had but the most casual observation of her, I didn't know whether she was alive or dead, and she was not in the least my starting point or example. Miss Birdseye was evolved entirely from my moral consciousness, like every other person I have ever drawn, and originated in my desire to make a figure who should embody in a sympathetic, pathetic, picturesque, and at the same time grotesque way, the humanitary and transcendental tendencies. . . . I wished to make this figure a woman, because it would be more touching, and an old, weary, battered and simple-minded woman because that deepened the effect. I elaborated her in my mind's eye—and after I had got going reminded myself that my creation would perhaps be identified with Miss Peabody—*that* I freely admit. So I have in mind the sense of being careful, at the same time that I didn't see what I could do but go my own way, according to my own fancy, and make my image as living as I saw it. . . . So I thought no more about Miss P. *at all,* but simply strove to realize my vision.[2]

   Despite this disclaimer, however, it is difficult to believe that James was not conscious of Miss Peabody in creating Miss Birdseye, perhaps more than he realized or would have cared to admit. James was never careless in naming his characters, and it cannot be ignored that a "birdseye" is an object of approximately the same shape and size as a pea. Moreover, there are a great many points of similarity between the life of Miss Peabody and that of Miss Birdseye. Miss Peabody was well known for her self-sacrificing devotion to innumerable humanitarian and reforming causes; in her later years, indeed, she was actively engaged in the women's movement and held meetings in the parlor of her Boston apartment, very much like Miss Birdseye.[3]

119

   The impression that James was conscious of actual personalities in the life of the time he writes about is also strengthened by the character of Dr. Mary Prance, whose conception suggests that it was inspired by Dr. Mary Walker. Like Dr. Prance, Dr. Walker was one of the first female doctors in the country. A petite, tender-hearted woman with a crusty, no-nonsense manner, Dr. Walker was prominent in the women's movement and attracted newspaper headlines by wearing men's clothing. The name Dr. Prance, moreover, strongly suggests a play on the name Dr. Walker.[4] In addition, James was almost certainly aware of the Spiritualist movement, and certain personalities involved in it, through his brother William, who by 1883 had become corresponding secretary of the British Society for Psychical Research.[5] It is known, too, that James had once attended a public performance in New York of the young, blonde, ringleted (and later notorious) Cora L. V. Hatch, whose "inspirational speaking" was similar in some respects to Verena Tarrant's, as Howard Kerr has pointed out in *Mediums, and Spirit-Rappers, and Roaring Radicals: Spiritualism in American Literature, 1850–1900.*[6]

Further still, the figure of Victoria Woodhull almost certainly looms in the background of *The Bostonians*. Verena Tarrant, the girl oratress, and her parents, whose lives have been patchy, bohemian, and not completely respectable, become credible if one remembers Victoria Woodhull's career, which mixed inspirational speaking with sensational journalism and women's rights with mesmeric healing and Spiritualism.[7] All of the bohemian movements in which Victoria Woodhull was immersed appear in the background of Selah Tarrant—his association with Spiritualism, his later role as a mesmeric healer, his period at a free love colony, his shuffling, migratory life and attention-seeking in the press. Victoria Woodhull comes to mind in James's description of Verena's childhood: "She had sat on the knees of somnambulists, and been passed from hand to hand by trance-speakers; she was familiar with every kind of 'cure,' and had grown up among lady-editors of newspapers advocating new religions, and people who disapproved of the marriage-tie" (p. 71).[8] The passage suggests the lightness with which James has touched the actual reforming bohemias of his day, making his bohemian characters seem both real and fanciful at once. "Really," William James wrote in a letter to Henry, "the *datum* seems to me to belong rather to the region of fancy, but the treatment to that of the most elaborate realism."[9]

One of the notable features of *The Bostonians* is its pictorial naturalism, its close attention to landscape and scene, which, undercutting the reformers' notions of a near-at-hand perfectability, come to suggest the joylessness of the New England milieu in its industrialized age. In his short story "A New England Winter" (1884), written shortly before the novel, James sketched the Boston landscape in a similar way, and the story seems like a preliminary sketch for *The Bostonians*. But neither James's use of scenic detail nor the actual people who provided clues for his characters explain the novel very fully; and they do not account at all for the mingled sense of romance and realism in *The Bostonians* which William James noted. Searching further into *The Bostonians,* and its conception of New England reformers and their deception, one is led back almost inevitably to Hawthorne's *The Blithedale Romance,* which is also set in Boston and its surrounding countryside and deals with the same subject. *The Bostonians* brings *The Blithedale Romance* almost necessarily to mind; and the two works in fact illuminate each other.

The relationship of *The Blithedale Romance* and *The Bostonians* has been treated previously by Marius Bewley in his chapter on the two novels in *The Complex Fate*.[10] Bewley argues that James must have intended *The Bostonians* as a corrected version of *The Blithedale Romance*. They have in common, he points out, the subject of New England reformers and philanthropists in successive generations, and certain of James's characters give the impression of having been redrawn from Hawthorne, with a more exact outlining of their relationships. Zenobia in particular establishes "the suffragist vocabulary" for Olive Chancellor, who, like Zenobia, dominates a young girl and suffers a martyrdom of a kind. Westervelt and Selah Tarrant have nearly identical natures and functions, and both give mesmeric performances which expose them as shams. Hollingsworth and Ransom both rescue a girl, held in a form of bondage, in a New England auditorium. The difference between Hawthorne's novel and James's, however, is the difference between Hawthorne's "shadows and confusions" and James's lucid social relationships, which have been made possible by exposure to a larger culture than Hawthorne had at his disposal.

Bewley's chapter appeared originally as an essay in *Scrutiny*, and in the following issue of the journal letters were exchanged between Bewley and Leon Edel over the position Bewley had taken.[11] Denying any important influence from Hawthorne, Edel cited a passage in James's *Notebooks* for 1883, which points to Daudet's *L'Evangéliste* as the source and inspiration for *The Bostonians*. In this passage James wrote: "Daudet's *Evangéliste* has given me the idea of this thing. . . . I wished to write a very *American* tale, a tale very characteristic of our social conditions, and I asked myself what was the most salient and peculiar point in our social life. The answer was: the situation of women, the decline of the sentiment of sex, the agitation on their behalf."[12] Bewley had himself cited this passage, explaining that it was a "distraction" from the real source for James's novel in Hawthorne; but Edel insists in his rebuttal that the com-

121

ment about Daudet is conclusive, and cannot be waved aside. In a more recent discussion, in *The Grasping Imagination,* Buitenhuis has sided with Edel, and described Bewley as "misguided" in attempting to account for *The Bostonians* in relation to Hawthorne. His own account of the novel centers upon Daudet, and he gives the impression that Hawthorne's influence, relative to the French one, was very minor indeed.

It seems to me that in diminishing the role of *The Blithedale Romance,* reducing it even to the point of irrelevance, Edel and Buitenhuis overlook a great deal. Bewley fails to take Daudet and the French naturalists fully enough into account; but at least his intuition of the central importance of Hawthorne to *The Bostonians* places James's novel in its tradition. His general sense of what has occurred, that a transposition of character types has taken place, is sound. In appropriating Hawthorne's characters, however, James also appropriated his themes, and more needs to be said—the subject is almost untouched by Bewley—about the thematic connections between *The Blithedale Romance* and *The Bostonians.* Both deal with appearance and reality, reform and sham; but even further, they reveal the same theme of a communal self-deception, and employ the motif of masquerade to imply a disguise of the self. James remarked in his *Notebooks* that he wished to "write a very *American* tale, a tale very characteristic of our social conditions," and although Hawthorne did not provide him with his contemporary social surfaces, he did furnish clues as to how they could be treated imaginatively. In *The Bostonians* James both affiliated himself with Hawthorne as a psychologist and at the same time brought him into his own criticism of American democracy.

The social conditions James examines in *The Bostonians,* as I have mentioned, have been traced with a naturalistic exactness. His characters are perceived, the sense of their lives conveyed, by their gestures, their clothes, their apartments. In the opening scene, for example, Olive Chancellor is revealed in a small detail before she appears. She will keep her guests waiting in her downstairs parlor for about ten minutes; but not ten exactly, her sisters says, more likely nine or

122

eleven. She turns what should be the pleasure of the social act into a morbid scrupling over minutes. When she comes down, James's description of her—her eyes that are like "green ice," and her cold, limp handshake—suggests a personal coldness, a coldness given a sexual connotation before the scene is over by the association of Olive with advanced age. Although she is in her twenties, she gives Ransom the impression of being already old, and her sister, Mrs. Luna, refers to her as "a dear, old thing" (p. 80). Adelaide Luna, who is the physical and temperamental opposite of her sister (Olive avoids men while Adelaide chases them), is also defined by her appearance and garments; she wears a frivolous shawl, and is shown in the characteristic attitude of putting on her elbow-length gloves, "as if arrayed for the street" (p. 79). Later, Mrs. Farrinder, a prominent feminist, is introduced, and seems captured in essence in the image of her having "a pair of folded arms" (p. 24). In her different way she has, like Olive Chancellor, a quality of rigid exactitude. "She had a terrible regularity of feature," James observes, "which seemed to ask how a countenance could fail to be noble of which the measurements were so correct" (p. 24). In the entourage of these reformers, but of a different mold, is Verena Tarrant, whose vivacity (and sexual vividness) is intimated in the detail of her red hair, and, in the opening scene, of the red fan she continually flutters before her.

The apartments of Boston are revealing, and Olive Chancellor's is so particularly. On his first visit, as he waits in the parlor for Olive to appear, Ransom notices "the books that were everywhere, on little shelves like brackets (as if a book were a statuette)" (p. 14). The suggestion is given that a strict, bookish mentality rules her experience, confining it within brackets, and taking the place of art. Her parlor is "strenuous," and so is her window view of the Charles River, a "hard, cold void" broken by the prospect of "chimneys and steeples, straight, sordid tubes of factories and engine shops, or spare, heavenward finger of the New England meeting house" (p. 149). Olive Chancellor's parlor has special importance as the novel's initial setting: it recurs as setting later when the Boston women who are in the movement spend summer evenings there discussing reform while they look out toward the bleak bay, and again when Verena

123

spends her first winter at Olive's home. They live almost in isolation, enjoying the wintry view of approaching dusk: "as the afternoon closed, the ugly picture was tinted with a clear, cold rosiness" (p. 149). Miss Birdseye's parlor has the same purely linear shape as Olive's; and it comments on her life, like the building itself, which is said to have "a peculiar look of being both new and faded—a kind of modern fatigue—like certain articles of commerce which are sold at reduction as shopworn" (p. 31). Apart from these strenuous parlors, no "society" exists in Boston; at least none is shown as existing, and there is no implication that any does.

Against this austere background, the feminists have been depicted as having a priestly role. They gather at the Tremont Temple and have the appearance of worshipping under the morally strenuous "bust of Beethoven," and Miss Birdseye, who had once brought the Bible to the slaves in the South, says that the statute book must be their Bible now. At one point James describes Olive and Verena in the attitude of votaries of a religious cause: "The two young women took their way through the early darkness, pacing quietly side by side, in their winter robes, like women consecrated to some holy office" (p. 132). Indeed, Olive asks Verena not to marry, since priests never married, "and what you and I dream of doing demands of us a kind of priesthood" (p. 116). This priesthood, however, has an ominous quality in a scene which takes place outside the Tarrant home in Cambridge. Olive draws Verena near her in the chill night air, flinging over her with one hand the fold of her cloak, and asks her to promise that she will never marry. As Olive does, Mr. Pardon steps out onto the veranda, and with an irony of which he is unconscious, shouts to them: "You ladies had better look out, or you'll freeze together!" (p. 114).

James notes in "A New England Winter" that a prominent feature of contemporary Boston is its absence of men, and in *The Bostonians* he has imagined a world in which men have faded in both the social and the political life. For heightened effect, the Boston men who appear in the novel, all of them weak figures, have been given the names of the strongly dominant patristic fathers. Mrs. Farrinder has a husband so superfluous that almost the only thing said of him is that "his name was Amariah." Amariah is a name that appears in postexilic priest lists in the Old Testament; but Matthias Pardon, the newspaperman, has a biblical name, too, since Matthias, who replaced Judas, was the last of the apostles. Pardon's conversation is interspersed with such expressions as "goodness gracious" and "mercy on us," and his sexual faintness is intimated, as it is with Olive Chancellor, in the idea of premature old age. His hair, for example, is described as being "precociously" white. Like Pardon, who is a lackey of the women's cause in the press, the other young men of Boston shown in the novel seem subordinate to women. Henry Burrage, a well-to-do dilettante (his rooms at Cambridge are decorated with intaglios and Spanish altar cloths), has his mother do his courting for him, and is linked with Pardon in the "white" vest he wears (p. 219), and with Amariah Farrinder, who is shown trailing behind his wife in a "white" overcoat (p. 361).

The denial of sexuality and the pretension of priesthood also come to involve the bohemian characters in the novel. In *Hawthorne* James objected that he found in *The Blithedale Romance* "no sketching of odd figures . . . no reproduction of strange types of radicalism," and in *The Bostonians* he supplied what he found missing in Hawthorne's novel.[13] The Tarrants, who have, like Olive herself, a priestly pretension, imply a whole social stratum of American bohemianism. Dr. Tarrant has allied himself with innumerable movements —with the Cayuga Community (and its "free unions"), Spiritualism, and mesmeric healing. The waterproof he habitually wears (indoors and out) denotes him as a priest of regenerating ideas. Just before Verena begins her inspirational speaking at Miss Birdseye's apartment, Tarrant invokes the presence of "the spirit" with hierophantic gestures, the sleeves of his waterproof falling over his hands like a robe: " 'It will come, my good girl, it will come. Just let it work—just let it gather. The spirit, you know; you've got to let the spirit come out when it will.' He threw up his arms at moments, to rid himself of the wings of his long waterproof, which fell forward over his hands" (p. 50). Mrs. Tarrant, too, wears "a flowing mantle, which resembled her husband's waterproof—a garment which, when she turned to her daughter or talked about her, might have passed for the robe of a sort of priestess of maternity" (p. 95). In the period during which the couple practiced spiritual séances, they were said to have resembled "two augurs behind the altar" (p. 62).

The dubious priesthood of Olive Chancellor and the others is an aspect of the cultural or social conditions James noted that he wished to examine in *The Bostonians*.[14] By social conditions, James meant primarily the leveling effect, and confusions of value, in a democracy. James had treated democracy satirically in a series of stories of the late 1870s and early 1880s. In "The Point of View" (1882), for example, Louis Leverett returns from Paris to his native Boston to find his old rooms on West Cedar Street occupied by "a mesmeric healer." Writing to his friend Harvard Tremont, he remarks that "there is no mystery in corners; there is no light and shade in types. The people are haggard and joyless; they look as if they had no passions, no tastes, no senses. . . . They are diluted in the great . . . bath of Democracy!"[15]

126

James's earlier male characters with antidemocratic biases in his short stories (Louis Leverett and M. Lejaune in "The Point of View," and Count Vogelstein in "Pandora") culminate in Basil Ransom in *The Bostonians*. Like them, Ransom is treated with irony, and yet his barbed remarks about democracy often have some point. Moreover, he is flanked by figures like Pardon and Tarrant, who certainly do not reflect well on democracy. There is a lustiness in James's assaultive description of Tarrant as an American democrat who haunts the public streets, railway stations, horsecars, newspaper offices, and hotel lobbies, at the last of which, together with "rows of shaggy-backed men in strange hats," he writes letters "at a table inlaid with advertisements" (p. 88). Of Pardon, James remarks that "everything to him was very much the same, he had no sense of proportion or quality; but the newest thing was what came nearest exciting in his mind the sentiment of respect" (p. 106).

James's characters illustrate the tendency of democracy to reduce life to a common level, where distinctions become vague, and even sexuality becomes anomalous. When he observed in his notebook entry that one of the most salient features of the American scene was "the decline of the sentiment of sex," he meant the whole body of instincts, emotions, and attitudes attached to the idea of sexual differentiation, and a passional response to life. Sexual distinctness was a striking feature of European society and art, but in America sexual distinctness paled; and James associated this sexual pallor with a faded pleasure in life and imagination. The industrialized backgrounds of Boston and New York in the novel comment on the quality of their life—the work orientation of these cities rather than pleasure in the senses. But democracy, too, with its opposition to personal or typal distinctions, contributed to the decline of the sentiment of sex. Dr. Prance is symptomatic of her world in her sexual vagueness; she is biologically female, but her purely practical, professional approach to life makes her seem like a man. Even on a holiday, when she is at Cape Cod, she behaves as a male doctor might, going fishing by herself.

Basil Ransom, the critic of democracy in the novel, is not a European, but as a Southerner he comes from a more aristocratic order than the democratized North. James does not use Ransom as his spokesman; in fact, Ransom is often treated satirically. But he does use him at times to remind the reader of democratic humbug. Verena's speaking at Mrs. Burrage's apartment seems to Ransom "perfected humbug" (p. 271), which it is. Miss Birdseye, in whose displaced spectacles the moral history of Boston is reflected, cannot distinguish between what merits her support and what does not. When Ransom is introduced to her, she gives him "a delicate, dirty, democratic little hand, looking at him kindly, as she could not help doing, but without the smallest discrimination against the others who might not have the good fortune (which might possibly involve an injustice) to be present on such an interesting occasion" (p. 22).

The reforming parlors of democratic Boston have been drawn by James so that they suggest a whole community given over to professions of altruism and a search for a new perfectability; and in this way Boston becomes a larger, urbanized version of Hawthorne's colony of reformers in *The Blithedale Romance*. The resemblance is increased by the fact that both of these reforming worlds contain basic elements of illusion. Professor Westervelt and Dr. Tarrant are the most conspicuous instances of sham in their respective novels,

127

but they are not isolated cases of it; they also serve notice of its presence in their adoptive communities. The colonists at Blithedale have endeavored to free themselves from society's errors and falsehoods, and to make their lives illustrations of the "new truths"; but near the close of the book Zenobia declares that she has found at Blithedale "nothing but self, self, self" (p. 311).[16] She announces that "there are no new truths, much as we have prided ourselves on finding some" (p. 320), and her words are echoed in *The Bostonians* when Olive Chancellor asks Ransom if he does not believe in the "new truths," and he replies that he has never found any but "old truths."[17] By the end, the Blithedale colony comes apart like an exploded illusion, and in *The Bostonians* the final scene at the Music Hall in Boston communicates a sense of repudiated assumptions, not only those of Olive Chancellor, but also those of the community she serves.

128   In his treatment of communal illusion at Blithedale, Hawthorne employs an elaborate motif of masquerade and disguise, most particularly a disguise of the self; and in *The Bostonians* James orchestrates Hawthorne's motif in a more urban setting and in a more urbane way. Blithedale represents for its founders a new beginning, where "the reformation of the world" (p. 12) will come about, and brotherhood and selflessness will finally prevail. But before long their ideal collapses under the pressure of reality, and ego assertion is shown as being more deeply rooted in the human personality than altruism. All of the principal characters, in fact, are guilty of violating the sanctity of another. Miles Coverdale is in this respect something more than merely a narrator-spectator, since he illustrates the egotistic tendency of the Blithedale colony. Examining himself at one point, he acknowledges that "that cold tendency, between instinct and intellect, which made me pry with a speculative interest into people's passions and impulses, appeared to have gone far toward unhumanizing my heart" (p. 220). And in the vocabulary of the predator, he refers to his custom of entering into other people's minds and making their individualities "my prey" (p. 118). Priscilla herself (although he claims at the end to have been "in love" with her) is not exempt from his inquiries, which Hawthorne has ex-

pressed in a curiously Freudian imagery. "No doubt it was a kind of sacrilege in me," Coverdale concedes, "to attempt to come within her maidenly mystery; but as she appeared to be tossed aside by other friends, or carelessly let fall, like a flower which they had done with, I could not resist the impulse to take just one peep beneath her folded petals" (pp. 178–79). His natural home is a furtive spy place in the forest, a pine tree eyrie—a word which means both a habitation on a height and a lofty nest for birds of prey.

Coverdale's role as a vampire of the beings of others, however, is but one angle from which a character's attempt to impose a dominance over the identity of another has been shown. In order to clear her way to Hollingsworth, Zenobia violates Priscilla's ingenuous trust in her, placing her in the hands of Westervelt, who will "waste" her soul as his psychological subject. And Hollingsworth exploits Zenobia's love for him in order to further his improbable, self-centered scheme for rehabilitating criminals, learning by the end that he ought to have begun by reforming himself. The Blithedale colony, which was to usher in "the millennium of love" (p. 30) and to be a "Paradise anew" (p. 8), comes to seem like the most misguided of illusions.

129

The pervasive sense of illusion and masquerade in Hawthorne's novel takes a number of different forms. Zenobia's name, for example, is a kind of "mask." As Coverdale explains, "it is merely her public name; a sort of mask in which she comes before the world" (p. 5). Westervelt's handsome face is masklike, and is altered radically when he puts on a pair of spectacles. Hawthorne's masking imagery calls attention to the difference between outward appearance and inward truth and reality; to roles that are adopted or assumed, as in a stage masque or pastoral. When Coverdale first arrives at Blithedale, he is greeted by Zenobia, who will, she announces, play the part of hostess. Someone then inquires if they all have their parts assigned, and Coverdale says that he will "play a part, with Zenobia and the rest of the amateurs, in our pastoral" (p. 57), and later he will look ahead to the time when "our pastoral shall be quite played out" (p. 109). He sees the other characters "upon [his] mental stage, as in a drama" (p. 233), and Zenobia in particular is characterized as seeming like an "actress." To Coverdale, arriving at Blithedale, her presence "caused our heroic enterprise to show like an illusion, a masquerade, a counterfeit Arcadia" (p. 25).

Near the end, a masquerade is acted out literally in the woods beyond Blithedale, as Silas Foster, the materialist, looks on skeptically. An antic dance of Blithedale colonists in costume ends with a shower of sere autumn leaves upon them, marking a somber end to their "performance." And it is in this passage that Zenobia tells Hollingsworth: "You are a better masquerader than the witches and gypsies yonder; for your disguise is a self-deception" (p. 321). Shortly afterward she makes her valedictory announcement that she is "weary of this place, and sick to death of playing at philanthropy and progress. Of all varieties of mock-life, we have surely blundered into the very emptiest mockery in our effort to establish the one true system" (p. 324).

130   In *The Bostonians* James has assimilated and restated Hawthorne's themes in *The Blithedale Romance* of masquerade, illusion, and participation in mock-life. With James's characters, the masking theme is implied in the "public" nature of their lives, which can be noted in their apartments—in Olive's "queer, corridor-shaped drawing-room" (p. 12) and in Miss Birdseye's parlor, of the same shape, which has the "similitude of an enormous street-car" (p. 25). At various times James's characters have the effect of wearing *public* masks. Mrs. Farrinder, for example, is said to have an "eminently public manner" and a "fine placid mask" (p. 44) of a face. James remarks that "there was a lithographic smoothness about her, and a mixture of the American matron and the public character" (p. 24). Miss Birdseye also has a public face: "She had a sad, soft, pale face, which (and it was the effect of her whole head) looked as if it had been soaked, blurred, and made vague by exposure to some slow dissolvent. The long practice of philanthropy had not given accent to her features; it had rubbed out their transitions, their meanings. The waves of sympathy, of enthusiasm, had wrought upon them in the same way in which the waves of time finally modify the surface of old marble busts, gradually washing away their sharpness, their details" (p. 21). When Verena speaks at Miss Birdseye's apartment,

she seems, in the gaslight, with her white gown and pale complexion, like "a moving statue" (p. 49). All of these images—statues, busts, and lithographs—are *public* representations of the self, and, in effect, are masks.

The masking effect in *The Bostonians* can be noticed particularly in the impression created by gaslight or lamplight. As it falls over the faces of the reformers, the gaslight has the effect of seeming to transfigure them nobly while it actually washes out their features. When Olive rides in a carriage with Basil Ransom toward Miss Birdseye's, she speaks with intensity about "emancipation," and as she does so the illumination of a streetlamp bleaches her face white, making it seem like a "spectral" mask, an incident which foreshadows the masking effect in the scene which immediately follows. At Miss Birdseye's, the glare of gaslight makes the room "white and featureless" (p. 24), yet at the same time gives the illusion of endowing it with an atmosphere in which things seem larger than life. As Miss Birdseye approaches, it transforms her "familiar, her comical shape, and made the poor little humanitary hack seem already a martyr" (pp. 31–32). The *public* gaslight (which James associates with the lecture hall, or the theater or stage) has the effect of depriving the reformers of any authentically *personal* identity. For that reason, having only a *public* identity, Olive Chancellor has "absolutely no figure" (p. 15), and Miss Birdseye is an "essentially formless old woman, who had no more outline than a bundle of hay" (p. 23). The garment she wears is indicative of her life: a loosely fitting black jacket with deep pockets stuffed with correspondence, it is totally public. She belongs to every sort of league "that had been founded for almost any purpose whatever" (p. 22), and is described as being confused and entangled. Her gestures are "irrelevant."

The illusion implied in the reformers' public identities is captured well in James's observation that Miss Birdseye "never had any needs but moral needs" (p. 23)—as if she had no needs as a woman. The denial of the private or personal, together with an implication of illusion or deception, is also present when Verena is about to speak at Miss Birdseye's and Dr. Tarrant "looked around at the company with all his teeth, and said that these flattering allusions were not so embarrassing as they might otherwise be, inasmuch as any success that he and his daughter might have had was so thoroughly impersonal: he insisted on that word. . . . It was some power outside—it seemed to flow through her" (p. 46). It is obvious, however, that this mysterious outward power is her own intrinsically appealing youth, naiveté, and sexual charisma. "It was an intensely personal exhibition," Ransom concludes, "and the person making it happened to be fascinating" (p. 51). Tarrant's pretension of being disinterested, and involved in his daughter's success in merely an impersonal way, reflects on many of the characters present, and the questionable nature of their motives.

James's use of a masking effect in *The Bostonians,* particularly as it is seen in the adoption of public rather than private identities, is closely related to another theme, that of victimization, and in the same way the two themes are related in *The Blithedale Romance.* At Blithedale, where selflessness is ostensibly to be established, almost all of the principal characters attempt to bring others under the domination of their own egos. While they are working at repairing a stone fence, Hollingsworth asks Coverdale to pledge himself to his humanitarian project, which would mean a virtual surrender of his life, indeed of his very being, to Hollingsworth's ambition. A "strenuous exercise of opposing will" (p. 193) ensues, in which Coverdale is able to refuse compliance only by the most arduous summoning of inner strength. Hollingsworth's attempt to "possess" Coverdale, or to bring him under his will, is reproduced in the relationships of the other characters. In particular, Priscilla, the frail snow-maiden, falls under the dominance of several of the others—of Zenobia, Hollingsworth, and Westervelt. A final contest of opposing wills, for possession of Priscilla, takes place between Hollingsworth and Westervelt, with Hollingsworth rescuing her from the mesmerist who bears the signet of the devil.

A similar pattern of a struggle for domination and possession of another is also apparent in *The Bostonians.* James's democratic reformers all profess a high-minded altruism, but one of the conspicuous features of the work is an undercurrent of exploitation. Pardon makes exploitative use of the privacy of the individuals he interviews

132

for the newspaper, the people he interviews being described by James as "his victims." Dr. Tarrant has a similar victimizing role, since he publicizes the "spiritual gifts" of his child, exploiting both the public and his daughter herself. Together, they give an indication of the temptation to exploit or seek selfish power over others in a democratic community. When the novel opens, Verena lives under the domination of her father as a kind of Veiled Lady exhibited in Boston. Thereafter, others attempt to dominate her—two suitors of slight sexual endowment, Pardon and Burrage, and more importantly, Olive Chancellor and Basil Ransom. The struggle for domination comes to center upon these latter two; between them it is "war to the knife, it was a question of which should pull hardest" (p. 322).

Ransom and Olive Chancellor are virtually polar opposites, but they have in common that their modes of thought have been conditioned by cultures which effectively ended with the Civil War. Puritan and royalist, they seek to dominate Verena, and, in their different degrees, to stifle her freedom of development.[18] Olive's hardly visible smile is described in the opening scene as seeming like "a thin ray of moonlight resting upon the wall of a prison" (p. 5), and it is the prison of conscience in which she would confine Verena. But Ransom is also a jailer of sorts, since he is a male chauvinist in the extreme, and would restrict Verena to the confines of his parlor and kitchen. And with Ransom as with Olive Chancellor, there is a discrepancy between habits of thought and reality. He is called an intellectual who has "read everything," but he seems to have read only Carlyle, and his articles are rejected by journals as being at least two hundred years behind the times. One of the more strangely humorous moments in the novel occurs when he is fired with confidence in his future, and suddenly prepared for matrimony, on the basis of having an article accepted by an apparently obscure journal, *The Rational Review*. The discrepancy between Ransom's royalist pretensions and his real situation can be seen in his powerlessness in New York, where he is a lawyer without clients, a toothless lion. But despite this element of unreality in his thinking, Ransom has some important redeeming traits, particularly in his having some resemblance to a man.

133

Unlike the young men of Boston depicted in the novel, he has some toughness of mind, is virile, and possesses a masculine sexual aura.[19] By the end of the work, despite the clash of their differences, Verena and Basil are recognizably in love; and love between the sexes is affirmed as a norm of civilization, as the inner torment and cold, virginal estrangement of Olive is felt as an aberration.

At the beginning of the novel, however, Olive Chancellor has the money, causes, and persuasion to attract Verena, and as she does she also contemplates a means to "bind them together for life" (p. 95). Olive is concerned chiefly at this stage of the work with wresting Verena from Pardon and Burrage, and James begins here to make recurrent use of the words *victim, sacrifice,* and *possession.* When she is at the Tarrant house in Cambridge, Olive is seized by the desire to "take a more complete possession of the girl" (p. 111), and outside she tells Verena that she must be ready, for the sake of their cause, to "sacrifice"—by which she means her life. The moment is heightened by an accompanying imagery of a cold prison cell and sharp knives: the sky in the background seems "a sparkling wintry vault, where the stars were like myriad points of ice. The air was silent and sharp, and the vague snow looked cruel" (p. 113). The sacrificial implication of this scene is repeated, in different ways, elsewhere. In turning Verena over to Olive for their own monetary advantage, the Tarrants claim to be "willing to sacrifice her to the highest good" (p. 141), and Verena, staying with Olive, thinks that "there was no sacrifice to which she would not have consented" (p. 140) in order to prove herself worthy.

As Verena falls more deeply under Olive's domination, a variation of her experience is enacted in New York between Olive's sister, Mrs. Luna, and Basil Ransom. Mrs. Luna pursues Ransom and attempts to trap him into matrimony, offering the bribe of her money when she realizes that he is vulnerable in his reduced circumstances. Like Olive, she thinks above reality, seeing Ransom in the romantically heroic light of a fallen aristocrat after the French Revolution; in attempting to "possess" Ransom, she sees him less as he is than as an adjunct of her own aberrant imaginings. Her attempt to place Ransom under the control of her will also reflects what is taking place at the same time in Boston, where Olive's advantages place her in a position to exploit Verena's naiveté.[20]

Olive's domination of the girl has a distinctly Hawthornesque quality, since it is felt as a horrifying violation of her innocence, and at times has even been described in the vocabulary of an unnatural spell. "Verena was completely under the charm," James writes at one point. "The fine web of authority, of dependence, that her strenuous companion had woven about her, was now as dense as a suit of golden mail" (p. 143). Ironically, Olive regards Ransom as exercising a spell from which Verena must be "saved," and late in the work, referring to Ransom's increasing influence, she calls Verena "the victim of an atrocious spell" (p. 343)—which she is, Olive's own.

Although Olive claims to be motivated by the public interest, her motives are not necessarily altruistic, and there is more than a slight hint in *The Bostonians* that she is gripped by a dark obsession. At the beginning Mrs. Luna speaks of the "weird meetings" Olive attends, and Ransom replies: "You speak as if it were a rendezvous of witches on the Brocken" (p. 3). Although humorous, the exchange introduces the motif of the Witches' Sabbath, held on the Brocken in the Alps, where young maidens were "sacrificed." The allusion, moreover, introduces a motif from *Faust* (where a Witches' Sabbath on the Brocken is held), which recurs later with the implication of Olive as a female Faust, tormented by her totally mentalized life and, in effect, tempted by Mephistopheles' vision of the seduction of a young maiden.

One of James's critics has observed recently that since *The Bostonians* was written before the age of Freud, it would be of little use to try to search into Olive's sexuality, especially since a close attachment such as hers to Verena was common among women in the Victorian period.[21] But by assuming that James could not have grasped the sexual implication of Olive's attraction to Verena, he does not examine James's conception fully. James was well acquainted with the mores of upper-class life in England and France in the 1880s, and it is certainly possible, whether before the age of Freud or not, that he was conscious of the existence of overt or latent homosexuality.[22]

He would, in any case, have been aware of lesbian sexuality in the work of the French naturalists, since it was present overtly in Zola's *Nana* (1880), which James read and reviewed, and well before that in "La Fille aux Yeux d'Or" (1835) of Balzac, of whom James once wrote that he sometimes presented aspects of human sexuality not usually acknowledged to exist by English readers.[23] And, as we shall see, there is evidence in *The Bostonians* that James did indeed, quite knowingly although of course discreetly, indicate a lesbian orientation in Olive.

Furtive sexuality is implied at a number of points in *The Bostonians*. Despite his professed loftiness of motive, a cloaked sexuality is noticed in Dr. Tarrant—in his shadowy past at the "free-love" colony, in his relationship to the lonely women he visits as a mesmeric healer, and even in his "stroking" of his daughter at the beginning of her public performances, which carries an unsavory suggestion of incest. And it should be remembered that it is Tarrant who precedes and prepares for Olive as Verena's sponsor. Of the clues which intimate Olive's sexual nature, one appears in the scene where Verena performs at Miss Birdseye's apartment and is described in the imagery of a gypsy girl. "If she had produced a pair of castanets or a tambourine," Ransom reflects, "such accessories would have been quite in keeping. . . . [He] would have thought she looked like an Oriental, if it were not that Orientals were dark; and if she had only had a goat she would have resembled Esmeralda, though he had but a vague recollection of who Esmeralda had been" (p. 49). Esmeralda of course is a character in Hugo's *The Hunchback of Notre Dame,* a beautiful gypsy girl of sixteen who performs in public and captivates everyone with her singing and dancing. Unfortunately, she also captivates the priest-alchemist Claude Frollo, who spirits her away to the Gothic tower of Notre Dame, where she is held in a vampire's bondage. The following passage illustrates the intensity of the priest's love-damnation:

> No head was lifted as high and as proudly as mine. . . . Science was all in all to me. In spite, however, of my determination to acknowledge no other influence, that power of nature, which . . . I had hoped to crush

for life, had more than once convulsively shaken the chain of those iron vows which bind me, miserable man that I am, to the cold stones of the altar. . . . O maiden! . . . take pity on me; thou deemest thyself miserable. Alas! thou knowest not what misery is. It is to love a woman—to be a priest. . . —to love with all the energies of your soul—to feel that you would give for the least of her smiles your blood, your life, your character, your salvation, immortality and eternity, this world and the next—to regret that you are not a king, an emperor, an archangel, that you might throw a greater slave at her feet; to clasp her night and day in your sleeping, and in your waking dreams. . . —to think of that delicious form till you writhe for whole nights on the floor of your cell, and to see all the endearments which you have reserved for her in imagination end in torture—these are pincers heated in the fire of hell . . . love, jealousy, despair![24]

It is precisely when Olive first sees Verena, as she performs at Miss Birdseye's, that the allusion to Esmeralda occurs, and in Hugo's novel it is when Claude Frollo first sees Esmeralda dance in the street that he becomes carried away by a longing, unpermitted him as a priest, that becomes a jealous, possessive torment. Surely this allusion hints at the inner springs of Olive's sexuality. She may suffer without understanding the sexual basis of her possessive torment, but the reader need not be as much in the dark, and I do not think that James was.

The allusion to Esmeralda deepens the sense of Olive Chancellor as being involved in masquerade and deception, particularly self-deception. At the beginning Mrs. Luna describes her as being full of rectitude, but at various points in the work her rectitude is revealed as a form of self-deception. She rides the streetcar because she identifies with the suffering masses, who are obliged to ride it; but she really hates the streetcar, as well as the masses. The Tarrants turn their daughter over to her, to share her "narrow drawing-room" (p. 1), on her assurance that Verena "should have every opportunity for a free expansion" (p. 141), which she will certainly not have living under Olive's dominance. Finally, her adoption of Verena as her protégé, to help in the emancipation of women, is not motivated by

137

the altruism she claims. In turning Verena away from "life," Olive will wither her soul; and in this way she is a much more sophisticated, more plausibly motivated, version of Hawthorne's Westervelt. It seems hardly a coincidence that Olive's losing her hold over Verena at a public exhibition of her inspirational faculties at the Music Hall in Boston should call to mind the scene at the village lyceum in *The Blithedale Romance,* where Hollingsworth rises from his seat in the auditorium to wrest Priscilla from the sinister spell of a wizard.

It is James's subtle and deeply ingenious refinement on Hawthorne's romance archetype of the innocent maiden, who performs in public under the auspices of a wizard, and the threatened violation of her soul, that gives *The Bostonians* its romance quality within the novel's elaborate realism. In rethinking Hawthorne's themes in *The Blithedale Romance*—the deception of New England reformers, their engagement in a form of "mock-life"—James both allied himself with Hawthorne as a psychologist and at the same time involved him in his own criticism of democracy, the social milieu in which a professed altruism concealing an exploitation of others becomes credible. *The Blithedale Romance* and *The Bostonians* illuminate each other insofar as they show a thematic continuity but an extreme difference in handling of a common subject. Taken together, they demonstrate James's urbanization of Hawthorne's rustic vision into the comedy of manners. Hawthorne's dark fable of a whole community that espouses brotherhood and selflessness but is concerned with victimization has the nature of a moral abstraction. *The Bostonians,* on the other hand, is brilliantly concrete in its handling of human relationships, and suggests what James, with his greater social awareness, had found still relevant in *The Blithedale Romance*—that Hawthorne had written an unconscious allegory of democracy.

138

9 The Blithedale Romance and The Bostonians: The Pattern of Transformation

In *Novelists in a Changing World*, Donald David Stone has shown how the careers of Meredith and James during the 1880s demonstrate the breakup of the Victorian order, Meredith's novels confirming a harmonious social integration after it no longer existed, and James's giving importance to the individual rather than to the larger social unit to which he belongs. Stone is exceptionally well informed about the English Victorian novel, but his discussion of *The Bostonians* gives, it seems to me, a misleading impression that James's novel can be best understood in relation to its English rather than its American background. Indeed, he gives only slight attention to the American literary background of *The Bostonians* and makes the Hawthorne relation seem unimportant, or even nonexistent.

Stone argues that while James intended a very American tale, what he in fact produced was a novel "distinctly Victorian in style." To support his claims he points out the use, unusual for James, of an omniscient narrator who frequently intrudes on his narration, sometimes to look into a character's mind or to admit that he does not know what his character is thinking, and of a "closed" ending that was more acceptable to an English audience than James's previously "open" ones. He points out, too, that James's satire in the novel has a Dickensian quality which is especially evident in his depiction of the group at Miss Birdseye's apartment. These "Dickensian regulars" seem to preexist rather than to develop in the manner of James's more usual characters. He also notes that the novel's heroine, in her passivity, "seems derived from Trollope's heroines,"[1] a conclusion he could hardly have reached if he had given more attention to James's American literary background. In particular, Stone overlooks the transformations that were occurring in the American novel after the Civil War—both the transfer of concept from Hawthorne to Howells and James, and between Howells and James themselves.

As the new American realism emerged after the Civil War, an interplay of character conception and theme between Howells and James was frequent. James found in Howells an "unerring" sense of American character, and at various times took clues from him in his own treatment of native themes. It was Howells who created "the American girl," first as Kitty Ellison (*A Chance Acquaintance*, 1871), and again as Florida Vervain (*A Foregone Conclusion*, 1873), this time in an international setting, before James created her more enduringly in *Daisy Miller* (1878). Moreover, *A Foregone Conclusion*—in its conception of a romantic, doomed central figure in Italy, contrasted with a more marginal male character who cannot commit himself deeply to life—also anticipates *Roderick Hudson*. It would be possible to elaborate upon thematic ties between Howells and James, but only one instance of their shared concerns and common themes in the 1880s need be mentioned here—their mutual interest during the decade in neurotic young New England women.

Marcia Gaylord (*A Modern Instance*, 1882), the high-strung daughter of a rigid and forbidding father who comes out of a Calvinist background, is the most striking example of this type, but she is only one character among a group of others. Alice Pasmer (*April Hopes*, 1888) and Annie Kilburn (*Annie Kilburn*, 1888) have restless New England consciences; and Helen Harkness (*A Woman's Reason*, 1883) literally admits that she cannot be happy until she has known misfortune and self-sacrifice. In *Dr. Breen's Practice* (1881) there are several neurotic New England women, one of whom has driven herself until she has become a nervous invalid. Grace Breen's mother is de-

140

scribed as "an old lady, who had once kept a very vigilant conscience for herself; but after making her life unhappy with it for some three-score years, now applied it entirely for the exasperation and condemnation of others. She especially devoted it to fretting a New England girl's naturally morbid sense of duty in her daughter." Grace Breen takes up the practice of medicine not because she enjoys tending the sick (in fact, she does not at all), but because she feels that an arduous altruism is a social duty. "In the end," Howells writes, "she was a Puritan; belated, misdated, if the reader will, cast upon good works which the Puritans formerly found in a creed."[2] Howells's portrayals during the 1880s of young New England women who have a neurotic tendency, or are driven by a sense of duty to the point of self-sacrifice, have a quite definite relevance to James's conception of Olive Chancellor in *The Bostonians*.

The interplay between Howells and James, however, is complicated by the interest they both showed in Hawthorne. Howells took particular pride in Hawthorne as an American writer who could be compared to the best of England's novelists and referred to him often as having set a standard for younger American writers. "When you've a fame as great as Hawthorne's," Howells wrote to James in 1869, as they were both beginning their careers, "you won't forget who was the first, warmest and truest of your admirers, will you?"[3] Howells also studied Hawthorne as a guide to American experience, and his own fiction suggests Hawthorne's influence at various points. It is particularly noticeable in *The Undiscovered Country*.

Howells's assimilation of *The Blithedale Romance* in *The Undiscovered Country* (1880) is part of a larger pattern of transformation, but it is especially significant because it is involved in a transformation of *The Blithedale Romance* by both Howells and James. The heroine of *The Undiscovered Country*, Egeria Boynton, is a descendant, in realistic version, of Hawthorne's Priscilla in *The Blithedale Romance*. Like Priscilla, she acts as the passive trance-medium of a mesmerist and is exhibited in public before being liberated into the world of actuality. Both *The Blithedale Romance* and *The Undiscovered Country* are set in Boston and the countryside beyond it, and are concerned with forms of sham life, illustrated in part by the public performances of mes-

141

merists and Spiritualists. When Hawthorne's Coverdale attends a public performance given by Professor Westervelt, who speaks of holding "intercourse with spirits," he remarks that "the epoch of rapping spirits, and all the wonders that followed in their train—such as tables upset by invisible agencies, bells self-tolled at funerals, and ghostly music performed on jew's harps—had not yet arrived" (p. 283).[4] Which is to say that they already had when Hawthorne was writing *The Blithedale Romance*, a criticism of his own period.

In 1850 the Fox sisters of Rochester, New York ("the Rochester Rappings"), began a series of séances in New York City and thereafter toured the United States and Europe. Hawthorne knew of them, as he did also of Daniel Dunglas Home, who even as a youth gained fame in New England as a Spiritualist able to produce rappings, table movings, and other psychic phenomena. In *Victoria's Heyday*, J. B. Priestley has described the Spiritualist craze in New England, which then swept to England at the beginning of the 1850s:

> Beginning with the Fox sisters, Kate and Margaret, from 1848 onwards, America produced hundreds of mediums, some of them children, all of them holding regular séances. In every town there were darkened rooms in which luminous spirit faces appeared, and musical instruments played themselves, strange voices were heard prophesying, hands materialized from nowhere, and the faithful shivered in drafts of Arctic air. . . . New revelations were needed, and the Eastern states of America . . . were buzzing with strange cults and Utopias. Young D. D. Home was only another of these spirit miracle-workers, though it was not long before he became the most impressive of them. . . . During the next two years, visiting many New England towns and being lionized everywhere, Home went from strength to strength, making furniture float around, materializing spirit hands, and levitating not only tables but himself too.[5]

Hawthorne wrote skeptically of the new Spiritualism in his *American Notebooks* and in *The Blithedale Romance* treated it as an evasion of reality. He describes the Veiled Lady ironically as "a phenomenon in the mesmerist line; one of the earliest that had indicated the birth of a new science, or the revival of an old humbug" (p. 1), and Westervelt, who exhibits her, is bogus both in his credentials and in his outward appearance, which changes completely when he puts on a pair of spectacles. As Westervelt tells his audience of the new Spiritualism, Coverdale remarks: "It was eloquent, ingenious, plausible, with a delusive show of spirituality, yet really imbued throughout with a cold and dead materialism" (p. 85). In *The Undiscovered Country* Howells treats the same phenomenon of Spiritualism, relating it, as Hawthorne had done, to the theme of deception, but placing it in the context of post–Civil War Boston. Howells's novel opens upon the scene of a Boston séance, complete with a materialization of spirit hands, and there is about it all an atmosphere of humbug. The street, house, and characters present are depicted as symptoms of a social decay, a disintegration of Boston's former culture, a decline of religious integrity into bohemian eccentricity.

Present at this scene is Egeria Boynton, a pale, blonde maiden dressed, not unlike Priscilla (as the Veiled Lady) in a "theatrical robe of white serge." Her father is with her, a short man with small hands, "a mouth of delicacy and refinement, and a smile of infantine sweetness" (p. 4).[6] His "exquisite . . . child-like" smile implies his credulous nature before the rest of the novel confirms it. Before Dr. Boynton places his daughter in a mesmeric trance and the séance begins, other characters arrive, including Mrs. LeRoy, the landlady; Mr. Weatherby, who has a special interest in levitation; and Mr. Eccles (who has a name with ecclesiastical connotations), a "scientist" of Spiritualism who, when he opens **his** mouth to speak, reveals a "lavish display of an upper and lower set of artificial teeth" (p. 17). Howells refers in this section to his "dental smile," and, in an image that seems to depersonalize him, to his "setting his artificial teeth to smile"; and he is thus made deliberately reminiscent of Westervelt, whose smile reveals a gold band running along the upper part of his teeth that suddenly makes his whole being seem a sham. Present at the séance too is Ford, a skeptical journalist, who finds the performance a hoax and thereafter decides to expose its fraudulence publicly. He enters here into a struggle with Dr. Boynton which continues through the rest of the novel and is in fact a contest to see which of them shall dominate and possess Egeria. The complicated struggle of will depicted in *The Blithedale Romance* has been reduced in *The Undiscovered Country* to this focal issue.

Ford is Howells's own variation of Hollingsworth as a rescuer of Priscilla from Westervelt, but rather than being a crank philanthropist, he is a crank journalist, out of harmony with Boston life. He is caustic, virile, hard-minded, and extremely critical of his fellow Bostonians (significantly, Ford is not originally from Boston), who seem to him to belong to an "effeminized" age. His one friendship, an incongruous one, is with Phillips, whose connoisseur's existence implies a decline of force and coherence in the culture of Boston itself. Phillips's father had been in wholesale trade and had left him well enough provided for that he can live a leisured life, and indulge his taste for exquisite things like bric-a-brac, paintings, and colonial clocks. At one point Ford tells Phillips that he and Mr. Eccles are much alike. "He is a brother dilettante, it seems. He dabbles in ghosts as you dabble in bricabrac" (p. 85). Eccles and Phillips are, indeed, symptomatic of the decline of purposive energy in Boston in the aftermath of its heroic age.

This early section of *The Undiscovered Country* reveals not only how Howells interpreted Hawthorne's characters in terms of social realism, but also how his characters prepare for James's in *The Bostonians*. Howells's mesmerist and his daughter who perform at gatherings in Boston anticipate James's conception of Dr. Tarrant and his daughter Verena; Phillips prepares for James's somewhat effeminized young Bostonian men like Burrage and Gracie; Ford looks forward to Basil Ransom, another crank journalist and outsider-critic of Boston's culture who "rescues" a performing maiden. James's satire and characters are incomparably more vivid, but the diagram of their relationships has already been furnished by Howells. In his discussion of *The Blithedale Romance* and *The Bostonians* in *The Complex Fate*, Bewley leaves out *The Undiscovered Country* as a revealing middle stage of adaptation. Had he included it, he would have been able to assemble an even more persuasive case—and given sharper outline to the pattern of transformation.

After this early section of *The Undiscovered Country*, Howells be-

144

gins to develop the theme of his heroine's dormant nature, a conception of her that involves a fairy-tale element, a version of Sleeping Beauty. Ford's belligerency toward the Spiritualists before long results in a victory for him, when he forces Mrs. LeRoy to admit that she had produced the supernatural manifestations at the séance. Afterward, Ford and Phillips engage in a discussion of Egeria's nature which has the effect of emphasizing further her affinity with Hawthorne's Priscilla, the innocent participant in Westervelt's public performances:

> "The girl [Phillips says] is such a deliciously abnormal creature. It is girlhood at odds with itself. If she had been her father's 'subject' ever since childhood, of course none of the ordinary young girl interests have entered into her life. She hasn't known the delight of dress and dancing; she hasn't had 'attentions.' . . . It means that she's kept a child-like simplicity, and she could go on, and help out her father's purposes, no matter how tricky they were, with no more sense of guilt than a child who makes believe talk with imaginary visitors. Yes *[she] could be innocent in the midst of fraud.* Come, I call that a pretty conjecture!"
>
> "My dear fellow [Ford replies], *I'm proud of that conjecture. It was worthy of Hawthorne.*" (Pp. 109–10, italics mine)

145

At the same time, Dr. Boynton and Egeria leave Boston and eventually find shelter in a community of Shakers. This later section reads more like a romance than a novel of manners, a romance with a Shakespearean quality in which characters undergo sea changes and make new recognitions. Howells insinuates the idea of an "unnaturalness" in the Shakers' life, which necessitates celibacy and renunciation of the world. Egeria is not meant for such renunciation, as even her name implies, since the original Egeria of Roman religion was affiliated with nature and fecundity, being the goddess of fountains and streams, and also of childbirth. After Ford meets Egeria in Boston, he is shown still thinking about her, as he is seated on a bench in the Public Garden, next to a fountain; and later Egeria herself is depicted by other streams and fountains, particularly in the woods near the Shaker settlement, where she has been joined by

Ford, and their attraction to each other is subtly and skillfully evoked by the blooming of nature around them.

At the Shaker settlement, both Egeria and her father experience illnesses, after the crises of which they reach new understandings of themselves. Dr. Boynton's long struggle of will with Ford for the possession of Egeria ends with his belated recognition that he has, without full understanding, been using his daughter as a trance-medium for selfish ends, hoping through her to establish communication with his wife, who died when Egeria was born. He describes himself here as having used his daughter as a "subject for psychological experiment," and so seems like a benign version of Dr. Rappaccini: "At last, 'Yes,' he groaned, with an indescribable intensity of contrition in his tone, 'I see what you mean! I seized upon a simple, loving nature, good and sweet in its earthliness, and sacred in it, and alienated it from all its possible happiness to the uses of my ambition. I have played the vampire!'" (p. 318).

But if Dr. Boynton has been too credulous, Ford has been too cynical; the self-centeredness of both is corrected finally by a larger human understanding. The novel moves, thus, from aberration to normality, from illusion to reality; it concludes with the marriage of Egeria and Ford, and their settling down in Boston as Ford becomes an unprosperous, but less abrasive and more socially adjusted, inventor. In this ending Howells shares with Hawthorne a skepticism of utopias and a very firm sense of human limitations. *The Blithedale Romance* and *The Undiscovered Country* correspond, furthermore, in the use they both make of the pastoral mode to explore illusion and reality, their narratives moving back and forth between Boston and the surrounding countryside as assumptions are tested. Hawthorne's pastoral is tragically oriented, while Howells's is not; yet both work toward conservative visions that are critical of the "new truths" of their periods.

Six years before Howells wrote *The Undiscovered Country*, James published his story "Professor Fargo" (1874), which also draws from *The Blithedale Romance* and deals with a mesmerist who gives public performances in New England. And it is possible that "Pro-

146

fessor Fargo" may have suggested to Howells the possibility of adapting the mesmerist-and-maiden archetype in *The Undiscovered Country*.[7] Professor Fargo, in any case, reappears in a new version in *The Bostonians*. Professor Westervelt-become-Professor Fargo now becomes Dr. Tarrant, a paternal vampire who exhibits his daughter in public as a girl whose speech is inspired. In his paternal relation he is also a variant of Dr. Boynton, and comes recognizably out of the world Howells created in *The Undiscovered Country*. Tarrant can remember the "darkened room, the waiting circle, the little taps on the table and wall, . . . the music in the air, the rain of flowers" (p. 62). Mrs. Tarrant cherishes the same memories of those days when she assisted the supernatural as "the spirit hand" at séances— "those exciting days of his mediumship, when the table, sometimes, wouldn't rise from the ground, the sofa wouldn't float through the air, and the soft hand of a loved one was not so alert as it ought to have been to visit the circle" (p. 61). Exposed as a medium, Tarrant has since become a mesmeric healer, with a clientele of older, lonely women.

147

Although Tarrant is subjected to James's urbane satire, his romance origins are still perceptible. Westervelt's display of gold-banded upper teeth is remembered in Tarrant's smile, "which made his mouth enormous, developed two wrinkles as long as the wings of a bat, on either side of it, and showed a set of big, even, carnivorous teeth" (p. 38). The bat image is fitting, since Tarrant's relationship to his daughter is vampiric and defiling: "Tarrant's grotesque manipulations . . . seemed a dishonour to the passive maiden" (p. 50). In Tarrant, James evokes the idea of a spurious priesthood, deception, and exploitation, which is then explored more fully in the character of Olive Chancellor. Rather than dwelling on the father-daughter relationship, as Howells had done in *The Undiscovered Country,* James shifts his center of interest to Miss Chancellor, to whom Dr. Tarrant, in an extraordinary scene, "sells" his daughter. Verena thus passes from one version of exploitation, treated in a broadly comic manner, to another, treated with far greater refinement. This relationship becomes the psychological case or "study" of the novel.

James found the "germ" for Olive Chancellor in Alphonse Daudet's *L'Evangéliste* (1883), which attacks religious fanaticism, particularly the conversion to its purposes of the young and innocent. In his critical sketch of Daudet's career, written in 1883 and later collected in *Partial Portraits,* James refers to its principal character, Madame Autheman, as a "theological vampire." His other comments make it clear that he found in the novel "a great opportunity" missed:

> Daudet's weakness has been simply a want of acquaintance with his subject. Proposing to himself to describe a particular phase of French Protestantism, he had "got up" certain of his facts with commendable zeal; but he has not felt or understood the matter, has looked at it solely from the outside, sought to make it above all things grotesque and extravagant. . . . Madame Autheman strikes me as quite automatic; and psychologically she is a blank. One does not see the operation of her character. She must have had a soul, and a very curious one. It was a great opportunity for a piece of spiritual portraiture; but we know nothing about Madame Autheman's inner springs, and I think we fail to believe in her. I should go so far as to say that we get little more of an inside view, as the phrase is, of Eline Ebsen; we are not shown the spiritual steps by which she went over to the enemy—vividly, admirably as the outward signs and consequences of this disaster are depicted.[8]

But even if seen only from the outside, Madame Autheman is a figure one remembers, a cold and unrelenting woman driven by destructive impulses concealed from her by her own Calvinist fervor. The conception of a woman with something of Madame Autheman's temperament in a New England setting, and of an innocent girl whom she converts to her cause, provided James with an opportunity for "spiritual portraiture," which would also comment on the life of Boston. James's version of Madame Autheman would have greater inwardness and plausibility, and the stages by which the girl becomes associated with her and becomes her protégé would be carefully traced. Rather than being a religious crusader, Olive Chancellor would be dedicated to the holy work of women's emancipation, her morbid psychology conditioned by New England Calvinism. In this way *L'Evangéliste* was indeed conceptually important to James, but it was so partly as a point of departure.[9] As he began to give a distinctively American outline to Olive and her relationship to Verena, he was drawn, as he had been many times in the past, to the psychological themes of Hawthorne.

Immediately upon meeting Olive Chancellor, Ransom asks himself why she is morbid, and why her morbidness is "typical." The answer, it is implied, is that she has been molded by a New England conscience that interferes with an ease of response to life. Olive cannot be "happy" until her nerves are frayed. She is morbid also and more particularly, because her impulses are self-destructive. "The most secret, the most sacred hope of her nature," James remarks, "was that she might some day . . . be a martyr and die for something" (p. 9). She has practically a martyr fixation, seeing martyr figures in unlikely people. Miss Birdseye has "always had for Olive a kind of aroma of martyrdom" (p. 153). At one point she can even think of Verena as being like a heroic martyr, Joan of Arc. Her fascination with martyrdom seems like a secular version of the Puritan effort to atone for sin; but most of all, it suggests that her habits of thought are unreal, and will lead to her unhappiness. She not only dreams of martyrdom, but also courts it. It is *she* who invites Ransom to visit her in Boston, knowing that she may be asking for difficulties by doing so, and it is *she* who introduces Ransom to Verena. Earlier in her life she had tried to befriend shop girls, whom she views in her imagination as the "downtrodden," but they have always rejected her for a young man named "Charlie." Yet she persists with Verena in this same course, which has always ended in disappointment, and will again, for the same reasons.

Eventually she achieves martyrdom in a figurative sense. Verena leaves her for Ransom, and she suffers the worst personal torment she has ever known. At the Boston Music Hall, that temple of severe culture in which she and the others have "worshipped," she has to face an angry mob. With her morbid dread of speaking before the public, this final act is very much like a martyrdom. "If he had observed her," James remarks, "it might have seemed to him that she

149

hoped to find the fierce expiation she sought for in exposure to the thousands she had disappointed and deceived, in offering herself to be trampled to death and torn to pieces. She might have suggested to him . . . even the sacrificial figure of Hypatia, whirled through the furious mob of Alexandria" (pp. 376–77).

James's allusion to Hypatia is literary as well as historical, referring to Charles Kingsley's novel *Hypatia* (1853), a work better known in the Victorian age than it is today, in which Hypatia is a votary of the Neoplatonic school of philosophy, "supreme Reason," as opposed to religion, which stresses the emotions and the soul. Kingsley described Hypatia as being coldly virginal, estranged from men or a surrender to love. In his chapter on *Hypatia* in *Heroines of Fiction,* Howells calls Hypatia "arrogant in mind, holding matrimony in high scorn. . . . her philosophy cares only for things of the mind. . . . Hypatia's fatal mistake [was in] trying to transcend her own nature. . . . She was a sort of Alexandrian Margaret Fuller." [10] Margaret Fuller is an interesting association for Howells to have made. She was of course an ardent feminist, and a very striking example of the young New England woman who, deeply read in Goethe and the German idealistic philosophers, had adopted the Transcendental view of the world. Her culture was so strenuous that she grated on Hawthorne's nerves; and he surely had her in mind, at least in part, in his portrait of the high-strung Zenobia.

The connection between the warm-blooded and womanly Zenobia and Olive Chancellor, the Boston spinster with "pale lips and cold eyes," may not be immediately obvious; but a close relationship and discernible line of descent does exist. As the most notable feminist in the American fiction of Hawthorne's period, Zenobia is a character against whom one can measure Olive Chancellor and her intensities. Zenobia's advocacy of women's rights takes a peculiar form, since it exists as a kind of passionate abstraction. Asked about women's rights, she snaps that "women possess no rights" (p. 201), and when she speaks of society's injustices to women, her voice is always humorless. "Did you ever see a happy woman in your life?" she asks, adding, "How can she be happy after discovering that fate has assigned her but one single event, which she must contrive to

150

make the substance of her life?" (pp. 81–82). When Olive Chancellor speaks of society's wrong to women, she uses the same, self-dramatizing vocabulary. " 'I always feel it—everywhere—night and day. I feel it *here*'; and Olive laid her hand solemnly on her heart. 'I feel it as a deep, unforgettable wrong; I feel it as one feels a stain that is on one's honour' " (p. 132).

Zenobia and Olive Chancellor both possess an inner strenuousness that seems to push them beyond their limits. Coverdale's private reflections about Zenobia apply as well to Olive. "What puzzled me," he remarks, "was the fact, that women, however intellectually superior, so seldom disquiet themselves about the rights of their sex, unless their own individual affections chance to lie in idleness, or are ill at ease. . . . I could measure Zenobia's inward trouble by the animosity with which she now took up the general quarrel of woman against man" (p. 171). A victim of unrequited love, Zenobia imperiously commits suicide, going to a self-imposed "martyrdom" (Hawthorne's word) that had been foretold earlier in the work; and Olive Chancellor, whose inner nature is "like a skiff in a stormy sea" (p. 7), also imposes upon herself martyrdom of a kind. In their intensities and neuroticism, they are women of New England who seem virtually to welcome the exaltation of suffering.

Olive Chancellor is not only herself deceived; she would impose her self-deception on Verena until the younger woman's life would become as austere, unfulfilled, and joyless as her own. In this sense she is a vampire who will feed on the youth and freshness of Verena as her only *real* life, while Verena will be left to dwell upon the wrongs to womanhood by men. At her apartment, during their first winter together, she explains to Verena what sort of life she envisions for her:

"Do you understand German? Do you know 'Faust'?" said Olive. " '*Entsagen sollst du, sollst entsagen!*' "

"I don't know German; I should like so to study it; I want to know everything."

"We will work at it together—we will study everything," Olive almost panted.

. . . At the same time she asked the meaning of the German words. " 'Thou shalt renounce, refrain, abstain!' " Olive answered. (Pp. 72–73)[11]

Olive Chancellor and Basil Ransom engage in a struggle of will for the possession of Verena, with Olive appealing to her mind and Ransom to her heart. Like Egeria Boynton, Verena has a dormant nature that is womanly and sexual. Egeria's name affiliated her with nature, with fountains and streams, and Verena has a vernal name and is compared to a "naiad" (p. 51), the nymph who lived in and gave life to fountains and streams. She is called "an inspired maiden, a young lady from whose lips eloquence flowed in streams" (p. 63), and later her personal success seems to wrap itself about her "with a glamour like the silver mist that surrounds a fountain" (p. 228). Verena's association with nature becomes important when (following a pattern in *The Undiscovered Country*) James shifts his setting from the city to the countryside to Miss Chancellor's summer house at Marmion on Cape Cod. With this shift, James begins to work in the pastoral mode, evoking values which are wholly different from those of Boston's intellectualized life. During his first visit at Olive Chancellor's apartment, Ransom jestingly describes himself as a "Boeotian"—a rude, unlettered person from the agrarian South. *Boeotian* is synonymous with countrified or boorish, but it also refers to the ancient Boeotians, as they appear in literature, who loved agricultural and pastoral pursuits. At Marmion Verena too is given Boeotian associations, particularly when she is compared to Corinna, the Boeotian lyric poet of the fifth century B.C. who was noted for her beauty. She is called "a New England Corinna with a mission instead of a lyre" (p. 223). In an earlier meeting between Ransom and Verena, which Verena has kept secret from Olive, Verena appears very natural and at ease, and speaks in a "gay, friendly, trustful tone —the tone of facile intercourse, the tone in which happy, flower-crowned maidens may have talked to sunburnt young men in the golden age" (p. 190). At Marmion this pastoral motif, quietly insinuated early in the novel, is given new emphasis, and one begins to

note allusions to Arcadia, the Virgilian countryside of idyllic plea-
sures that is preferred to a more complex urban existence.

What James actually suggests in this section as a contrast to Boston, although critics seem not to have noticed it, is Italy. When
Ransom arrives in Cape Cod by afternoon train, his impressions of
the countryside seem curiously Mediterranean. "The ripeness of
summer lay upon the land. . . . There was a kind of soft scrubbiness
in the landscape, and a sweetness, begotten of low horizons, of mild
air, with a possibility of summer haze, of unregarded inlets, where
on August mornings the water must be brightly blue. . . . the
drowsy Cape, the languid Cape, the Cape not of storms, but of eter-
nal peace." James then adds that Ransom "had heard that the Cape
was the Italy, so to speak, of Massachusetts" (p. 230).

Moreover, the woods behind Olive Chancellor's summer house
suggest the play of the senses and art and are made to seem Italian-
ate. In a compromise arrangement, Verena agrees to go for a walk in
the woods with Ransom, but only for a brief, specified period of
time which she has agreed upon with Olive. "They sometimes
followed bosky uplands, where accident had grouped the trees with
odd effects of 'style,' and where in grassy intervals and fragrant
nooks of rest they came out upon sudden patches of Arcady. In such
places Verena listened to her companion with a watch in her hand"
(p. 321). This image shows Verena poised between two cultures—
the Boeotian one that is at ease with nature and is unself-conscious,
and the other represented by the angular Miss Chancellor and the
world view implied in the strict timepiece Verena holds.

Important in this section also is Miss Chancellor's garden. It is
a "back-garden" in which the activity of public involvement and a
preoccupation with change have been stilled and are replaced by a
sense of what is unchanging in the human condition. The breezes
which blow through it are "idle," and there is time here to recover a
larger perspective of human experience and illusion, to which art
gives outline. Ransom "thought Miss Chancellor's back-garden a
delightful spot, and his jaded senses tasted the breeze—the idle,
wandering summerwind—that stirred the vine-leaves over his head.

153

The hazy shores on the other side of the water, . . . (they seemed powdered with silver, a sort of midsummer light), suggested to him a land of dreams, a country in a picture. . . . the situation in which he now found himself pleased him almost as much as if it had been a striking work of art" (p. 302). This association of the garden with art and illusion is relevant to Miss Birdseye's appearance in it. In a spirit of kindliness, James suggests again that she has lived with illusion (her mistaken impressions continue to the end), but in this garden setting her humanity and generous spirit are also strongly felt and she becomes touching, as her death is touching, whereas in the narrower perspective of Boston she had seemed merely a philanthropic hack.

Stone has described this section as a "slip" on the part of James; it is, he says, stylistically different from the earlier part because of "the poignancy that accidentally breaks into the novel."[12] But the poignancy of this section is not "accidental," in respect either to Miss Birdseye or to Miss Chancellor. In Boston, Miss Chancellor had stood for a perfection of the universe, but here she learns about imperfection in herself, and thus, for a time at least, becomes humanized. Her recognition comes one afternoon when Verena goes to see Ransom to tell him that she will remain with Olive and see him no more. It is the great test of her attachment to Olive, and she fails it; instead of severing her relations with Ransom, she spends the entire afternoon with him, aboard a sailboat on the estuary. Before Verena returns after sunset, "Olive lived over, in her miserable musings, her life for the last two years, . . . how it had all rested on an illusion of which the very thought made her feel faint and sick. What was before her now was the reality, with the beautiful, indifferent sky pouring down its complacent rays upon it. The reality was simply that Verena had been more to her than she ever was to Verena" (p. 344). When Verena returns, Olive's suffering is projected with a psychological intensity that makes one feel a compassion for her that had not been felt previously.

Verena enters from the back-garden into the parlor, which is now dim, and here she finds Olive waiting for her:

Olive stopped short, and for a minute the two women remained as they were in the dimness . . . and Olive took her hand with an irresistible impulse of compassion and reassurance. From the way it lay in her own she guessed her whole feeling—saw it was a kind of shame, shame for her own weakness, her swift surrender. . . . they were beyond each other's help now. Verena leaned her head back and closed her eyes, and for an hour, as nightfall settled in the room, neither of the young women spoke. Distinctly, it was a kind of shame. After a while the parlor-maid . . . appeared with a lamp; but Olive motioned her frantically away. She wished to keep the darkness. It was a kind of shame. (Pp. 346–47)

In Boston, Olive was described as having no "figure," and as being thus like Miss Birdseye, a public person without form. But in the scene above, Olive has been touched by what is personal, an experience as timeless as love unrequited, and in this extremely *personal* moment her woman's life suddenly achieves shape and becomes distinct. The deepest truth about Olive as a human being, her vulnerability and loneliness, is brought out by James in this passage with an intense reality. It is the reality behind the appearance.

Olive loses Verena at Marmion before she loses her finally at the Music Hall in Boston, where Verena does not deliver her address entitled "A Woman's Reason,"[13] going off instead with Ransom, apparently into nowhere, or at least to a life that is not strongly specified. James's ending completes the pattern of a rescue into actuality which appears in *The Blithedale Romance* and *The Undiscovered Country*, and confirms how deeply he was working with American sources, and how much *The Bostonians* is implicated in a complex pattern of transformation in nineteenth-century American fiction. Despite certain resemblances it has with the English Victorian novel, and its immediate source in Daudet's *L'Evangéliste*, *The Bostonians* is revealed most fully by its American background.

The Blithedale Romance, *The Undiscovered Country*, and *The Bostonians* occur in something like a direct line of descent, and demonstrate a transition from the romance to the romance-novel to a fully realized novel of manners. All are set in and around Boston and move back and forth from the city to the country; and in doing so they employ some version of pastoral to organize their themes and to comment on New England's life, particularly on the phenomenon of the new utopian formulas. Hawthorne's pastoral, dealing with a search for universal brotherhood, ends with a tragic sense of the essential separateness of human beings from one another; his theme is centered, romantically, on the individual and his isolation. Reflecting his different attitudes, Howells's pastoral works toward a reconciliation to community and finds sanity and health in normality and the democratic average. James's novel, written in a different spirit still, is an antidemocratic satire of manners which makes cultural comparisons and illuminates the fallacies behind the "truths" which a particular culture regards as absolute. The rigidities and intellectualization which the culture of Boston imposes come, indeed, to prevent James's characters from being able to perceive reality.

156

In his "correction" of *The Blithedale Romance*, James has also subjected Hawthrone and his age to a modern understanding. Miss Birdseye is called a battered monument to the heroic age in New England, and her death, in old age, in Marmion leaves an impression of James's own personal farewell to the heroic tradition of New England. Early in the work Miss Birdseye is said to have no personal needs, only moral ones, words which bring to mind James's remark about Emerson in his review of the Emerson-Carlyle correspondence in 1883. "Nothing is more striking in Emerson's letters," James remarks, "than the way in which people are measured exclusively by their moral standards, designated by moral terms, described according to their morality. There was nothing else to describe them by." [14] Later, Miss Birdseye is called exquisitely "provincial," a word James used in his biography to characterize Hawthorne's genius. In *The Bostonians* James has consciously distanced himself from Hawthorne and his preoccupation with tragic isolation as an absolute of human experience, an absolute that is also an expression of New England's Puritan heritage, and that in the next generation produces an Olive Chancellor. Olive is so tormented by mind that she suffers the fate of certain other of James's characters—the deprivation of life. *The*

Bostonians, on the other hand, is centered not on a single absolute, but on the possibilities before James's characters of experiencing life well or fully, or of failing of their chance. James's characters live and die by their perceptions, and Olive Chancellor is the great reminder in the novel of what failed perception means, as she longs for a martyrdom—and needlessly, having already been martyred by the culture of Boston.

10 Conclusion: The End of James's Earlier Period

Although complete unto itself as a work of art, *The Bostonians* begins a novel trilogy that includes *The Princess Casamassima* (1886) and *The Tragic Muse* (1890) and concerns itself with the public versus the private or esthetic life. The priority James gives to the esthetic life in the trilogy is anticipated early in the 1880s in *The Portrait of a Lady,* whose invalid hero, a kind of artist manqué, measures life against the fineness and large disinterestedness of art. In the trilogy, however, the conflict between the public and the private life becomes a focal issue. In *The Bostonians* James deals most obviously with the clash between reforming politics and public causes, and a personal fulfillment made possible through privacy; but he also intimates a tie between the private and the esthetic life. His story, "A New England Winter," comments on the women of Boston who give themselves to committees rather than to "society," and in *The Bostonians* they appear, in another version, as the women who gather at Olive Chancellor's apartment, wasting the warmth and beauty of summer evenings discussing reform while "life" passes them by. The absence of the pictorial spectacle of a "society" is felt in *The Bostonians* as an esthetic ugliness; and this impression is deepened by the presence of such characters—with vulgarly externalized lives—as Pardon (a shoddy journalist rather than an artist) and Selah Tarrant

Conclusion

(an exploiter who soils his daughter's distinctness and grace by offering her as an article of commerce). By contrast, the motif of Italy at the end suggests an entirely different set of values—the drama of purely private and personal relationships against a background of nature and art, a spectacle that has esthetic form and "style."

In this respect, a revealing scene takes place at the Cambridge apartment of Mr. Burrage. Earlier gatherings had occurred in Boston apartments, but this gathering has nothing to do with politics or reform. It is a musical evening that, bathed in the red glow of fireplace light, is evoked with the suggestion of considerable richness. The passage I have in mind follows:

I must add, however, that there was a moment when [Olive] came near being happy—or, at any rate, reflected that it was a pity she could not be so. Mrs. Burrage asked her son to play "some little thing," and he sat down to his piano and revealed a talent that might well have gratified the lady's pride. Olive was extremely susceptible to music, and it was impossible for her not to be soothed and beguiled by the young man's charming art. . . . His guests scattered in the red firelight, listening, silent, in comfortable attitudes; there was a faint fragrance from the burning logs, which mingled with the perfume of Schubert, and Mendelssohn; the covered lamps made a glow here and there, and the cabinets and brackets gleamed—some ivory carving or cinquecento cup. It was given to Olive, under these circumstances, for half an hour, to surrender herself, to enjoy the music, to admit that Mr. Burrage played with exquisite taste, to feel as if the situation were a kind of truce. Civilization, under such an influence, in such a setting, appeared to have done its work; harmony ruled the scene; human life ceased to be a battle. She went so far as to ask herself why one should have a quarrel with it; the relations between men and women, in that picturesque grouping, had not the air of being internecine. (P. 130)[1]

The contrast in this scene between the discordant energies of politics and the enriching harmonies of art is quite evident.

The tie between the private life and esthetic enrichment implied in *The Bostonians* becomes explicit in *The Princess Casamassima,* a proletarian novel that is suffused with James's estheticism. Its hero, Hyacinth Robinson, is inwardly divided. He embodies the class conflict of his parents, aristocrat and commoner, each of whom has wronged the other. Hyacinth's tastes reveal an innate refinement, molded by an aristocratic order, and yet his lower-class conditions and deprivations call for revolt against such a system. Eventually he becomes drawn into the London underworld of political radicalism and pledges his life to its egalitarian ideals. This pledge, in conflict as it is with his commitment to the life of culture, which an aristocratically ordered society fosters, leads finally to his suicide.

Hyacinth's temperament, however, is felt more convincingly in its esthetic than in its political orientation; and, in fact, James has shaded the ending to intensify the pathos of Hyacinth's lonely and sacrificial death, so that the reader is influenced to feel indignation at the meddling of the radicals. An impression is given that their notions of a vastly better social order emerging from the destruction of the old are visionary, and that even if they were not would count as nothing compared to the boy's chance for "life," the possibility of his enlargement through participation in the life of culture. The ending emphasizes not so much Hyacinth's inner conflict as the issue of "life," as against its politicized waste and destruction. The Princess Casamassima appears in the novel to reinforce the idea of political passions that are a form of destructive self-deception. In her illusion about herself, and in her adoption of a young protégé, whose life she will sacrifice to her own neurotic drives, she has a close affinity with Olive Chancellor in *The Bostonians*. And with even stronger emphasis than in *The Bostonians*, *The Princess Casamassima* announces James's allegiance to the ideals of privacy and esthetic enrichment.

In *The Tragic Muse*, the concluding work of the trilogy, the private versus the public life is again at issue; but it is intimated that the issue has now been settled. The novel's hero, Nick Dormer, is a portrait painter who must struggle against the bribes that he is offered to forsake his artist's vocation (about which he feels some uncertainty) for the security of an enlarged role in English politics and an important position in society. Gabriel Nash appears as a kind of

160

archangel who awakens the wavering, or drowsing, Dormer to life —to the life of the creative spirit. Nash and the actress Miriam Rooth complement each other as artist figures, since she represents the creative spirit guided by training and self-denial to a clearly focused professional definition, while he represents the creative spirit in essence, and is therefore not subject to definition. Near the end Nick Dormer has Gabriel Nash sit for a portrait, but after a first sitting he does not appear again; his likeness cannot be completed because the creative spirit he embodies takes a thousand shapes but no single one. Dormer even has the impression that what he has committed to canvas will gradually lose its substantiality: "[Dormer] couldn't catch it in the act, but he could have a suspicion, when he glanced at it, that the hand of time was rubbing it away little by little (for all the world as in some delicate Hawthorne tale), making the surface indistinct and bare—bare of all resemblance to the model. Of course the moral of the Hawthorne tale would be that the personage would come back some day when the last adumbration should have vanished."[2]

James's allusion to Hawthorne is appropriate since *The Tragic Muse* (which has the nature of allegory) shows James moving into a new relationship to him, one in which the artist has an outsider's role in society. By the first third of the novel, it begins to become apparent that Dormer will abandon a political for an artistic vocation; and attention is thereafter drawn to the question, or problem, of the life of the artist. Throughout the work the importance of "duty" is urged on Dormer—by Julia Dallow, his fiancée, Lady Agnes, his anxious mother, and Mr. Carteret, his potential benefactor —but by the end Gabriel Nash has the last word. "We must recognize our particular form," he declares, speaking of the artist, "the instrument that each of us—each of us who carries anything—carries in his being. Mastering his instrument, learning to play it in perfection —that's what I call duty, what I call success." The "success" of the artist's vocation, however, entails a great price. Miriam Rooth and Nick Dormer are contrasting figures in a sense because, while she will practice her art in public, and win popular recognition, he will be alone with his art. Nash tells him that he has previously cared for

161

life and society, but that he has now "chosen the path of solitude and concentration."[3]

It is particularly relevant that Dormer should be a painter of portraits, since the portrait suggests the portrait art of the novel. James indeed speaks, as he might of literary portraiture, of the complexity of the portrait, which involves the artist's giving definition to his subject at the same time that he gives definition to his own special perspective on experience, and therefore to himself. Dormer's taking up his rightful place as a portrait painter intimates James's own identification with him and his sharing in Dormer's ambiguous situation—his "success" in perfecting his art, and his outsider's relation to the active world. Dormer's situation (and James's contemplative response to his own) becomes the subject of many of James's later stories dealing with the paradoxes of the artist and his vocation. In "The Lesson of the Master" (1888), written shortly before *The Tragic Muse,* Paul Overt learns the ambiguous lesson (doubly ambiguous because it may not be true) that the artist must relinquish his life in order to invest it in his work, an ironic sort of "success" that Gabriel Nash enunciates to Dormer. It is this later phase of James's career—with its preoccupation with the artist, its 1890s mood of alienation, its obliquities of style that suggest an immersion in a self-made world—that *The Bostonians* ultimately reaches toward.

The Bostonians was the last novel James completed that was set on American soil and contains his most elaborate restatement of Hawthorne's themes. It is a culminating work of James's formative period and reflects both on his apprenticeship under Hawthorne and on his steadily developing differentiation of his own art from his predecessor's. At the same time, it looks forward to a new period of permanent residence abroad. The trilogy *The Bostonians* initiates illustrates James's passage into expatriation, the closing out of a large, earlier phase of his career.

Hawthorne's effect on James's imagination may still be noticed in his later career—in certain of his preoccupations of the 1890s; in his last, unfinished novel, *The Sense of the Past,* where James returns to the theme of an American claimant to an old English house (which

162

Conclusion

he had taken originally from Hawthorne's *Our Old Home*); and, most particularly, in *The Wings of the Dove* and *The Golden Bowl,* which have a Hawthornesque quality of moral fables.[4] The novels of the major phase give the impression, indeed, that James reached a new reconciliation with Hawthorne, in contrast to the adversary relation of the 1880s.

But this later phase falls outside the scope of my study, which treats the development of James's art in its special relation to Hawthorne from the beginning to a middle point in his career, a period of notable kinship and yet marked conflict between them. The kinship of Hawthorne and James is implicit in their peculiarly American preoccupations—in the unusually important attention they give to the individual and the inner life. The forms of experience they treat, and their character types, are often strikingly similar—the victimizer and his innocent, unworldly victim; the character who suffers from an obsession; the coldly detached psychological investigator who 163 lacks reverence for the being of another; the spectator who cannot participate fully in life; the egotist; and the artist or the esthetic solitary. Hawthorne and James belong distinctively to the same tradition. In the second volume of *Heroines of Fiction,* Howells suggested Hawthorne's uniqueness by comparing him to his English contemporary Dickens. "While Dickens was writing in England," Howells remarks, "Hawthorne was writing in America; and for all the ostensible reasons the romances of Hawthorne ought to have been rude, shapeless, . . . the novels of Dickens ought to have been fastidiously elect in method and material." Yet the opposite was true. Hawthorne's art, Howells continues, "sprang from a sensitiveness of nerve in the English race that it had never known in its English home"; was special in "its greater refinement, its subtler beauty, and its delicate perfection of form."[5] Howells's characterization of Hawthorne could as well apply to James, whose tales have a psychological acuteness and sensitivity to nuance more nearly comparable to Hawthorne's than to any other writer's.

Because of this affinity of sensibility, James gravitated to Hawthorne frequently in the conception of his tales. Hawthorne had established prototype models, showing how moral and psychological experience could be treated with "the great dramatic chiaroscuro," and James often projects his characters' experience with a similar, sharply felt intensity. Like Hawthorne, he is concerned with his characters' inner states, their moments of recognition or of acutely felt life. In praising Hawthorne in his biography, James referred to his familiarity with "the deeper psychology," a phrase he did not explain fully, but by which he seems to have meant the dramatic projection of deep, inner life. Hawthorne writes with an eerie acquaintance with his characters' inmost beings, the darkness and mystery of their groping consciousness. This "deeper psychology" cannot be found in Thackeray or Trollope. It is the distinctive property of Hawthorne, a possessor of "souls," and in James one finds a similar dramatic projection of deep inner life. In incorporating Hawthorne's "deeper psychology" into the novel of manners, James extended an American mode of perception.

164   Yet there was as much conflict as kinship in James's relation to Hawthorne, and the New England tradition. Coming as he did at the end of the New England tradition, James was continually critical of it. In the emerging realism in which they were engaged, both James and Howells were conscious of New England as a distinct culture, which they subjected to inspection and appraisal. Both frequently explain their characters' motives and reactions in terms of the culture of New England, or of Boston. In many of his novels, Howells was especially interested in Boston types, and in what might be called "the Boston psychology." In *A Chance Acquaintance,* one of Howells's earliest novels, Miles Arbuton illustrates the stifling effect of Boston on spontaneous or natural emotion. A coldness is said "perpetually to hover in Mr. Arbuton's atmosphere"; he has "high and difficult tastes," and shrinks from a coarse exposure to the immediate world around him.[6] In *The Undiscovered Country,* Phillips, a collector of bric-a-brac, is symptomatic of a culture that has maintained its formality but lost its force. Howells studies the cultural decline of Boston almost as a scientist observes an organism in decay. In *The Minister's Charge*, the Reverend Sewell has a pastorate in Boston, but as a spiritual leader he is symptomatic of modern conditions, having ethical scruples rather than spiritual inwardness.

Conclusion

Bromfield Corey, who belongs to the old Brahmin caste and whose culture once placed him at the forefront of Boston's life, has receded into the background and is losing his vision in both a literal and figurative sense. Moving beyond Boston to the New England countryside, Howells notes further symptoms of decay. In *Annie Kilburn*, he observes the emergence of a new social type in the businessman Gerrish, who has shunted aside Putney, a lawyer of Brahmin stock, now a periodic alcoholic. When the old Puritan temper is still felt, it is likely to exist in a decadent or neurotic form, as in *A Modern Instance*, in which Squire Gaylord and his daughter Marcia relate to one another neurotically in their sexual repressions.

The culture of New England was as important to James's fiction as it was to that of Howells. In treating it he was often conscious of Hawthorne, the conflicts of whose characters have a broadly cultural typicality James was able to incorporate into his studies of New Englanders at home and abroad. The conflict in *The Scarlet Letter* between a yearned-for sensuousness and an immutably decreed austerity furnishes the diagram for the experience of many of James's New Englanders, including a procession of inwardly divided male characters such as Longmore in "Madame de Mauves" and Winterbourne in *Daisy Miller*. Hawthorne sometimes refers to his puritans as "men of iron," implying both an unusually rigorous spiritual vision and an inflexible narrowness; and in James these "men of iron" become such figures as Mr. Babcock in *The American*, whose conscience will not allow him a relaxed enjoyment of Europe, and Mr. Wentworth in *The Europeans*, who seems to be undergoing a martyrdom not of fire but of freezing. Mr. Wentworth in particular illustrates how James was able to accommodate Hawthorne's "men of iron" in his novels and tales of contemporary manners, adapting his conception to a comic vision.

In his early conceptions of the New England girl, James also takes clues from Hawthorne, and the spotless New England maiden he created. Often a pale wraith, Hawthorne's New England maiden is contrasted with a "dark" and worldly woman; and this contrast can be noticed in James's earliest conception of his American girls in the late 1860s. His young women who are worldly (and potentially "dangerous") tend to have either dark names or dark hair and complexions (like Miriam in "A Landscape-Painter"), while his sheltered heroines are characteristically pale or blonde (like Martha, the American girl, in "The Last of the Valerii"). These heroines appear, however, before James's fully developed realism;[7] by the mid-1870s, James begins to give a stronger social outline to the New England maiden Hawthorne created.

Of Hawthorne's maidens, Phoebe, with her radiant freshness, most nearly establishes "the American girl"; Hawthorne in fact suggests specifically that it is not with the past of the Puritan Pyncheons that she belongs, but with the American present and future. In her fearlessness, she is the ancestress of Daisy Miller and Bessie Alden. A more sainted figure, Hilda is also influential, since she implies typically American experience and illustrates the career of the American girl in Italy. Charlotte Evans, in "Travelling Companions," is an early version of her; she goes about unescorted in Italy, and after experiencing suffering, enters St. Peter's in Rome to offer up "half-prayers," while remaining a Protestant believer. In Mary Garland, in *Roderick Hudson,* the Hilda figure is made plausible as a modern New England girl, the descendant of a line of clergymen. Like Hilda's, her exposure to European corruption is at second hand, in her case through Hudson. She herself remains untainted; faced with the temptations of a large freedom and a complicated reality, she declares herself from "the very heart of New England," and remains faithful to its ideals.

In the 1870s "the American girl," descendant of Hawthorne's radiant New England maiden, began to preoccupy both James and Howells; and as time went on, their conceptions show an increasingly critical scrutiny of her.[8] Howells's Kitty Ellison in *A Chance Acquaintance,* although not actually from New England, has a quality of freshness and spotlessness that places her in a line of descent from Hawthorne's Phoebe. In describing her Howells speaks of "the unsnubbed fearlessness of a heart which did not suspect a sense of social difference in others, or imagine itself misprized for anything but a fault," words which also make one think of James's "immaculately" ingenuous Daisy Miller.[9] But by the 1880s, Howells' buoyant and graceful conceptions of American girls are followed by his depiction of New England girls who are in some way maladjusted or neurotic. In Marcia Gaylord, of *A Modern Instance,* the New England girl is studied in her strenuous repressions and sexually prompted hysteria, her refusals of understanding that make her "innocence" a fright.

In a similar way James moves from his spare drawings of ingenuous American girls, like Bessie Alden and Daisy Miller, to the more complicated Isabel Archer, whom he subjects to the most elaborate psychological scrutiny. Although she comes from Albany, Isabel has her spiritual origins in New England; and it is exactly her "spotlessness" (her moral heroism and sexual fears) that confuses her perception of reality. In her different way, Olive Chancellor is also a version —a dark one, surely—of "the American girl," a young woman whose neurotic fixations are symptomatic of Calvinism in decay. In his portrayal of her James entered into the mainstream of American realism in the 1880s. At the same time that Olive Chancellor was sequestered in her intense Boston parlor reading Goethe on wintry nights, and subject to such fits of tragic shyness that there were times when she could not meet her own eyes in the mirror, Bartley Hubbard ran off from his hysteric wife Marcia, to be shot down later in the dirt street of a raw Western town, and Huck Finn lit out for the territory, to drift down the Mississippi River with an ethnic companion toward a freedom as transitory as boyhood. Together these works give a socially defined picture of American society in its industrialized age, as well as a sense of its underlying tensions, and mood of the individual's alienation.

The evolution of Hawthorne's Phoebe to James's Isabel Archer and Olive Chancellor is indicative of the large differences which exist between Hawthorne's romance conceptions and James's socialized ones. The difference between them is the difference between archetypal insights into American psychological experience in a context partly of fantasy, and a readjustment of perspective to an anchored world in which characters' behavior is accounted for with an elabo-

167

rate thoroughness and credibility. And in this respect James was indeed at variance with Hawthorne, and could regard himself as his adversary and "corrector."

James's conflict with Hawthorne, however, involved more than his allegiance to realism. His international viewpoint and more purely "esthetic" sensibility also form part of their disagreement. It is significant that in *The Europeans* the artist Felix speaks of New England's failure "to enjoy," words repeated only a short time later in *Hawthorne*, in James's characterization of Hawthorne's world. The first volume of his correspondence records the rapture with which James discovered Italy, with its ubiquitous presence of history and art, its sensuous and pictorial spectacle. There were more than a dozen periods thereafter when James resided in Italy, and it enters into his work as the diametrical opposite of New England.[10] Hawthorne too had resided in Italy, and *The Marble Faun,* which comes out of that period, laid the foundations of American experience in Italy for later writers; but there is an important difference between the responses to Italy of Hawthorne and James. In *The Marble Faun* Hawthorne drew from Madame de Staël's *Corinne* in the conflict of cultures he dramatizes; but in bringing New England to Italy, he reversed Madame de Staël's priorities. While she had celebrated Italian sunlight and sensuousness, Hawthorne ponders this sensuousness only to reject it, finally, as error, and to cast his characters' experience in terms of a somber Protestant morality. James is able to accommodate Hawthorne's Italy, which, in his fiction, frequently stands for the idea of tragic knowledge; yet he also rehabilitates Madame de Staël's sensuous Italy. His own vision contemplates open possibilities before his characters (even if they are not always able to realize such possibilities, or to move beyond their fates), alternative ways of apprehending experience. Such potentially open possibilities are not present in Hawthorne as they are in James; however yearned for, or richly evoked, they have been foreclosed by Hawthorne's vision of somber necessity.

At the risk of oversimplifying, one way to compare Hawthorne and James is in their different preoccupation with conscience and

Conclusion

consciousness. The New England conscience is deeply embedded in Hawthorne's imagination, and James too has been called an observer of "fine consciences"; James's concern, however, is less with conscience than with consciousness, particularly with different modes of consciousness (and points of view). In his earlier fiction James is aware of evil, but his recognition of it does not preempt a many-sided vision. If frustration lies in wait for many of James's characters (as it does), the possibility of self-enlargement is still real, or is felt to be. Although experience may be hazardous (what Conrad would later call "the destructive element"), it also contains the potentiality of larger life, or expanded consciousness. To the grave, skeptical Hawthorne such a notion of enlarged consciousness, existing as a kind of absolute good in itself, did not obtain, and accordingly, his characters cannot move far out into the world in the hope of embracing such an ideal.

In *Hawthorne* James stresses Hawthorne's chilled recoil from the immediate world around him, and describes *The Scarlet Letter* as "passionless," at least in the sense that its passion is curiously disembodied. The gross world would contaminate and defile it. James was stirred by the profane world in a way that Hawthorne was not; and despite their important affinities, Hawthorne and James were also divided by temperamental differences, particularly in their responses to the immediate world before them. Because of these differences James was able at many points in his career to define himself against Hawthorne. In "Benvolio" James reimagined Hawthorne's archetype of Dr. Rappaccini and his daughter in a way that invites a comparison between himself as an American writer and Hawthorne, implying that the New England world which had nourished Hawthorne could not sustain his own imaginative life. Again, in *Hawthorne,* James makes an implicit comparison between himself and Hawthorne, whose notation of the actual world around him was vague because he was not absorbed by it, as James was. And in assimilating *The Blithedale Romance* into *The Bostonians,* to underscore themes he shared with Hawthorne, James also made Hawthorne's material reflect his own more worldly attitudes—his sense of the limitations of the New England mind, his concern with manners, and the possibilities of esthetic enrichment represented for him much more by Italy than by Boston.

James's relationship to Hawthorne was thus complex and many-sided and involved both close kinship and essential conflict, affinity and dissent, agreement and disavowal. The psychological chords struck by Hawthorne are sounded again by James. The individual's selfhood has unusual importance in Hawthorne, as it does again in James; it is part of James's distinctively national consciousness which, in *Hawthorne,* he reminded himself that he should guard against betraying. As American writers, Hawthorne and James have many similarities, certainly in the sense they both give of being out of phase with their native environment, of being estranged by their recoil from a materialistic civilization. Their fiction, continually interested in moral problems, has an extraordinary delicacy that reveals what T. S. Eliot called an "awareness of spiritual reality." In his concern with form and meticulous detail, Flaubert prepares in many ways for James; and yet James had serious reservations about Flaubert, whose view of life he found "mean." From "A Passionate Pilgrim" to *The Portrait of a Lady,* with its "imagination of loving," a spiritual ideal can be felt in James's fiction, and it seems at times a kind of reality above reality. This spiritual sense in James that is not exactly Christian and involves no dogma often impels him toward symbolic contours in his fiction, just as Hawthorne creates such contours in the romance.[11] Such a tendency reveals a tension in James's fiction between romance abstraction and realistic objectivity that is relevant to his relationship to Hawthorne. Again and again James attempts to disavow the native tradition of Hawthorne; and again and again he is drawn back to it. It might be claimed that in transforming Hawthorne's romance conceptions into realism, James had repudiated Hawthorne—which is true, but only in a certain sense. For in dwelling upon Hawthorne's themes, James reveals the hold Hawthorne exerted over his imagination. There were other writers from whom James learned—among them Balzac, Turgenev, and George Eliot—and I have not slighted their influence. But there was no writer from whom James drew more frequently, or with greater

Conclusion

moral relevance, than Hawthorne. Hawthorne's influence forms such a steady pattern in James's formative period that it overshadows any other single one.

With figures like Dr. Tarrant and his daughter Verena, one has the impression of characters who come out of a romance world but have already passed into realism; and one has this impression repeatedly in James's earlier period in his adaptive use of Hawthorne's romance archetypes. The Rappaccini archetype, for example, appears in James's apprenticeship before he employs it to shape his conception of Dr. Sloper and Gilbert Osmond in their relation to their daughters. The garden-and-Fall archetype of *The Marble Faun* appears in various forms before it occurs, with a resonant suggestiveness, in *Roderick Hudson* and *The Portrait of a Lady*. The mesmerist-and-maiden archetype of *The Blithedale Romance* appears early in "Professor Fargo" before it is reimagined elaborately in *The Bostonians*. Such repeated, significant use of Hawthorne's archetypes—garden-and-Fall, doctor-and-daughter, mesmerist-and-maiden—binds James inescapably, even if reluctantly, to Hawthorne.

In recent years, Harold Bloom has been concerned with what he calls "the anxiety of influence," the inevitability of one artist's effect on another. Surely the relationship of Hawthorne and James is a striking instance of this. It was an imaginative encounter between psychological novelists of approximately equal stature, between master and master, and there is nothing in that period with which to compare its interlocked involvement of imaginations. James was Hawthorne's heir, and yet his unceasing critic and adversary. To come to maturity, to establish his own vision, it was necessary for him to overthrow Hawthorne—as it was necessary for him to overthrow his father, Mr. Emerson, and their world. In Freudian terms, James's revision of Hawthorne into realism was a kind of kin slaying, a sacrilegious act, which was redeemed by the new understanding James brought to the modern novel. The reaction of James's urbane intelligence upon Hawthorne's powerfully archetypal mind helps to demonstrate how the American psychological tradition came into being in the nineteenth century.

Notes

Index

Notes

1. Nathaniel Hawthorne to Horatio Bridge, quoted in F. O. Matthiessen, *American Renaissance* (New York: Oxford University Press, 1941), p. 287; Herman Melville to Nathaniel Hawthorne, ibid.

2. Herman Melville, "Hawthorne and His Mosses," *The Literary World* (August 17 and 24, 1850), reprinted in Willard Thorp, *Herman Melville: Representative Selections, with Introduction, Bibliography, and Notes* (New York: American Book Company, 1938), pp. 333–34, 341.

3. To a lesser degree, and in a less crucial way, the same is true of Howells. The most literal and surface-measuring of the young realists, he faced enormous difficulties in writing about American social reality when no previous models existed, and he often searched in Hawthorne's fiction for clues to the psychologies of his New Englanders. Ben Halleck in *A Modern Instance,* for example, has affinities in the type of conflict he suffers with Hawthorne's Dimmesdale; a clergyman of the old orthodoxy, he is at the end torn between his desire for Marcia, which he feels is tantamount to adultery, and his spiritual vocation, which is unfulfilling. In other cases Howells has compared his characters specifically to prototypes in Hawthorne. The Reverend Peck, an obsessed philanthropist in *Annie Kilburn,* is compared by the heroine to Hawthorne's Hollingsworth. In *The World of Chance* the literary man Kane, who pries into other people's minds and is unable to enter very fully into the life around him, is compared to Miles Coverdale in *The Blithedale Romance.*

Hawthorne's stories and novels have also been incorporated, in a more important way, into Howells's conceptions of his novels. *The Son of Royal Langbrith,* for example, which deals with the expiation of a curse upon a New England house and family, seems a more realistically drawn version of *The House of the Seven Gables.* In each work the founder of the house has committed some injury to another person, defrauding him and his heirs. In *The House of the Seven Gables,* the founding figure is reproduced in type later in Judge Pyncheon, a hypocrite of virtue who has a respected position in the community. Howells's Royal Langbrith is a comparable figure. Publicly esteemed, he has actually defrauded his business partner, Hawberk, an inventor whose fortunes, like Matthew Maule's, thereafter decline. Langbrith dies as suddenly and mysteriously as Judge Pyncheon, and *The Son of Royal Langbrith* ends with a partial expiation of the curse upon the house, in the marriage between the heirs of the two families in conflict, James Langbrith and Hope Hawberk. They leave a guilt-ridden past (like Hawthorne's Holgrave and Phoebe) to enter a present containing fewer illusions.

In another of Howells's novels, intriguing resemblances can be noticed with Hawthorne's story "My Kinsman, Major Molineux." Lemuel Barker in *The Minister's Charge* is a country youth who comes to Boston on the mistaken notion that he has a patron in the unfamiliar city in the Reverend Sewell. Disillusioned by Sewell after his first meeting with him, Barker wanders through Boston at night, is robbed by confidence men, sexually enticed and jeered by city girls, and seems to wander in a labyrinth of mocking laughter. His arrival in Boston duplicates that of Robin in "My Kinsman, Major Molineux": like Robin, he finds an older moral order to have vanished, and eventually leaves the city alone, chastened by his experience. Howells's novel is framed, too, like Hawthorne's tale, by a historical moment separating past and present—in this case the Civil War, a dividing line in American experience. Lemuel has an exemplum quality (his birth on the Fourth of July, and his loss of his father in the Civil War, help to suggest his exemplary nature); and his experience comes to demonstrate the disappearance of former religious sureties and social coherence, and the individual's new isolation in the city.

The Shadow of a Dream is focused by Hawthorne's imagery and themes in a central scene where Howells's character Faulkner is depicted in a morally resonant, atmospheric garden that suggests a poignantly ruined innocence. After his death, moreover, this focal setting is reintroduced as a garden in the West, from which Faulkner came. The Faulkner mansion is described as being in the heart of the town, in "the midst of ample lawns and gardens." Howells comments that "it all looked much older than anything in the East, from the soft-coal smoke with which wall and mansion and garden trees were blackened." Howells, *The Shadow of a Dream,* in *"The Shadow of a Dream" and "An Imperative Duty"* (1890; rpt. New York: Twayne, 1962), p. 103. This original garden, now blackened by coal smoke, implies the changes that have occurred in America since Faulkner's youth—the coming of the railroads, the emergence of a new industrialism, the replacement of natural impulse by repression and neurosis. Through these gardens Howells insinuates a quality of fable or allegory and introduces the rich suggestiveness of romance into his novel.

Other instances of Hawthorne's effect on Howells's conceptions and art might be elaborated; but important here is that Howells's assimilation of Hawthorne's romance into his realism coincided with James's assimilation of Hawthorne during the same period. Undoubtedly Howells and James were aware of adaptations from Hawthorne occurring in the other's work, although they do not comment upon this subject specifically in their correspondence.

4. Henry James, *Hawthorne* (1879; rpt. Ithaca: Cornell University Press, 1956). All parenthetical page references are to this edition.

5. T. S. Eliot, quoted in Matthiessen, *American Renaissance*, p. 356; ibid., p. 292; and F. O. Matthiessen, *The James Family: A Group Biography* (1947; rpt. New York: Alfred A. Knopf, 1961), p. 482. Matthiessen's words are later echoed by Edmund Wilson: "[James] was to revert in the *Golden Bowl,* his last completed novel, to a symbolism that goes straight back to Hawthorne: the golden bowl itself and the curio dealer who sells it belong certainly to the world of *The Birth-Mark* and *The Minister's Black Veil.*" Edmund Wilson, introduction to James's *Hawthorne,* in *The Shock of Recognition,* ed. Edmund Wilson (New York: Farrar, Straus & Cudahy, 1955), p. 426.

6. Marius Bewley, *The Complex Fate* (London: Chatto and Windus, 1952), pp. 5, 6.

7. Peter Buitenhuis, *The Grasping Imagination: The American Writings of Henry James* (Toronto: University of Toronto Press, 1970).

8. Henry James to Thomas Sergeant Perry, September 20, 1867, in Leon Edel, ed., *The Letters of Henry James: Vol. 1, 1843–1875* (Cambridge, Mass.: Harvard University Press, 1974), p. 77.

9. Henry James to The James Family, November 1, 1875, ibid., p. 484.

10. Northrop Frye, "The Four Forms of Fiction," in *Discussions of the Novel,* ed. Roger Sale (Boston: D. C. Heath, 1960), p. 4.

2. JAMES'S APPRENTICESHIP: THE HAWTHORNE ASPECT

1. Rebecca West, *Henry James* (New York: Henry Holt, 1916), p. 25; and F. R. Leavis, *The Great Tradition* (1948; rpt. New York: Doubleday Anchor, 1954), p. 159. Elsewhere in the book, Leavis writes that James "is related to Hawthorne . . . closely. . . . A study of the very early work shows Hawthorne as a major influence—as *the* major influence" (p. 21, n. 13).

2. All parenthetical page references to "The Story of a Year" are from Leon Edel, ed., *The Complete Tales of Henry James,* vol. 1, 1864–1868 (London: Rupert Hart-Davis, 1962). Subsequent parenthetical page references to "A Landscape Painter," "The Story of a Masterpiece," and "De Grey: A Romance" are from the same edition and volume.

3. Matthiessen, *American Renaissance,* p. 292.

4. Parenthetical page references to "A Light Man" are from *The Complete Tales of Henry James,* vol. 2, 1868–1872. Subsequent parenthetical page references to "Travelling Companions" and "A Passionate Pilgrim" are to the same edition and volume.

5. Nathaniel Hawthorne, *English Notebooks,* in *The Writings of Nathaniel Hawthorne,* Old Manse Edition (Boston: Houghton, Mifflin, 1900), 19: 237; and *Our Old Home,* ibid., 11: 15, 16, 19, 21.

6. The romance of Clement and Margaret Searle is also related ironically to Shakespeare's *The Passionate Pilgrim,* the cycle of poems celebrating an awakening to love and human fulfillment, after which James took his title.

7. Parenthetical page references to "The Madonna of the Future" are from *The Complete Tales of Henry James,* vol. 3, 1873–1875. Subsequent parenthetical page references to "The Last of the Valerii," "Professor Fargo," "Madame de Mauves," and "Benvolio" are to the same edition and volume.

8. Honoré de Balzac, "Le Chef d'oeuvre inconnu," in *The Works of Honoré de Balzac* (Freeport, N.Y.: Books for Libraries, 1971), 1: 26, 17.

9. The mesmerist-wizard who holds a maiden in thrall also appears elsewhere in Hawthorne's fiction. Matthew Maule in *The House of the Seven Gables* subjects Alice Pyncheon to his will through his mesmeric powers and is seen in her funeral procession "gnashing his teeth" in bitter regret that she has escaped him.

10. Leon Edel, *Henry James, The Untried Years: 1843–1870* (Philadelphia: J. B. Lippincott, 1953), p. 275; and T. S. Eliot, "The Hawthorne Aspect," *The Little Review,* 5 (August 1918), reprinted in *Critics on Henry James,* ed. J. Don Vann (Coral Gables: University of Miami Press, 1972), p. 34.

3. *RODERICK HUDSON:* THE MERGING OF OPPOSITE TRADITIONS

1. Henry James to Charles Eliot Norton, March 31, 1873, in Leon Edel, ed., *The Letters of Henry James: Vol. 1, 1834–1875* (Cambridge, Mass.: Harvard University Press, 1974), p. 362.

2. Henry James, "Hawthorne's French and Italian Journals," *The Nation,* March 14, 1872, reprinted in Leon Edel, ed., *The American Essays of Henry James* (New York: Vintage, 1956), pp. 4, 5, 7–8, 10, 11.

3. For discussions of Turgenev and James, see Oscar Cargill, *The Novels of Henry James* (New York: Macmillan, 1961); Cornelia P. Kelley, *The Early Development of Henry James* (1930; rpt. Urbana: University of Illinois, 1965); and, most particularly, Daniel Lerner, "The Influence of Turgenev on Henry James," *Slavonic and East European Review,* 20 (December 1941), 28–54. Royal A. Gettmann's *Turgenev in England and America* (Urbana: University of Illinois Press, 1941) is also revealing, particularly in showing the extent of Turgenev's popularity and influence in America after the Civil War.

4. Henry James, "Ivan Turgéniéff," *North American Review,* 118 (April 1874), included in *French Poets and Novelists* (1878; rpt. New York: Grosset & Dunlap, 1964), p. 250.

5. Ibid., pp. 212, 216, 217, 220.

6. Henry James, "Eugene Pickering," in Leon Edel, ed., *The Complete Tales of Henry James,* vol. 3, 1873–1875 (London: Rupert Hart-Davis, 1962), p. 335.

7. Parenthetical page references are to Ivan Turgenev, *Smoke*, in *The Novels of Ivan Turgenev* (New York: AMS Press, 1970), vol. 5.

8. Parenthetical page references to *Roderick Hudson* are from Henry James, *Roderick Hudson* (1875; rpt. New York: Harper Torchbook, 1960).

9. Quoted in Gettmann, *Turgenev in England and America*, p. 74.

10. Henry James, "Ivan Turgénieff," *Atlantic Monthly*, 53 (January 1884), included in *Partial Portraits* (1888; rpt. Ann Arbor: University of Michigan Press, 1970), pp. 298–99.

4. *THE EUROPEANS* AND *DAISY MILLER:* MOTIFS TRANSFIGURED

1. Parenthetical page references are to *Daisy Miller: A Study*, in Leon Edel, ed., *The Complete Tales of Henry James*, vol. 4, 1876–1882, (London: Rupert Hart-Davis, 1962), pp. 141–208; and *The Europeans*, in Henry James, *Washington Square/The Europeans* (New York: Dell, 1959).

2. An early allusion to Gertrude and envisioned romance occurs when Felix, looking out upon the Boston street, is reminded of "mid-May's eldest child," a phrase from Keats's poem "Ode to a Nightingale." The late-blooming Gertrude first appears in the Wentworth garden, her eyes restless and yet "dull," since youth cannot bloom "Here, where men sit and hear each other groan; / Where palsy shakes a few, sad, last gray hairs, / Where youth grows pale, and spectre-thin and dies; / . . . Where Beauty cannot keep her lustrous eyes."

3. All parenthetical page references to *The Blithedale Romance* are from Nathaniel Hawthorne, *The Writings of Nathaniel Hawthorne*, Old Manse Edition, (Boston: Houghton, Mifflin, 1900), vol. 8.

4. Oscar Cargill, *The Novels of Henry James* (New York: Macmillan, 1961), pp. 67–68.

5. It is not quite certain if James had read the novel. In a letter to Howells dated February 3, 1876, James mentions that he has noticed *Private Theatricals* in serial form in the *Atlantic Monthly*, but would prefer to read and review it later when it appears as a book. Because of a threatened lawsuit, Howells did not publish the novel in book form during his lifetime; it was published posthumously, in 1921, as *Mrs. Farrell*. But James might still have read it in serial form; and he had, at least, glanced it over and formed some impression of what it was about. See Leon Edel, ed., *The Letters of Henry James: Vol. 2, 1875–1883* (Cambridge, Mass.: Harvard University Press, 1975), p. 23.

Certain parallels between *Private Theatricals* and *The Europeans* are, in any case, rather striking, and in both novels Hawthorne's Zenobia can be discerned in the distant background. Zenobia comes to mind in Howells's depiction of Belle Farrell as a worldly "dark lady," with a temperament combining nature and artifice, who enters into an Arcadian adventure in rural New England. She has been given an exotic quality by Howells, who writes: "A dim mirage of Oriental fancies rose before Easton, with sterile hills, gleaming lakes, cities, temples of old faith, and priestesses who had the dark eyes, the loose overshadowing hair, the dusky bloom of Mrs. Farrell" (Howells, *Mrs. Farrell* [New York: Harper & Brothers, 1921], p. 50). Similarly, James describes Eugenia's "great abundance of . . . dark hair . . . that suggested some Southern or Eastern, some remotely foreign, woman. She had a large collection of earrings . . . and they seemed to give a point to her Oriental or exotic aspect" (p. 209).

Howells contrasts the bohemian Mrs. Farrell, who seems out of place in the New England countryside, with a New England girl who belongs—Rachael Woodward, "a born saint [who accepts] self-sacrifice as if it were her birthright" (p. 124). Rachael is sincere and faithful, the "pale charm of her character" (p. 240) containing no trace of variability or shadow. In *The Europeans* Eugenia is contrasted with the paleness of the Wentworth sisters, particularly the self-sacrificing Charlotte. Howells explores the notions of "duty" and "enjoyment" which his differing female characters suggest; these contrasts are dramatized by James shortly afterward in *The Europeans*.

6. Parenthetical page references to *The Marble Faun* are from *The Complete Novels and Selected Tales of Nathaniel Hawthorne* (New York: Modern Library, 1937), pp. 589–858.

7. F. W. Dupee, *Henry James* (New York: William Sloane Associates, 1951), pp. 110–11.

5. JAMES'S *HAWTHORNE:* CRITICISM AS SELF-DEFINITION

1. Henry James to William James, February 13, 1870, in Leon Edel, ed., *The Letters of Henry James: Vol. 1, 1843–1875* (Cambridge, Mass.: Harvard University Press, 1974), p. 205.

2. Leon Edel, *Henry James, 1870–1881: The Conquest of London* (Philadelphia: Lippincott, 1962), p. 342.

3. George Parsons Lathrop, A Study of Hawthorne (Boston: James R. Osgood, 1876).

4. "G. P. Lathrop will *hate [Hawthorne],* and me for writing it; though I couldn't have done so without the aid (for dates and facts) of his own singularly foolish and pretentious little volume." Henry James to Thomas Sergeant Perry, September 19, 1879, in Leon Edel, ed., *The Letters of Henry James, Vol. 2: 1875–1883* (Cambridge, Mass.: Harvard University Press, 1975), p. 255. Lathrop's book has a painfully sanctimonious tone. In treating the stories he dwells upon Hawthorne's "immense sorrow over sin"; and asking himself what guiding principle can be found in the tales, he concludes that it is "an unsectarian religiousness, which ever stirred below the clear surface of his language like the bubling spring at the bottom of a forest pool" (p. 152). He compares Hawthorne to Balzac and the French realists and is "grateful" that Hawthorne avoided their handling of sexual matters. In the section on Hawthorne abroad he seems to have James personally in mind and to be "correcting" him

when he remarks on "that almost faulty abstention from assuming the European tone which has made Hawthorne the traveller appear to certain readers a little crude, —that very air of being the uncritical and slightly puzzled American is precisely the source of his most delightful accuracies of interpretation" (p. 252).

Parenthetical page references are to Henry James, *Hawthorne* (1879; rpt. Ithaca: Cornell University Press, 1956).

5. Lionel Trilling, "Our Hawthorne," in *Hawthorne Centenary Essays,* ed. Roy Harvey Pearce (Columbus: Ohio State University Press, 1964), pp. 431, 434–35.

6. In his essay "Charles Baudelaire" (1876), James compares Baudelaire to Hawthorne: "A good way to embrace Baudelaire at a glance is to say that he was, in his treatment of evil, exactly what Hawthorne was not—Hawthorne who felt the thing at its source, deep in the human consciousness." Henry James, "Charles Baudelaire," in *French Poets and Novelists* (1878; rpt. New York: Grosset & Dunlap, 1964), p. 61. There is a contradiction in James's crediting Hawthorne here with a deeply felt sense of evil, while in *Hawthorne,* written only two years later, he speaks of his sense of evil as having a merely *imported* quality, as an entity treated ironically, for esthetic pleasure and contemplation.

7. Lathrop, A Study of Hawthorne, p. 231.

8. Tony Tanner, Introduction, *Hawthorne,* by Henry James (New York: St. Martin's Press, 1967).

9. Henry James, "Nathaniel Hawthorne," in *Library of the World's Best Literature,* ed. Charles Dudley Warner (New York: 1897), vol. 12, reprinted in Leon Edel, ed., *The American Essays of Henry James* (New York: Vintage, 1956), pp. 13, 22, 23.

10. Henry James, "The Hawthorne Centenary," in *American Essays,* p. 27.

11. Henry James, *Notes of a Son and Brother,* in *Autobiography,* ed. F. W. Dupee (New York: Criterion Books, 1956), p. 478.

12. Ibid., p. 480.

13. Ibid.

14. Lyall H. Powers, *Henry James: An Introduction and Interpretation* (New York: Holt, Rinehart and Winston, 1970), p. 15.

6. *WASHINGTON SQUARE:* ROMANCE SHADOWS IN THE DRAWING ROOM

1. Henry James to William Dean Howells, January 31, 1880, in Leon Edel, ed., *The Letters of Henry James: Vol. 2., 1875–1883* (Cambridge, Mass.: Harvard University Press, 1975), p. 268; Peter Buitenhuis, *The Grasping Imagination: The American Writings of Henry James* (Toronto: University of Toronto Press, 1970), pp. 107, 108.

2. F. O. Matthiessen and Kenneth Murdock, eds., *The Notebooks of Henry James* (1947; rpt. New York: George Braziller, 1955), pp. 12–13.

3. Cornelia Kelley, *The Early Development of Henry James* (1930; rpt. Urbana: University of Illinois Press, 1965).

4. Henry James, "The Lesson of Balzac," in *The Future of the Novel,* ed. Leon Edel (New York: Vintage, 1956), pp. 102, 104.

5. Quoted in Kelley, *Early Development,* pp. 29–30. James's review appeared in the *North American Review* 100 (January 1865).

6. Ibid., pp. 280–81.

7. Ibid., p. 281.

8. More might be said of the larger aspect. But there are also specific correspondences, as, for example, in the use made of the houses in both works. The house in *Eugénie Grandet* is always central to Eugénie's confined experience of life and at the end embraces her fate. "She has all the nobility of suffering . . . but also the stiffness of the old maid and the mean habits that arise in the petty confines of provincial life. In spite of her eight hundred francs a year, she lives just as poor Eugénie Grandet once lived, lighting the fire in her bedroom only on the days of the year when her father had permitted a fire in the living room, and putting it out on a certain day according to the strict regulations which had been laid down in her youth. She dresses as her mother had dressed. The house in Saumur, without sun or warmth, full of shadows and melancholy, tells the story of her life" (Honoré de Balzac, *Eugénie Grandet,* in *Eugénie Grandet/The Curé of Tours* [Boston: Houghton, Mifflin, 1964], p. 179). The house on Washington Square also dominates the action of James's novel, most of the scenes being set there, and this concentration upon fixity of place creates a sense of Catherine's restriction and confinement from the world without. At the end it seems an almost empty house, haunted by memories of the past.

9. James, "Lesson of Balzac," pp. 115, 118–19.

10. Henry James, "Honoré de Balzac," in *French Poets and Novelists* (1878; rpt. New York: Grosset & Dunlap, 1964), pp. 84, 89.

11. R. P. Blackmur, Introduction, *Washington Square/The Europeans* by Henry James (New York: Dell, 1969), p. 10.

12. Richard Poirier, *The Comic Sense of Henry James* (New York: Oxford University Press, 1960), p. 180.

13. Henry James to William Dean Howells, January 31, 1880, in *Letters,* 2: 268.

14. Elsewhere, James also refers to "Rappaccini's Daughter" as one of his favorite of Hawthorne's tales: "[Stories] like 'Roger Malvin's Burial,' 'Rappaccini's Daughter,' 'Young Goodman Brown' are 'moralities' without the moral, as it were; small, cold apologues, frosty and exquisite." Henry James, "Nathaniel Hawthorne," in Leon Edel, ed., *The American Essays of Henry James* (New York: Vintage, 1956), p. 14.

15. Parenthetical page references are to *Washington Square,* in F. O. Matthiessen ed., *The American Novels and Stories of Henry James* (New York: Alfred A. Knopf, 1947).

16. Florence Dombey is treated with the cruelty of underappreciation by her father in *Dombey and Son,* and Mirah Lapidoth is exploited and misused by her father in *Daniel Deronda,* but in neither case is a psychological "game" played.

17. Henry James, An International Incident," in Leon Edel, ed., *The Complete Tales of Henry James,* vol. 4, 1876–1882 (London: Rupert Hart-Davis, 1962), p. 250.

7. *THE PORTRAIT OF A LADY:* THE GREAT DRAMATIC CHIAROSCURO

1. *The Portrait of a Lady* is indebted in certain respects to Turgenev, particularly in its having the form of the "dramatic novel," which Turgenev pioneered. Like many of Turgenev's novels, *The Portrait of a Lady* begins with a strong central situation, and the appearance in a particular setting of an outsider, and proceeds to an ending that is "open." Its "open" ending substitutes for a traditional "closed" one a strong concluding impression that closes the circle of the action studied while yet suggesting that the life of the characters continues beyond the ending itself.

In his preface to *The Portrait of a Lady,* James again paid tribute to Turgenev's "beautiful genius," his preoccupation with form and a sharply focused center of moral interest. In the same passage he discusses his own decision to make Isabel Archer, and her consciousness, the center of interest in his novel; everything else, and every other character, would have "an interest contributive only to the greater one." "Such is the aspect that to-day *The Portrait* wears for me," he continues, "a structure reared with an 'architectural' competence, as Turgéniéff would have said, that makes it, to the author's own sense, the most proportioned of his productions after *The Ambassadors.*" *The Novels and Tales of Henry James,* New York Edition (New York: Charles Scribner's Sons, 1909), 3: xvi.

2. Henry James, "The Novels of George Eliot," *Atlantic Monthly,* 18 (October 1866), reprinted in Gordon S. Haight, ed., *A Century of George Eliot Criticism* (Boston: Houghton, Mifflin, 1965), pp. 51, 52.

3. Henry James, "George Eliot's 'Middlemarch'," *The Galaxy,* March 1873, reprinted in Henry James, *The Future of the Novel,* ed. Leon Edel (New York: Vintage, 1956), p. 89; Henry James to William James, January 8, 1873, in Leon Edel, ed., *The Letters of Henry James: Vol. 1, 1843–1875* (Cambridge, Mass.: Harvard University Press, 1974), p. 323; Henry James to Grace Norton, ibid., p. 351.

4. James, "George Eliot's 'Middlemarch'," *Future of the Novel,* p. 83.

5. Henry James to William James, June 22, 1876, in Leon Edel, ed., *The Letters of Henry James: Vol. 2, 1875–1883* (Cambridge, Mass.: Harvard University Press, 1975), p. 55; Henry James to Alice James, February 22, 1876, ibid., p. 30.

6. Henry James, "Daniel Deronda: A Conversation," *Atlantic Monthly,* 38 (December 1876), reprinted in *Partial Portraits* (1888; rpt. Ann Arbor: University of Michigan Press, 1970), pp. 73, 78, 87.

7. F. R. Leavis, *The Great Tradition,* (1948; rpt. New York: Doubleday Anchor, 1954), pp. 136–44.

8. George Eliot, *Middlemarch* (1872; rpt. Baltimore: Penguin, 1965), p. 30.

9. George Eliot, *Daniel Deronda* (1876; rpt. Baltimore: Penguin, 1967), pp. 53, 101, 199.

183

10. Ibid., p. 70.

11. Parenthetical page references to *The Portrait of a Lady* are from *The Novels and Tales of Henry James*, New York Edition (New York: Charles Scribner's Sons, 1909).

12. Eliot, *Daniel Deronda*, pp. 183, 365, 736.

13. Ibid., p. 477.

14. Ibid., p. 646.

15. Nathaniel Hawthorne, "Rappaccini's Daughter," in *Mosses from an Old Manse, The Writings of Nathaniel Hawthorne*, Old Manse Edition (Boston: Houghton, Mifflin, 1900), 4: 135, 152, 175.

16. Interestingly, the courtyard has a certain resemblance to the courtyard of the palazzo in Rome where Miriam, in *The Marble Faun*, has her studio. In this studio above the cloistered court, with its strewn fragments of antique statues and little fountain that "echoes plaintively," Miriam works at sketches that show an obsession with a "dark woman" estranged from her former innocence.

8. *THE BLITHEDALE ROMANCE* AND *THE BOSTONIANS:* FROM RURAL TRAGEDY TO URBAN SATIRE

1. Quoted in Leon Edel, *Henry James 1882–1895: The Middle Years* (Philadelphia: J. B. Lippincott, 1962), pp. 102–03; letter to Howells quoted in ibid., p. 103.

2. Quoted in F. O. Matthiessen, *The James Family: A Group Biography* (1947; rpt. New York: Alfred A. Knopf, 1961), p. 326.

3. Elizabeth Peabody, with whom James was personally acquainted (see Leon Edel, ed., *The Letters of Henry James: Vol. 2, 1875–1883* [Cambridge, Mass.: Harvard University Press, 1975], p. 170), had many resemblances to Miss Birdseye. Like Miss Birdseye, who finds a genius "under every bush," Miss Peabody aided the talented and unrecognized—Jones Very, for example, and Hawthorne, who was then an anonymous author of stories in the *New England Magazine.* Her bookshop press published at cost several of Hawthorne's early books as well as Channing's "Emancipation," Margaret Fuller's "Conversations," *The Dial,* and a number of the Abolitionists' tracts.

In the 1860s Miss Peabody attended almost all the antislavery meetings in Concord and Boston, including one where her life was endangered by an angry mob. In *The Bostonians* Miss Birdseye was affiliated with the Abolitionists and was supposed to have brought the Bible to the Negro slaves in the South; and while Miss Peabody had not done this, she very nearly had. She received the family of John Brown at her home after his raid on Harper's Ferry and went about Boston collecting money, clothing, and hospital supplies for them to take to the prison at Charles Town. After Brown's execution, she journeyed to Virginia to plead for the lives of the remaining prisoners who had taken part in the raid. When the Civil War broke out two years later Miss Peabody went to Washington, where she organized an orphanage for Negro children, many of whom she found roaming the streets, separated from their parents in the South, abandoned, and sometimes starving or dying of disease. During the war she founded a Negro children's school and recruited and trained its teachers.

By the late 1870s Miss Peabody had become actively involved in the women's movement. Like Miss Birdseye, she held women's suffrage meetings in her home and attended meetings of the movement elsewhere in the city. She was a familiar figure in the Boston of that time, a woman in her late seventies, rather heavyset, somewhat careless of her appearance, her eyesight failing (she had developed cataracts), her cap blown askew by the cold Boston winds as she made her way to a women's rights meeting.

Miss Peabody was by then a beloved figure, and not less so because she was sometimes gullible in her efforts to help others. She sponsored the lectures in Boston, for example, of a Dr. Kraitsir, a Hungarian emigré who had a theory of language that would "unlock all tongues," which proved to be unworkable, and she helped to raise funds to send Kraitsir to Hungary to take part in revolutionary activities; but once there he became a "leader" without followers, and the political letters he promised never materialized. In 1883, in another instance of her naiveté, Miss Peabody sponsored Sarah "Winnemucca" Hopkins in Boston. She hired halls and gave lectures with her about the suffering of the Piutes, the Indian tribe to which "Winnemucca" belonged. The funds that Miss Peabody raised for the relief of the Piutes were forwarded faithfully to "Winnemucca," who used them to enrich herself rather than her people. *185*

In *The Bostonians* James characterizes Miss Birdseye as an indiscriminate humanitarian, "whose charity began at home and ended nowhere" (p. 22), a sometimes gullible woman who has herself talked about by befriending a "Hungarian," who absconds with her possessions. If James evolved the character of Miss Birdseye entirely from his "moral consciousness," then his moral consciousness proved to be infallible, for the resemblance between Miss Peabody and Miss Birdseye, point by point, is extraordinary. It is not surprising that James was accused of drawing a "portrait from life."

4. Dr. Mary Walker, from Oswego, New York, began her medical practice in upstate New York in the 1850s. She served in the medical corps of the Union army during the Civil War and in 1866 lectured in England and Scotland in behalf of women's rights. In London she captured the attention of newspapers, not so much for her advocacy of the vote for women, and "equal pay for equal work," as for the men's clothing she wore. It is likely that James had read of her in the English press, or in American newspapers, since she continued to lecture in America in the 1870s and sometimes made headlines.

In *The Bostonians* Dr. Prance does not wear men's clothing, or belong to the women's movement, but there is something masculine—in a crusty, comical way—in her stronger interest in practical medicine than in love or romance, in her bluff, no-nonsense approach to life. There is even a humorous suggestion that Dr. Prance and Miss Birdseye, who occupy the same house, are an ersatz husband and wife, an "odd couple." Dr. Mary Walker's life has been detailed by Charles Snyder in his biography *Dr. Mary Walker* (New York: Vantage Press, 1962).

5. The Spiritualist phenomenon in nineteenth-century America, and its relevance to the Jameses, has been treated by Martha Banta in *Henry James and the Occult: The Great Expansion* (Bloomington: Indiana University Press, 1972). She is primarily concerned with James's ghostly tales of the 1890s, but also traces the origins of the Spiritualist movement (pp. 9–36), which began in mid–nineteenth-century America and quickly spread to England. The Society for Psychical Research was founded in London in 1882, and William James was a corresponding member; in 1884 he was instrumental in establishing the American branch. During this time William James began to investigate the claims of a Mrs. Piper, a Boston medium, that she was able to communicate with individuals who had passed over into the "Summerland," a term Henry James uses in *The Bostonians* as the subject of Mrs. Ada T. P. Foat's lectures.

6. (Urbana: University of Illinois Press, 1972). Kerr points out that the name of the popular Spiritualist lecturer, Ada Hoyt Foye, may have influenced James's naming of Ada T. P. Foat, a name whose double middle initials also make one think of Cora L. V. Hatch, a young Spiritualist speaker whom James had seen perform in New York in 1863. Then twenty-three years old, Cora L. V. Hatch continued to perform as a medium for another decade. Her manner at Clinton Hall, where James saw her, was similar in some ways to Verena's performance, with a period of silent waiting for inspiration, followed by a torrent of Spiritualistic clichés and an advocacy of the emancipation of women. Her background also contained similarities with Verena's. She had been a "child medium" managed by her father; later, she married a physician and mesmeric healer and appeared under his guidance before large crowds in Boston and New York.

Cora Hatch later achieved a dubious notoriety in the press, after divorcing her husband and accusing him of holding her in thrall and misappropriating her earnings. Hatch replied in a volume entitled *Spiritualists' Iniquities Unmasked* that his innocent but magnetically susceptible wife had fallen under the control of demonically possessed Spiritualists bent on making her the spokeswoman for their free-love doctrines. Hatch's revelations helped to incite the popular revulsion against Spiritualism at the end of the 1850s, reflected in Bayard Taylor's "Confessions of a Medium" (1860), a melodrama of a trance-maiden's victimization that anticipated James's "Professor Fargo."

7. In 1883, when James began to plan *The Bostonians*, Victoria Woodhull almost certainly came to his attention, since it was then that she "crashed" London society by marrying John Biddulph Martin, a British baronet, and created a stir. It has been speculated that James's story "The Siege of London" (1883), which deals with a middle-aged American woman, Mrs. Headway, who seeks to live down her notorious past and marry into English society, was inspired by the Woodhull-Martin marriage.

Victoria Woodhull, née Claflin, was born in a small Ohio town in 1838, and bred, as her biographer Emanie Sachs remarks, "in poverty and chicanery." In the late 1840s she treked with her family across the Midwest, announcing herself a medium and treating patients "for the cure of disease." When she was sixteen years old she met and married Dr. Channing Woodhull (his doctor title did not necessarily mean that he had much medical training), and he became her manager as they traveled in a wagon selling an "elixir of life."

Meanwhile, Victoria's younger sister, Tennessee, had also come forward as a girl Spiritualist. In Canada, the Claflins opened a cancer clinic, which was forced to close when Tennessee was charged with manslaughter. Scandal followed them to Cincinnati, where Tennessee figured in blackmail and adultery suits; and they then appeared in Chicago, and later in St. Louis, as practitioners of "magnetic healing." In St. Louis, Victoria met Colonel James Blood, president of the Society of Spiritualists, who became her lover, and like Dr. Woodhull before him, acted as her agent and manager. During this period particularly Victoria Woodhull became closely associated with the free-love movement, which flourished at that time and had its own colonies and newspapers.

By the beginning of the 1870s she had become quite possibly the most notorious woman in America. During this time the Claflin sisters met Commodore Vanderbilt in New York, and the beautiful Tennessee came to his aid with her "magnetic healing" (which, interestingly, involved a stroking and caressing of the patient's body), and her attentions affected his rapid recovery. Soon the Claflin sisters went into Wall Street as speculators—unprecedented for women—and, advised by Vanderbilt, made a fortune. They then started a newspaper, *Woodhull & Claflin's Weekly,* the masthead of which read: "PROGRESS! FREE THOUGHT! UNTRAMMELLED LIVES!" The paper offered a strange combination of financial news and articles on Spiritualism and free love. Indeed, Victoria Woodhull lectured on these subjects, as well as on women's rights, at Steinway Hall in New York and on other platforms across the country. "Her private life," her biographer writes, "blazed in the courts, the newspapers, her own paper, and on the platform." In *The Bostonians* Selah Tarrant may seem singular in his odd alliance with a number of different bohemian movements and his worship of publicity and exposure in the press, but there is something salient in his oddity, coming, as he does, directly out of the world Victoria Woodhull publicized.

187

8. Parenthetical page references to *The Bostonians* are to the Dial Press edition (New York: Dial Press, 1945).

9. William James to Henry James, Spring 1886, quoted in Matthiessen, *The James Family,* p. 328.

10. Marius Bewley, *The Complex Fate* (London: Chatto and Windus, 1952), pp. 11–30.

11. Marius Bewley and Leon Edel, "Correspondence," *Scrutiny,* 17 (Spring 1950), 53–60.

12. F. O. Matthiessen and Kenneth Murdock, eds., *The Notebooks of Henry James* (1947; rpt. New York: George Braziller, 1955), p. 47.

13. Henry James, *Hawthorne* (1879; rpt. Ithaca: Cornell University Press, 1956), p. 69.

14. Tarrant's priestly role is emphasized further by his name *Selah,* a word indi-

cating a pause that occurs repeatedly in the Book of Psalms, in which the Hebrews are allied heroically with God as his chosen people. Another member of the Tarrants' circle, Mr. Pardon, also has a name with priestly connotations, since a pardoner was a traveling medieval priest who acted as a fund-raiser for religious causes by selling indulgences—until the practice was stopped as fraudulent. Pardon would like to act as Verena's inspirational speaking-tour agent and share in the profits ("You see if she don't have quite a run"). The deity Tarrant and Pardon actually serve is the god of publicity.

15. Henry James, "The Point of View," in Leon Edel, ed., *The Complete Tales of Henry James*, vol. 4, 1876–1882 (London: Rupert Hart-Davis, 1962), pp. 501, 503.

16. Parenthetical page references to *The Blithedale Romance* are to *The Writings of Nathaniel Hawthorne*, Old Manse Edition (Boston: Houghton, Mifflin, 1900), vol. 8.

17. Similarly, the colonists at Blithedale undertake to "establish the one true system" (p. 324), and in *The Bostonians* Miss Birdseye takes her homeopathic medicine (like Coverdale), remarking: "Well, it's generally admitted now to be the one true system" (p. 303).

18. The comic strategy of puritan versus royalist is introduced by James quite specifically when he remarks that Ransom "had a longish pedigree (it had flowered at one time with English royalists and cavaliers), and he seemed at moments to be inhabited by some transmitted spirit of a robust but narrow ancestor" (p. 161).

19. It has been pointed out that Basil Ransom's last name indicates the role he is to play in the work—as a rescuer of Verena; but it might be noticed that his first name is also revealing, since the word *basil* is derived from the Greek *royal*, and in Greek and Italian traditions the basil plant was associated with the erotic. Moreover, basil has an association with the American South, from which Ransom comes, since it was commonly believed among the Creoles of Louisiana to have the power of attracting love; it appears in this context (particularly in chapter 9, entitled "The Traction of Basil") in George Washington Cable's *The Grandissimes* (1880), which James had read and reviewed.

20. Verena's situation as a maiden in need of rescue has been intimated quietly in this section in James's allusion to the opera *Lohengrin*, which Verena attends with Olive. In *Lohengrin* Ortrud is an evil enchantress, and Elsa a maiden in whose mind she has sown distrust of the "knight in shining armor" who is to champion and marry her.

An allusion of a similar kind appears later in the novel when Verena spends the summer at Olive's house at Marmion, an altered form of the village of Marion on Cape Cod. The change of name from Marion to Marmion forms an allusion to Walter Scott's historical poem. In Scott's *Marmion* Lord Marmion appears to have the upper hand as a wooer of the young maiden Constance de Beverly, but is killed in the battle of Flodden Field at the same time that Ralph de Wilton, whom she really loves, but has presumed dead, comes to claim her. This love motif is reintroduced by the poem-within-the-poem of "young Lochinvar" who, on the eve of her bridal to another, arrives to carry off the fair Ellen. Lochinvar's timely arrival (like Ralph de

Wilton's) underscores Verena's situation at Cape Cod, when Ransom appears just in time to rescue her from a lifelong bondage to Olive Chancellor.

Moreover, in the figures of the Abbess and the Novice Clare (the name Constance has taken) there is a suggestion of Olive and Verena. Had Ralph de Wilton not arrived to claim her, Constance would have been condemned to remain in the company of the youthful Abbess, who is described in the following way: "The Abbess was of noble blood, / But early took the veil and hood, / Ere upon life she cast a look, / Or knew the world she forsook. / . . . Black was her garb, her rigid rule / Reformed on the Benedictine school; / Her cheek was pale, her form was spare; / Vigils and penitence austere / Had early quenched the light of youth." The youthful Abbess seems extraordinarily like Olive Chancellor.

21. Donald David Stone, *Novelists in a Changing World* (Cambridge, Mass.: Harvard University Press, 1972), p. 278.

22. In a letter to Alice James dated April 25, 1880, Henry wrote that he had just left his friend Paul Zhukovsky (the probable model for Valentin in *The American*) in Naples, where he was living "in great intimacy" with Richard Wagner, and went on to refer to the "fantastic immoralities and aesthetics" of that circle. In a footnote, Edel comments that James "seems to have been greatly shocked to find his old Parisian friend in a veritable nest of homosexuals." *Letters*, 2: 288–89.

23. "La Fille aux Yeux d'Or" is the story of a young Creole beauty shut up in a secret, luxurious seraglio by her lesbian lover, an older woman.

24. Victor Hugo, *The Hunchback of Notre Dame* (New York: Dodd, Mead, 1947), p. 266.

189

9. THE BLITHEDALE ROMANCE AND THE BOSTONIANS: THE PATTERN OF TRANSFORMATION

1. Donald David Stone, *Novelists in a Changing World* (Cambridge, Mass.: Harvard University Press, 1972), pp. 278, 256.

2. William Dean Howells, *Dr. Breen's Practice* (1881; rpt. St. Clair Shores, Mich.: Scholarly Press, 1970), pp. 13, 270.

3. Mildred Howells, ed., *Life in Letters of William Dean Howells* (New York: Doubleday, 1928), 1: 144.

4. All parenthetical references to *The Blithedale Romance* are from Nathaniel Hawthorne, *The Writings of Nathaniel Hawthorne*, Old Manse Edition (Boston: Houghton, Mifflin, 1900).

5. J. B. Priestly, *Victoria's Heyday* (New York: Harper & Row, 1972), pp. 188–89.

6. Parenthetical page references to *The Undiscovered Country* are to William Dean Howells, *The Undiscovered Country* (Boston: Houghton, Mifflin, 1880).

7. In the first draft of *The Undiscovered Country*, Howells's journalist was named Gifford, like the colonel in "Professor Fargo." Later, Howells changed Gifford's name to Ford, perhaps because he knew that he could not use the same name James

had. This possibility further complicates the thematic interplay between James and Howells. Parenthetical references to *The Bostonians* are to the Dial Press edition (New York: Dial Press, 1945).

8. Henry James, "Alphonse Daudet," in *Partial Portraits* (1888; rpt. Ann Arbor: University of Michigan Press, 1970), p. 199.

9. In *The Grasping Imagination: The American Writings of Henry James* (Toronto: University of Toronto Press, 1970) Buitenhuis makes a number of good observations about James's drawing from *L'Evangéliste*: Madame Autheman suggests the role of Olive, and Eline Ebsen that of Verena, in her proselyte relation to Olive. "Madame Autheman's large town house in Paris gives the idea for the snug house on Charles Street; the Autheman chateau finds its American equivalent in the cottage on Cape Cod. . . . Even an apparently native touch like the 'immemorial waterproof' that Selah Tarrant perpetually wears, has its origins, seemingly, in the customary 'waterproofs plein de boue' of Madame Autheman's followers" (p. 144).

Madame Autheman gave James his initial conception of Olive Chancellor, and there are passages in *L'Evangéliste* where the physical resemblance between them is striking, particularly in Madame Autheman's thin lips and "smile, that imparted to her eyes, instead of an expression of warmth, a bluish light, like the reflection from a glacier." The association of Madame Autheman with coldness and old age (although she is still young) is also seen in Olive. Daudet writes of Madame Autheman and her group at one point: "This dream of apostleship of women arose in all their discussions. And why not priests, since there were women Bachelors and women doctors? The fact is, that with their faces fiery with zeal, or wan from exhaustion, and their plain black gowns which gave no indication of their sex, they might all have passed for old clergymen" ([Boston: Little, Brown, 1899], pp. 70, 77).

The sexual basis of Madame Autheman's neuroticism is implied throughout *L'Evangéliste*. Jilted as a young woman and unable to cope with the hazards of human relationships, she expends her enormous, concentrated energy in a "contempt for men and life." Cold and yet inwardly excitable, she becomes "absorbed in melancholy exaltation," words which fit Olive with precision. *L'Evangéliste* was expressly intended by Daudet as an "observation" on morbid psychology and was dedicated to Charcot, a predecessor of Freud who had studied the sexual basis of abnormal psychology. The influence of Charcot on Daudet's conception of Madame Autheman is fascinating to note, since it shows a Freudian notation of feminine psychology "before Freud." Charcot also indicates a point at which the psychological interests of William and Henry James touch. As Ralph Barton Perry points out in *The Thought and Character of William James*, William James was attending Charcot's lectures in Paris in 1882 when he received news of his father's last illness.

10. William Dean Howells, *Heroines of Fiction* (New York: Harper & Brothers, 1901), 2: 5, 6, 7, 9.

11. There is additional irony in these lines, since they occur in scene 4, part 1, of *Faust*, where Faust makes his compact with Mephistopheles. Further, it is Faust him-

self who speaks these lines, saying that abstinence and denial have been so unfulfilling that each morning he desires death. Examining Faust's book-lined study, Mephistopheles remarks: "What a place of martyrdom is here!"

12. Stone, *Novelists in a Changing World*, p. 263.

13. It might be noted that her address has the same title as Howells's novel *A
Woman's Reason* (1883), which deals with the morbid sense of duty in a young New
England woman. Its heroine, Helen Harkness, admits at one point that she cannot
be "happy" until she sacrifices herself, and suffers. In not delivering her address "A
Woman's Reason," Verena escapes the fate of Olive Chancellor.

14. Henry James, "The Correspondence of Carlyle and Emerson," *Century Magazine*, June 1883, reprinted in Leon Edel, ed., *The American Essays of Henry James*
(New York: Vintage, 1956), p. 46. Miss Birdseye is linked with Emerson specifically in the novel. James writes: "It was the perennial freshness of Miss Birdseye's
faith that had had such a contagion for these modern maidens, the unquenched flame
of her transcendentalism, the simplicity of her vision, the way in which . . . the only
thing that was still actual for her was the elevation of the species by the reading of
Emerson" (p. 153). Their shared trait of having no physical or personal, only moral,
needs is suggested elsewhere in James's review of James Elliot Cabot's *A Memoir of
Ralph Waldo Emerson* (1887), in which he remarks that Emerson "was altogether
passionless. . . . he had no personal, just as he had almost no physical wants."
"Emerson," in *American Essays*, p. 64.

191

10. CONCLUSION: THE END OF JAMES'S EARLIER PERIOD

1. Parenthetical references to *The Bostonians* are to the Dial Press edition (New
York: Dial Press, 1945).

2. Henry James, *The Tragic Muse* (1890; New York: Harper Torchbooks, 1960),
p. 597.

3. Ibid., pp. 309, 505.

4. In *Hawthorne* James had written slightingly of Hawthorne's use of allegory,
which he described as being one of the "lighter exercises" of the imagination. Yet in
The Wings of the Dove and *The Golden Bowl* James employs a Hawthornesque allegory, giving the novels the quality of delicate moral fables. Matthiessen has noted
that certain of James's earlier works also have an allegorical quality: "In several of his
earliest stories, as in *The Romance of Certain Old Clothes* and *Benvolio*, he had de-
pended on allegory in the manner of Hawthorne; and if we look closely at *Roderick
Hudson*, we realize that the novel is still essentially an allegory of the life of the artist.
As he went on to master all the skills of realism, he grew dissatisfied with allegory's
obvious devices; and yet, particularly towards the end of his career, realistic details
had become merely the covering for a content that was far from realistic." F. O.
Matthiessen, *Henry James, The Major Phase* (1944; rpt. New York: Oxford University Press, 1963), p. 71.

5. William Dean Howells, *Heroines of Fiction* (New York: Harper & Brothers, 1901), 1: 161.

6. William Dean Howells, *A Chance Acquaintance* (1874; rpt. St. Clair Shores, Mich.: Scholarly Press, 1970), pp. 75, 152.

7. A light versus dark patterning is sometimes still seen, however, in James's later women. Madame Merle in *The Portrait of a Lady* is darkly named, and there is a reminder of Hawthorne in the name, worldliness, and Jewish ancestry of Miriam Rooth in *The Tragic Muse*. In *The Wings of the Dove*, most of all, Hawthorne's feminine figures are reproduced in the pale, innocent Milly Theale, as compared to the dark, worldly Kate Croy.

8. A good, recent study of "the American girl" in nineteenth-century American literature is Paul John Eakin's *The New England Girl: Cultural Ideals in Hawthorne, Stowe, Howells and James* (Athens: University of Georgia Press, 1976).

9. Howells, *A Chance Acquaintance*, p. 66.

10. The cult of Italy in nineteenth-century America has been examined by Van Wyck Brooks in *The Dream of Arcadia: American Writers and Artists in Italy 1769–1915* (New York: E. P. Dutton, 1958); and Nathalia Wright in *American Novelists in Italy: The Discoverers: Allston to James* (Philadelphia: University of Pennsylvania Press, 1965). More specialized studies are: Carl Maves, *Sensuous Pessimism: Italy in the Works of Henry James* (Bloomington: Indiana University Press, 1973); and James Woodress, Jr., *Howells and Italy* (Durham, N.C.: Duke University Press, 1952).

11. F. R. Leavis writes: " 'Hawthorne,' says James in the early study he wrote for the English *Men of Letters* series, 'is perpetually looking for images which shall place themselves in picturesque correspondences with the spiritual facts with which he is concerned, and of course the search is of the very essence of poetry.' James's own constant and profound concern with spiritual facts expresses itself not only in what obviously demands to be called symbolism, but in the handling of character, episode and dialogue, and in the totality of the plot, so that when he seems to offer a novel of manners he gives us more than that and the 'poetry' is major." *The Great Tradition* (1948; rpt. New York: Doubleday Anchor, 1954), pp. 158–59.

Index

Index

Index

Index

196

Index

Index

Index

199

Index

Index

Index

Index